THE FOUNDATIONS OF SOVEREIGNTY

AND

OTHER ESSAYS

BY

HAROLD J. LASKI

AUTHOR OF "THE PROBLEM OF SOVEREIGNTY," "AUTHORITY IN THE
MODERN STATE," ETC.

THE LAWBOOK EXCHANGE, LTD.
Clark, New Jersey

ISBN 978-1-58477-330-6 (hardcover)
ISBN 978-1-61619-393-5 (paperback)

Lawbook Exchange edition 2003, 2014

The quality of this reprint is equivalent to the quality of the original work.

THE LAWBOOK EXCHANGE, LTD.
33 Terminal Avenue
Clark, New Jersey 07066-1321

*Please see our website for a selection of our other publications
and fine facsimile reprints of classic works of legal history:*
www.lawbookexchange.com

Library of Congress Cataloging-in-Publication Data

Laski, Harold Joseph, 1893-1950.
    The foundations of sovereignty and other essays / by Harold J. Laski.
        p. cm.
    Originally published: New York: Harcourt, Brace and Co., c1921
    Includes bibliographical references and index.
    ISBN 1-58477-330-8 (cloth: alk paper)
    1. State, The. 2. Sovereignty. 3. Political science. I. Title.

JC257 .L29 2003
320.1'5—dc2l   2002044372

Printed in the United States of America on acid-free paper

THE FOUNDATIONS OF SOVEREIGNTY

AND

OTHER ESSAYS

BY

HAROLD J. LASKI

AUTHOR OF "THE PROBLEM OF SOVEREIGNTY," "AUTHORITY IN THE
MODERN STATE," ETC.

NEW YORK

HARCOURT, BRACE AND COMPANY

1921

To My Friend
ROSCOE POUND
Dean of the Law School in Harvard University

WITH

Abiding Affection

PREFACE

I

The essays printed in this volume are part of an attempt at the reconstruction of political theory in terms of institutions more fitted to the needs we confront. Broadly speaking, they are part of the case for what is coming to be called the pluralistic state in contrast to the unified sovereignty of the present social organization. But they are only part of the case. The industrial and psychological inadequacy of the existing régime is briefly discussed in the second of these papers. Since that was written, the evidence given before the Royal Commission on the Coal Industry and the Inquiry into Dockers' Wages have shown that the institutional reconstruction will inevitably be more thorough-going than I there, writing in 1918, imagined. What evidence we have from the European continent, particularly from Russia and Germany, makes it evident that the classic system of representative government has reached its apogee. What we need above all is inventiveness in the social, legal, and political matters that are discussed in these essays.

It is a matter of no small interest to speculate upon the direction from which that inventiveness is likely to come. Despite the great service rendered by the philosophers to political science, they have studied rather the form than the substance of the state. This has meant an undue emphasis upon purpose as distinct from the fulfillment of purpose. It has led to an analysis of the

"pure instance," rather than an analysis of the actual
experiments with which history presents us. That is
why the attitude of the philosopher has been so similar
to that of the lawyer. The "rights" studied by the latter
take their origin from a set of historical circumstances
which the lawyer, from his standpoint naturally, is able
to ignore. They differ from the study of "right." But
it is upon the latter problem that our attention must
today be concentrated.

For we have found that a state in which sovereignty
is unified is morally inadequate and administratively
inefficient. It depends upon an intellectualist view of
the political process which is not, as Mr. Graham Wallas
has shown, borne out by the facts. It assumes that the
government is fully representative of the community without taking account of the way in which the characteristics of the economic system inevitably perverts the
governmental purpose to narrow and special ends. It
assumes that the problems of the modern state admit of
general solutions; the fact surely is that the essential
problem is the different way in which those general solutions can be administered. Nor can the average voter
be said to transcend his own interest by merging himself
into a larger whole with the result that a "general will"
is secured. Here we have been led astray by the facile
brilliance of Rousseau. The more carefully the political
process is analyzed, the more clearly does it appear that
we are simply confronted by a series of special wills
none of which can claim any necessary pre-eminence. In
particular, it does not sufficiently investigate the moral
character of governmental acts. The objectivity, for
example, of the interpretations issued by the British government during the railway crisis of 1919 can only be

fairly judged by the careful scrutiny of individual citizens. In politics, above all, there is no *a priori* rightness.

Nor is this all. The monistic state-philosophy too little investigates the relation of the citizen-body as a body capable of, but rarely exercising, judgment upon policy. The investigations of the Sankey Commission, for example, have shown how vast is the unrealized experience which lies waste in the autocratic management of industry. That waste is not less true of government departments. Once, at any point, work is divorced from responsibility the result is a balked disposition of which the consequence is to diminish the creativeness of the worker concerned. The hierarchical structure of the present state maximizes this loss. Nothing is more clear, for example, than the existence of a law of diminishing administrative returns. An official cannot be charged with business over a territory beyond a certain size without administering less efficiently for each addition to his work; and no amount of efficiency at a central office will morally compensate for the inferior interest in the result obtained of those who have had no effective share in making it. The appreciation of this is one of the most vital factors in Mr. Justice Sankey's scheme for the nationalization of British mines. And this is true not merely of industry alone. The departmental organization of every monistic state becomes over-centralized; and this, as Lamennais aptly said, results in apoplexy at the centre and anaemia at the extremities. For the inevitable consequence of centralization is an attempt to apply uniform and equal solutions to things neither uniform nor equal.

The pluralistic state is an attempt to remedy these defects by substituting coördination for a hierarchical

structure. Mainly it must be based upon a study of the
impulses which are at work in the business of production
and the channels we have erected for the satisfaction of
those impulses. We must start from the admission that
the allegiance of man is diverse and that where his loyalties conflict it is ultimately both safer and better for the
community that this instructed conscience should be the
source of his decision. It would follow that there is no
such thing as the sovereignty contemplated by law in any
sense which admits of practical political application. In
actual fact what we meet is a variety of interests, functional and territorial; and the way in which they are
related suggests the necessarily federal character of all
government. The main advantage of this federal structure is that it affords better channels for the operation
of an active consent upon the part of citizens than any
other method. Nor must this federalism be conceived in
merely spatial terms. It applies not less, say to the
government of the mines than to the government of
Ireland or of Massachusetts. Ultimately it suggests not
only a partition of sovereignty in terms of function but
also a complete revision of the accepted notion of property. Ultimately, also, it suggests a rough division
between the two great functions of production and consumption in which supreme power is divided between the
two. Where the interests of each touch upon the other,
it is clear enough that some mechanism of ultimate adjustment will be needed; but the main thing is to avoid a
system in which supreme power is concentrated at a
single point in the body public.

There is at bottom involved in this view a theory of
the nature of liberty. In Mr. Graham Wallas' admirable phrase, liberty is conceived as being the "capacity

of continuous initiative"; and it is suggested that this is
unattainable in a monistic state except for a small governing class. Liberty, it is argued, is derived from the
existence of avenues of creative activity for the mass of
citizens. It is obvious that the hierarchical structure
of our present order does not offer such opportunities
save to a small group of men. In the result we lose a
vast welter of experience while we balk the disposition
of many whose faculties are capable of far greater use
than that to which they are normally devoted. Above
all, the control of political power in the modern state
by a small group of property-owners must mean at the
bottom that the motives to effort upon which reliance is
based will be ineffective so soon as the majority of men
see through the façade by which they are screened.
Liberty, in short, is incompatible with the present system
of property; for its result is a concentration of power
which makes the political personality of the average citizen ineffective for any serious purpose.

II

These essays are part of a scaffolding from which
there is, I hope, eventually to emerge a general reconstruction of the state. But it may be useful at this
stage for me to indicate some of the sources in which I
have found deep comfort. I believe profoundly that no
attempt at reconstruction of our present institutions is
likely to be successful save in so far as it is deeply rooted
in historic knowledge. For that purpose we must go,
not merely to men like Maitland and Gierke, Figgis and
Mr. Justice Holmes, but to the actual texts themselves.
In things like the Conciliar Movement, the marvelous
edifice of Edmund Burke, the struggle for the Charter,

the early history of American federalism; in lesser men
like John Taylor of Caroline no less than in the great
thinkers like Hamilton himself will the clues to our problems be found.

Nor does the literature of our own time lack suggestiveness.　In law, men like Pound and Duguit; in economics, the superb edifice of Mr. and Mrs. Sidney Webb;
in history, the work of Tawney and Hovell and Mr. and
Mrs. Hammond; in administrative science, the books of
Mr. Graham Wallas and the analyses of Lord Haldane;
in politics, the brilliant, if too brief, suggestions of Mr.
G. D. H. Cole; all of these, in their sum, are the marks
of a movement which to the next generation will appear
not less influential than the work done a century ago
by the Utilitarians.　Its results are only less obvious
because it starts with the recognition of the great complexity involved in the facts of social structure.　They
are the more enduring for that very reason.

One remark at this point will not perhaps be out of
place.　The study of American history and politics has
barely been attempted in Great Britain.　Acton's magistral glance, of course, swept them within the range of
knowledge; and here and there an investigator like Doyle
or Payne has done work of high value.　But the relevance
of American political speculation to the general social
questions, the richness of American history as a source
of suggestiveness, has been badly neglected.　We in England, of course, know the *Federalist;* but we are too
inclined to regard the *Federalist* as unique in American
literature.　In fact, it is but a portion of a much vaster
effort which produced, between 1787 and 1840, a political
philosophy as rich and suggestive as any people can offer
in a similar period of time.　Since 1845, indeed, there

has been little of the first importance; though books like Mr. Herbert Croly's *Promise of American Life* and Mr. Walter Lippmann's *Preface to Politics* show that this is the accident of special economic conditions rather than exhaustion. The suggestiveness, indeed, has simply been transferred, perhaps in less ample measure, to the fields of history and law. No one who examines that literature of American sectionalism which has been produced through the genius of Professor Turner can fail to glean an insight of high value into the problems of organization. No one who studies the constitutional decisions of the Supreme Court of the United States, especially the great series associated with the name of Mr. Justice Holmes, but can gain a new understanding of the forces by which social relationships are molded.

I have dedicated this book to my former colleague Dean Pound; not merely in remembrance of my own full years at Harvard, but also as the least tribute I can offer to a Law School which is still, as it was in Maitland's time, the greatest educational experiment on the American continent. That it grows in creativeness is, as I have had full opportunity to observe, in largest measure the result of his influence.

I owe to various editors thanks for the permission generously accorded to reprint material which has already appeared in their pages.

HAROLD J. LASKI.

London School of Economics and Political Science.

CONTENTS

THE FOUNDATIONS OF
SOVEREIGNTY

I

WE too rarely inquire how greatly our institutions bear upon their face the marks of the environment they have inherited. Yet it is indubitable that the state, at least, is the offspring of a special set of historic circumstances. Man is, of course, a community-building animal; but it was not until the sixteenth century that the technique which surrounds the modern state came into existence. Sovereignty, in the sense of an ultimate territorial organ which knows no superior,[1] was to the middle ages an unthinkable thing. The basis of medieval organization was radically different. That at which it strove was unity and the road thereto lay through a system of groups which consistently surpassed the limits of geography. The territorial fact, indeed, was then, as now, an ultimately inescapable thing. No one can read the regulations of a medieval guild without the realization that the trader, at least, was passionately local; and even where the mercantilism of pre-Reformation times was limited by the maxims of canonist ethics and the obvious sources of economic supply, it was still shot through with vaguely nationalistic notions.

Yet the fact remains that the apparent simplicity of a world organized into a set of sovereign states was

[1] Cf. Zimmern, *Nationality and Government*, p. 56.

1

broadly unknown. Sovereignty, in the modern sense, is
the progenitor of impalpable barriers from which the
medieval thinker sought at all costs freedom. Our organization is inherited from the breakdown of that
Respublica Christiana by the thought of which he was
dominated. The notion therein implied was, at bottom,
the great legacy of imperial Rome; and it was not until
its impotence as a practical hypothesis was demonstrated
that more modern ideas could make their way. The
Respublica Christiana implied the worship of pervasive
unity. Everywhere plurality was taken as the merest
vesture beneath which men must penetrate if they would
discover the real secrets of the universe. It was the main
effort of the medieval thinker to find the essence of that
secret whereby the oneness of humanity in God might be
made manifest. Over and above the separate interests
of persons and of institutions there arose always the
majestic notion of the inclusive All which somehow tran-
scends the inconvenient variety of a shifting universe.
The *maxime unum*, so Dante thought,[2] is the *maxime
bonum*; and it was in shrinking from the infamous notion
of a dual universe that Boniface VIII could issue his
Unam Sanctam.[3] One law and one government were the
necessary corollary of its single, dominating purpose.[4]
That is why the medieval state is a church; for all men
were Christians, and before that basic unity of outlook all
differences were held as insignificant. It cannot be said
that the medieval mind thought intolerable the division
of the community into two separate spheres, but at least
it shrank therefrom. Some such picture Gelasius I may
have painted;[5] but in the later days of the Carolingian

2 *De Monarchia*, Ch. 15.
3 C I. Extrav, 1, 8.
4 *De Monarchia*, Cc. 3, 4.
5 *Epist.* X, 9.

empire men like Archbishop Hincmar and Jonas of Orleans could lay the foundations of wider claims which Gregory VII. and Innocent III. knew well how to bring to mature attainment.

Not, indeed, that the medieval thinker found reconciliation of church and state an easy thing. The idea of a separation of the eternal from the temporal order was never for long absent from his mind; and the great fact of increasingly separate kingdoms meant the acceptance of separate systems of law. A variety of legal systems implied a variety of governments to enforce them. In such a background, the notion of unity seemed like to vanish before hard facts. Yet it does not disappear. For the medieval mind became convinced that such disparity could find a reconciliation in a higher synthesis. The two great schools of political thought were seeking — at least from the struggle between empire and papacy — a solution in terms of unity. The solution broke down before the growth of nationalities on the one hand, and the persistent degeneration of Rome upon the other. Yet right down to the Conciliar Movement, at least, all Churchmen with high notions of the papal prerogative insisted that Rome is rightfully the mistress of the Christian world. This it is which permits the affirmation that the middle ages had a clear conception of sovereignty, even if its territorial aspect failed of development. For the *plenitudo potestatis* implied a full sovereignty over the affairs of men. The rule of Christ in heaven had to find its pale but real reflection in an earthly kingdom; and if Christ was King above, so, it was urged, must the Pope, as his vicar, rule below. The Emperor might bear the *imperium*, but he derived it mediately from the good offices of Rome. The two swords were ultimately in a single hand. Imperial power was nothing save the expression of papal convenience. *Jus divinum*, that is to say, postulated the universal sovereignty of the Church.

The dream is strange to us. Yet rare indeed is the medieval thinker who had the courage to urge that, as matter of historic record, Leo II had implicitly admitted the superior right of Charles the Great to govern. Rarer still is the publicist who dares to challenge the dream at its source. There are threats and acts with unexplored theory lurking at their root; as with the defiance of Norman William to the papal claims of suzerainty,[6] or that practical hate of solid financial loss which inspired the statutes of Provisors and Praemunire.[7] Gerard of York, indeed,[8] has a clear outline of a full theory hinging upon the divine right of kings. Ockham insists upon a world in which the Church is but a portion of the empire;[9] but it is still a unity of which he dreams. Marsiglio is Erastian enough; but he is pre-eminent because lonely in his Erastianism. The normal theory of those who challenged the Church in the name of the empire was the ancient notion of two separate powers each governing its due portion of the single Christian commonwealth. The powers, by most at least, were admittedly coördinate, and it was by their peaceful coöperation that unity could be achieved. That is the essence, for example, of the settlement at Worms.[10] It is even the essence of the solution Pierre Dubois had in mind, at an epoch when the fading power of Rome — though not, as Augustinus

[6] Stubbs, *Constit. History*, I, 305.
[7] 25 E. III. Ch. 4; E. III, St. 1, Ch. 1.
[8] Mon. Ger. Hist. *Libelli de Lite*, III, 663.
[9] *Octo Quaest.*, 1, Ch. 3–5, 20.
[10] And of the settlement after the Becket controversy. Stubbs, *Constit. Hist.*, II.

Triumphus shows us,[11] an epoch of fading claims — made possible more nationalistic dreams.[12] Let pope and emperor take their due share of an unified *imperium* which, for administrative purposes, was neatly and naturally divided between spiritual and secular in degree determined by the writer's party.

The motive, at least, is unmistakable. A world that recognized variety and difference seemed from its very basis to give promise only of anarchism. An ultimate unity of allegiance was a guarantee of order. That is why even so eminently Whig a thinker as Aquinas not only urges the supremacy of Rome but also warns against the popular rebellion for which he provides a sanction.[13] That is why, also, the movement of the middle ages is consistently away from the diversified allegiance which is inherent in the theory of feudal organization. A world of purely private rights — and this, at bottom, is the feudal world — gives no sanction for the safeguard of general interests. The whole importance, for example, of the Model Parliament of 1295 was the mechanism it provided for superseding the separate immunities of functional and territorial organizations. The modern state could not emerge until the universal interest of the community had obtained, at least in theory, an organ for the protection of its demands against the multifarious liberties and franchises which competed with its will.

The unity summarized in papal control went, for the adherents of Rome, at least, some distance to the accomplishment of this need. Medieval politics are a branch of theology; and so long as the ultimate concern was the

[11] Cf. Poole, *Illustrations of Medieval Thought*, 253 ff.
[12] De Recuperatione terrae sanctae. Cf. Figgis, *From Gerson to Grotius*, 31.
[13] *De Reg. Princ*, I, 3–6.

mechanism of salvation more earthly questions could
hardly hope to predominate. Yet within the unity typi-
fied by Rome a further unity must be conceded. If the
oneness of pope and emperor could be conceived, above
the seeming dualism of the world they govern, there were
few to doubt, and fewer still of eminence to suggest, that
the emperor was not the lord of the secular world. Rome
was the last of the great system of world-empires. Even
in pre-Christian times the conscious greatness of its mission might seem to defy the sceptic. It gained, at least
for theory, new sanction from the life of Christ, and,
after its transfer from Rome to Byzantium, it came to
Germany ordained of God. So might the empire still
rule, even if in appearance only, the lesser princes of the
world. Writers, indeed, interpreted differently the degree of the imperial power. The lawyers tended to make
the emperor in a full sense *dominus mundi;* [14] for the
categories of jurisprudence search always for the widest
content. Aeneas Sylvius, in his Germanic days, was full
of similar notions.[15] But to Ockham, with his native
English power to compromise, *imperium* was but a vague
suzerainty; [16] and the wisely generous Nicholas of Cusa
made imperial power no more than a zeal for the welfare
of all Christian men.[17]

II

That last thought is important; for it warns us against
the false simplicity which would summarize the political
thought of the middle ages in a single phrase. Not,
indeed, that such an ultimately desired unity of control

14 Cf. Baldus, II, Feud, 26, 1-13.
15 *De. Ort. et Auct.* Ch. 2.
16 Octo. q. II, Cs. 8. Dial. III, tr. 2, 1, 2, Chs. 26-8.
17 Nich. Cus. De Con., Cath. III, Ch. 4.

was not its pervading temper. But struggling alongside
that powerful current lesser but still significant streams
may be detected. The world did not stand still in awe
while the conflict between Guelf and Ghibelline was decided. The arrival of its peoples at nationhood was a
decisive factor in the Reformation; and the breakdown,
in its rigid form, of the feudal system marks the transition to a more complex economy. The ideas which survived did not, indeed, attain full growth. What was
mainly lacking to them was the administrative mechanisms by which alone their translation from concept to
fact might have been secured. The doctrines, as a consequence, are vague and inchoate, wan ghosts that seek
the substance of institutional form; and it is only from
such splendid failures as Arnold of Brescia, or some
accidently preserved sermon of John Ball, that we can
glean how vital they were to their proponents. They
represent in sum an effort towards a philosophy of
emancipation which, had it been able to secure effective
mechanisms, might well have challenged the medieval
notion of unity at its source. All theories of unified
allegiance are strong precisely because they hew their
way in a system whereby the common life of men is made
possible. Notions of liberty are always in more difficult
case. For their very basis is an admission that men,
not less as groups than as individuals, are united only
by partial bonds. They thus lack the simplicity that the
postulation of some universal centre of control makes
possible; and the loyalties they evoke will, as a consequence, come largely from men who feel the pressure of
the system that obtains. Yet, after all, they are a
struggle to attain in politics the realization of right.
They warn us, as we have grave need to be warned, that

the boundaries of law and morals are not identical.   They represent that final individualism of the human personality for which no system which seeks through law to attain a permanent stability can hope to find room.[18]

There is no medieval thinker who lacks some notion that the community as a whole must be master in its own house.   Power, so we can be told, issues only from the popular will;[19] and appeal will even be made to that fruitful source of mighty opposites the *Corpus Juris* to prove that no right can thereto be superior.[20]   Nor is the theory of a social contract wanting; it is in fact implied in the very substance of feudalism.   The prince's will may have the force of law; but Cicero has only to quote from the Twelve Tables the counter-assertion that the highest law derives from the welfare of the people,[21] to give the basis of an alternative doctrine.   *Populus major principe*, in fact, is a maxim that recurs continually in our texts.[22]   The legislative power is therefore interpreted as being bound by the limitations of popular need;[23] and deposition, even tyrannicide, are the remedies for misgovernment.   The medieval world, in fact, has a genuine conception of popular sovereignty.   As a consequence, the idea of representation is developed in a fashion almost startingly modern.   We hear of popular

[18] For an antithetic point of view, discussed in detail later, cf. Eustace Percy, *The Responsibilities of the League*, esp. pp. 275 f, and Mr. A. E. Zimmern's interesting but dubious defence of its position in the *New Statesman*, January 24, 1919, p. 460.

[19] Mars. Pad., I, 8, 12.   Nich. Cus. III, Ch. 4.

[20] L. 1. Dig., 1, 4; hist. 1, 2, 6. Cf. Aeneas Sylv., Ch. 8.

[21] Cf. Carlyle, *Medieval Polit. Theory*, Vol. I, Ch. 1.

[22] The references are innumerable. Cf. *John of Paris*, Ch. 11 and 16.   Ockham. Dialog. III, 2; I, 27.   Mars. Pad. I, 9.

[23] Ockham, Dial., III, 2; I. 30.

rights incapable of delegation to a part of the people.[24]
Nicholas of Cusa presents us with a parliamentary system
as an inherent element in the state.[25]　Marsiglio of Padua,
almost in the very manner of Rousseau, can see no genuine right to sovereignty save where its exercise is by an
assembly of the people as a whole.[26]

Nor is this all.　The medieval time is full of law;
and the notion of absolute power was carefully limited by
attention to the principles of abstract right.　It cannot,
indeed, be said that this doctrine was at all certain of
its ground.　Natural law was distinguished from the positive law which derived from government with a care
that suggests that the medieval publicist,[27] like the
modern thinker, was baffled by the conflict between ethical
demand and political need.　But it was at least seen
that positive law was a definitely human relationship; and
if the king made binding that which expressed his will,
at least the thought did not disappear that title of
positive law does not possess the right of natural law.[28]
It was, for instance, general medieval doctrine that all
princely acts which go beyond the moral purpose of the
state were null and void.　Bartolus himself, in refining
almost to vanishing point invasions of right, was still, at
the end, driven to admit that they were in truth beyond
destruction.[29]

It is worth while to reiterate that the structure of
medieval society gave emphasis to these notions.　The
attribution of a special instinct for freedom to the Teu-

---

[24] Mars. Pad. 1, 12.　Aquin. Summa. Theol., II, I, 105, a. 1.
[25] Nich. Cus., III, Ch. 4, 12–13.
[26] Mars. Pad., 1, 12–13.
[27] Aq. Summa Theol. II, 1, 90–2.
[28] Ockham, Dial., III, 2; I, Ch. 30.
[29] Bart. Comm. on Dig. Vet., Part I, p. 30, § 22.

tonic peoples is perhaps an unwise guess. But the pervasiveness of the contractual notion in feudalism cannot be without significance. If the lord had rights, he had also duties; and *diffidatio* was a reminder that feudalism and a democratic social contract would not be strange bedfellows. English kings were always making promises of good conduct; and even if they broke them with a striking carelessness, we at least have evidence in the Coronation oath and that strange attempt in Magna Charta at the legalization of rebellion,[30] to show us that the king and the law were not synonymous terms. Bracton himself, indeed, has told us that *lex* is *rex*;[31] his *universitas regni* may, on occasion, find warrant for the use of striking powers.[32] The articles of deposition against a Richard II who had striven to be '*entier empereur dans son roialme*' show a world to which the thought of kingly omnicompetence is still alien;[33] and it is followed by a constitutional experiment which still gives cause for wonder. Radicalism, in truth, was not unknown to the publicists of the medieval time.

Yet these democratic theories do not secure the validation of events. The reason is clear enough. To secure popular rights in any substantial fashion required administrative safeguards which hardly existed before the French Revolution. We can see even before the Reformation the growth of ideas more suited to the prevailing temper of the time. For the medieval period is full of privilege and barriers of a sort which stood in the way of natural territorial unity. The king, to take a natural

30 Ch. 61.
31 Bracton, f., 5b, 107. Cf. *Note-Book*, I, 29–33.
32 Bracton, f., 171b.
33 Rot. Par., III, 417–22.

focal point, emerges as an obvious centre of appeal; and
it is not difficult, by making his power capacious enough
to meet political need, to seek an outlet from inconvenient
immunities. Roman law added its organizing strength
to such apparent need. From the thought of communities we pass to that single community which is the state.
It needs, and gains, the powers which shield it from
destruction. It secures the rights which no law can
impair because, without them, it would cease to be a
state. We may hear of inalienable rights of popular
sovereignty; but metaphysical abstractions are hardly
strong enough to cope with the force of a dominating
personal will. The legists bring their logic to bear upon
the problem. It does not prove difficult to show that
natural limitations mean no more than moral limitations;
and thence it is but a step to urge omnipotence. So even
Wyclif's good man may own the whole world; but in the
face of its possession by graceless men, passive obedience
is his lot. The state is not, until the time of Hobbes,
formally held free from the bondage of moral law; but the
medieval thinker was baffled if the state refused obedience
to it. Doctrinaire Whiggism such as that of Aquinas
was bound to meet the fate of William FitzOsbert.[34]

What happened may perhaps be stated in a slightly
different fashion. The medieval state, it was seen, must
be explained; and variants upon the teleology of Aristotle
were the weapons most apt to the purpose. The individual may be an end in himself — for the Christian notion
of personal salvation has a significance no student of
the history of democracy may forget — but the state also
exists for its own separate purpose. Even with the competing purpose of the Church in view, men like John of

[34] Hoveden, IV, 5.

Paris [35] and Gerson [36] can argue that the purpose of the state is not less nobly moral; while Marsiglio charged it with the care of the good life in a way which seemed to render needless all ecclesiastic function.[37]   But if the state has purpose it must have rights wherewith to guard it; and those rights pass easily into a notion of supremacy.   It was thus an inevitable step to inquire into the technique whereby the purpose may be best effected.

The state, it is clear enough, must have the means of achieving its goal.   Nothing must stand in the path; and whatever the form of organization that obtains, some visible wielder of sovereignty, a people, a prince, an assembly, must be indicated.   The final power in the community is thus collected at a single point within its institutional structure.   To be a member of the community comes to mean to be a member of the state and subject to its claims.   But already its purposes are so wide that the claims of lesser groups are relatively unimportant.   State and society have become equated; or, rather, in the same way as with Hegel, the highest expression of the social purpose has become the state. *Salus populi* means the state's well-being, and the well-being of no other; for it is its nature to be an absorptive animal.   The state becomes self-sufficing, therefore to the state the unique allegiance of the individual is due. It ceases to think of superiority as existent outside itself. The state is that which has no superior, wherefore all other forms of social organization, as guilds for example, are subject to its control.   The dawning sense of nationalism was at hand to give that concept an enviable sharp-

---

[35] John Paris, Ch. 18.
[36] Cf. Schwab, *Johannes Gerson*, p. 88.
[37] Mars. Pad., I, Ch. 4–6.

ness of definition. There was thenceforth to be no lord
of the world, imperial or otherwise, for the simple reason
that there was no single world. There were England,
France, and Spain. The life of each was to be centralized within its ultimate sovereign. The realm of England,
as its Parliament declared, had ever been so free that it
had no earthly sovereign but God alone; [38] and when with
Byzantine majesty it was alleged by Henry VIII that
the realm of England had ever been an empire, it was a
final assertion of the right of the centralized Tudor state
to manage all matters that might arise within its territorial confines.[39]

The group was not destroyed, but put in fetters. The
state emerges, as the middle ages pass, as the institution
to which has been transferred the ideal of unity. The
medieval suspicion of pluralism as anarchic has never
deserted the modern world, but simply removed to the
new basis of all institutions. The change, indeed, came
with much doubt and hesitation. The lawyers, until
Bodin, remained uncertain whether there were not some
shadowy limits to its rights; at least they were uncertain
enough to make of office a property-concept about which
were collected safeguards subversive of complete power.
But the facts went faster than the theories. England
faced the chaos of civil war, and something akin to
personal sovereignty was, with the Tudors, thankfully
accepted as a relief from its manifold oppressions. So,
too, in different perspective, with France and Spain; and
if in Germany imperial centralization broke down, the
significant remedy was a plethora of centralized states.

Here, it may be suggested, is the permanent significance

[38] Cotton's Records, p. 348.
[39] 24 Hen. VIII, Ch. 12.

of Machiavelli. The medieval thinker grew to see that
the national state was necessary to achieve the perfect
life. But Machiavelli saw that to live well it must first
have the means to live; and he painted in relentless phrase
the arts of government. He summarized a development
perhaps longer than he knew. The wearisome search for
abstract right was largely impotent before concrete power
and grasping ambition. While the Councils of Basle
and of Constance were struggling with eternal principles,
the centralized bureaucracy of Rome could give a peace
which, if not ideal, was at least a breathing-space. Efficiency is ever more apt than right to action. Nor did
Machiavelli fail to notice that the power of popular
sovereignty was too unconscious to be capable of effective
exercise. He saw that achievement rested with the men
who, like Caesar Borgia, moved from the immediate purpose clearly seen to the power consciously at hand. He
sacrificed an interest in eternal right to the practical
rights that *de facto* power so easily obtained. Nor was
his volume other than a generalization from the hard
facts of his age.

The state thus became the heir of the *Respublica
Christiana;* yet what its power should be, events rather
than men were to determine. It had transcended all communities within its territory. It had secured some single
organ as the necessary channel for the expression of its
will. It had postulated as essential the direct allegiance
of the individual citizen. But there were still problems.
If the universal church no longer possessed the majesty of
old, it still was universal. What if it even yet stood
firmly against the invasion of its sovereign prerogative?
Nor is this all. The state was growing free from limitations of a legal kind upon its power. But moral limit

dies with slowness and men were still accustomed to the majesty of ethical claim. What was needed was a midsummer of high credit for the state. What was demanded was a crisis which should threaten its existence from without, and thus make deep appeal to that primitive herd-instinct which calls men to the defence of their own. Here the significance of nationality became apparent, for it gave to the glorification of the state an emotional penumbra it could have secured in no other fashion. All crises are unfavorable to liberty; and it was only through the medium of external attack that the state could shake itself free from the fetters that remained.

III

The needed solvent was provided by the Reformation. It is one of the outstanding paradoxes of history that a movement which sought ecclesiastical purification through the medium of the individual conscience should yet have resulted in a greater measure of state-power. Yet the paradox admits of simple explanation. Luther demanded of an obstinate church reforms it was unwilling to concede. Its refusal meant an appeal to the imperial power. But the emperor, with a complex foreign policy to manœuvre, hesitated at an increase of its problems. Thence Luther, by a simple evolution, was driven to make application to the prince of the empire. The Church, however, was divine; and an institution thus circumstanced only power similarly divine could change. Inevitably, therefore, Luther was compelled to re-assert the divine character of princely power. When to his claim was added the plea of territoriality in religion, all the materials were at hand for subsequent events. Luther's doctrines, doubt-

less, were a two-edged weapon; for, they admitted, as in
the Peasant's Revolt, interpretation in a democratic way
if men looked only to their theologic substance. The
peasant's defeat, and the warm welcome given by Luther
to their opponents' victory, emphasized the autocratic
aspect of his view. What at bottom had been asserted
was the right of the state, through the person of its
prince, to cleanse the Church of sin. Such claim implied
absorption; and Henry VIII did no more than give the
fullest expression that generation was to see of the new
Erastianism in action.

Yet, obviously enough, the Lutheran doctrine was
rather the chance weapon of a specialized encounter than
a generalization from a fully realized political philosophy.
The latter is the outcome of the Counter-Reformation.
Wars on behalf of religious principle brought death and
misery in their train. Political existence seemed in jeopardy unless the full allegiance of men to a unified state
could be secured beyond dispute. It might even, as Elizabeth saw in England, and the *Politiques* in France, be
necessary to admit the expediency of toleration so long
only as the right of the state to live as a self-sufficient
organization could be secured. And that, at bottom, is
the broad result of the second half of the sixteenth century. Each state adopts its special creed; and those who
differ are given a grudging right to their existence. But
right now has a special connotation. It is the right
conferred by an Act of Parliament, or of an edict registered by the Parliament and King of France. It is, that
is to say, a concession rendered by the state to some
group of its subjects whose destruction would be less
profitable than the exertion might warrant. The right,
that is to say, is in its nature legal. We have moved from

the medieval ground of universal ethical right to which the
state itself must bow, to a right of law which the state,
through its sovereign organ, is alike privileged to make
and to interpret.

Bodin expresses in the clearest fashion the theory to
which we have moved. His book, for that very reason,
is normally taken as the starting-point of modern politics;
for what he teaches is, with some difference of detail,
substantially the modern legal theory of the state. Nor
may we deny it a logical completeness within the narrow
realm it attempts to resume. "All the characteristics
of sovereignty," said Bodin,[40] "are contained in this, to
have power to give laws to each and everyone of his subjects, and to receive none from them." The sovereign
may be one or few or many, but unless it is an absolute
power, it lacks the marks of *majestas*. A long history
lies before those words. From Bodin and through
Hobbes to Austin, every legal analysis of the state has
depended upon their substance. Nor is it possible, in the
sphere of positive law, to refute it. *Jus est quod jussum
est* is of the essence of the state. There must be in every
organized political community some definite authority not
only habitually obeyed, but also itself beyond the reach
of authority. A law which secured the obedience of
men only on some chance whim of temper would obviously
lack the sanction which political life demands. A
sovereignty, moreover, which was divided between a number of coördinate authorities would lack for its commands
that generality of universal application by which alone
it can be distinguished from a private will. This it is
which Hobbes saw with relentless clearness; a will, to be
sovereign, must be all or nothing. This, too, is the head

[40] *De la Republique,* Bk., 1, Ch. 8.

and centre of Marshall's constitutional decisions. A sovereign people cannot suffer derogation from the effective power of its instruments. Habitual disobedience, a legal right of challenge, would reduce it to no more than that hopeful influence which Washington at once rightly and with care distinguished from government. A church or a trade-union has a will. But over the area they govern their wills are subject to appeal and therefore less than sovereign. The courts do not obey their mandates; or, rather, they look to state-texts before they give them confirmation.

So stated, Bodin's theory is unimpeachable. Yet we must not forget with what grave difficulty it made its way. To the question why men must obey the law, it answered only because the state so willed; and it therein forgot that the law, in its view, was no more than the command of the state. There were men unwilling to accept so simple a solution. Even Bodin himself, it may be remarked, has doubts of its adequacy; for he makes state-law morally bound by natural law and the law of God. Nor must we forget the general background of his argument. He was rescuing a state which seemed like to perish before the conflict of competing sects from the challenge to its existence their conflict implied. Huguenot and Ligueur alike prevented a peace a pervading and unimpeachable authority can alone secure; and when he gave his prince these attributes, he was in truth attempting their reconciliation. It is important to remember this very practical aspect of Bodin's work. He was not merely making a scientific analysis of the sovereign power. He was teaching also that a representative assembly — a States-General, for example — is no more than a useful organ for the registration of grievance.

He was interested in the prevalence of that brigandage
which, as he argued, the contemporary law of treason did
so much to promote. He has advice of value to offer to
his age on methods of preventing those revolutions to
which it was so lamentably prone. Bodin, in fact, was
above all a practical inquirer into the political sickness
of the time. The sovereignty he defined was conceived
less with a view to the metaphysics of his subject, than
as a weapon wherewith to make possible the special
remedies of which he was the advocate.

Nor was this all. To say, as Bodin said, that the
state must be obeyed because it is a state, was to reduce
the problem of political obedience within confines more
narrow than many were then willing to admit. Behind
the problem of legal superiority there was, for most, the
problem of that religious freedom legal superiority was
often so willing to deny. The basis of law, that is to
say, was still for most a theological-political inquiry.
Those who admitted the divinity of kings, as the Hugue-
nots after 1589, were mainly men who profited religiously
by their admission. It did not help a Calvinist in Holland
or a Jesuit in England to admit such doctrine. A Catholic answer, for example, to James I, or a defence of
Dutch resistance against the might of Spain was inevitably compelled to proceed upon different lines. Law,
for both, was compelled to assume a moral basis which
no purely legal fiat can pretend to claim. A law which
once derived from God or from the eternal principles
of nature could not easily suffer reduction to the confines
of a will too often that of a single human being. That
notion of some right anterior to the sovereign and acting
as the criterion of its substance has none, of course, of
the simplicity which attaches to Bodin's analysis. By its

very statement, indeed, it may be regarded as subversive of authority; for its primary implication is a doubt whether, before examination of its substance, the command should be obeyed.[41]

For, clearly, a Catholic like Rossaeus,[42] who sought a loophole for the admission of the papal power, could find no comfort in a doctrine which, in its final result, equated legality and right for the sake of peace. His starting-point, and it was that of Presbyterians such as Buchanan also, was that right was greater than peace. Struggling for a freedom that an admitted *a priori* pre-eminence of the state would have denied, what he sought was first to show that consent is of the essence of community, and next to argue that the only form in which consent is institutionally satisfactory is where sovereignty is admittedly popular in its nature. But popular sovereignty as an administrative problem will issue always in limitation upon the sovereign power that functions in the daily business of the state. Or, rather, it will be shown, as it is in substance argued by all the Monarchomachs, that the conception of unlimited power is impossible of equation with an ethical conception of right. This argument can take the most diverse forms. Francis Hotman, in the *Franco-Gallia*, sought to give the theory of popular sovereignty an historic basis by an analysis of previous French history in democratic terms. Althusius urged that ultimate power being always in the people, the active ruler is no more than what the delegation of his office makes him; and the chief magistrate of Emden must have been well acquainted with the narrow limits of a delegated power.

[41] Cf. my paper on the "Political Theory of James I" in the *Political Science Quarterly* for June, 1919.

[42] Cf. Figgis, *From Gerson to Grotius*, p. 182 f.

It is noteworthy — it is also natural — that all these counter-theories to Bodin's should mainly have sought the means of religious freedom. Had Bodin made the sovereign powerless in the realm of spiritual things, the passionate search for release from the toils of his logic would doubtless have been absent. But then his sovereign would have lacked *majestas,* which had been defined as omnicompetence. Yet, in truth, the history of England in the seventeenth century shows clearly that the acceptance of conditions upon which religious peace was possible made the theory of parliamentary sovereignty a commonplace within two generations. The source of the struggle, that is to say, against his doctrine lay in that sphere of experience in which men's deepest passions were then engaged. It needed only the great weariness of most, and a generous insight such as that of William III to secure the self-denying ordinance of the Toleration act. Thenceforth, the sovereignty of the English state had, for formal law, no barriers in its way. Nor was it without suggestiveness that the first revolutionary constitution of France should enounce a doctrine that is, in essence, indistinguishable from the English theory.[43]

IV

What, in fact, the removal of the religious problem seems to connote is the appearance of a ground where all possessed of citizenship may meet in common. That was the basis of Bodin's effort, and, at bottom, it is the large outlines of his theory that were accepted. But the problem was in fact more difficult than such statement would indicate. It made the state sovereign, but it did not de-

[43] Constit. of 1791, Art. II, 2.

fine the state with sharpness. Those, therefore, whom the pressure of events compelled to take refuge in more liberal theories, Althusius for example, discovered in the people as a whole the roots of the state. The Jesuit affection for popular sovereignty rests upon their clear conception that once the consent of the people to governmental acts may be regarded as but partial, the straight path lies open for papal interference. The doctrine of a social contract, in short, is, above all, a doctrine of limitation upon the governmental power. It was upon this that the acute mind of Hobbes seized. His stay upon the continent had doubtless given him acquaintance with the subtle fashion in which the papal defenders destroyed the serene confidence of the state in its sovereign separateness. His task it therefore was to make the social contract the vehicle of despotism. His is the first book in which a final specific of order is erected upon the basis of popular consent. How admirable his method was Sir Robert Filmer has testified when even his horror of the source in which Hobbes discovered power could not withhold admiration from the method of its exercise.[44] Yet the facts were stronger than the simplicity of Hobbes' formula.

It is clear from any primary analysis that the essence of the state turns upon the reciprocal relations of government and citizens. A state, after all, is fundamentally a territorial society divided into government and subjects. As matter of law that government may possess unlimited power; in actual fact there will always be a system of conditions it dare not attempt to transgress. Yet, often enough, a government will seek to pass beyond those boundaries. James II made that effort, and the result

44 Observations Concerning the Original of Government.

was the English Revolution.   The work of Locke only repeats the earlier protests of men like Sydney and 'Julian' Johnson.   There is some degree of popular consent which may not suffer degradation.   Locke seeks to wrest the palm of logical right from the brow of Hobbes by showing that the results of unlimited power destroy the possibility of its admission.   He realized well enough that the organ which transacts the daily business of the state will possess the main influence.   Sovereignty — Locke does not use the word — flows always towards the centre of administration.   That is why so much of Locke's thinking turned upon limitations of governmental power.   That was why, not only for himself, but for all his successors to the time of Rousseau, the legal theory of sovereignty proved always too narrow for final acceptance.   It would not work because the turning-point in political judgment was less the right to will than the substance of the thing willed by the organ to which ultimate power was confided.   Locke's view was satisfactory so long as Walpole gave England peace and Chatham gave her victories.   The effort of government fitted what of popular desires was discoverably articulate.   But after the attempt of George III to pervert constitutional forms to despotic purpose the view of Locke was in its turn inadequate.   A new formula was needed for a state of which the roots had spread beyond the voting audience.[45]

The birth of modern English radicalism that is symbolized by the foundation of the *Society for the Support of the Bill of Rights* saw the full recognition of Rousseau's influence.   The resident of a state in which the will of all had been narrowed to the expression of royal desire, his generous nature was revolted at a technique by which the

[45] Cf. my *Political Thought from Locke to Bentham*, Chs. 2 and 5.

popular good failed of general achievement. He wrote, accordingly, the antithesis of Hobbes' view. What impressed him was the fact that once the final power passes from the people's hands the will which secures expression is always a will that represents a special private interest. That will might, as in the France of Louis XV, be secure enough to win its way; but Rousseau did not stay at order as the final end. What he sought was justice; and his theory of the general will is the mechanism whereby justice may be attained. Its effect is immediate and striking. Priestley and Price in England go back at once to the full vigor of popular sovereignty for the roots of right. Law is no longer, for them, a command, but rather the expression of general consent to measures which satisfy general need. The inadequacy of legal right involves the rejection of the order it maintains. The great effort of Burke was his attempt to show that the legal order cannot thus easily be rejected. It is not, he urged, a simple question of supplanting inherited wrong. It is rather a problem of whether the novelties secured are likely, given the human materials with which we have to work, to be an improvement upon the accredited institutions of the past. What he denied in Rousseau was the latter's willingness to force political problems within a simple set of categories. Therein, most patently, Burke was right. The general will in which Rousseau put his confidence is impossible of discovery outside the parish. And Godwin, of Rousseau's disciples by far the most logical, was willing to draw the obvious conclusion and refuse the right of power outside the parish. Therein all action may be born of free consent. Once its boundaries are overpassed, the element of coercion enters. The will which operates does not merge our personality within

itself. For us it is restraint; and Godwin argued that
the limitation is ever exercised in the interest of private
selfishness.

Certainly the notion of a general will, as it is shaped
in Rousseau's hands, has little of value to contribute to
the problem. If it means that right must prevail, it
dwells in the realm of purpose without necessarily effecting its realization. If, as Rousseau would seem to imply,
it means majority-rule there are few of temper bold
enough to argue that majorities are always in the right.
But there is a more difficult problem which Rousseau
consistently evaded. The modern state must confide its
governance to relatively few hands. The prevailing will
is therefore, and inevitably, no more than a random
sample of that congery of wills of which it is composed.
And, for the purpose of law it is to that prevailing will
that sovereignty must be intrusted. Such a conclusion,
indeed, Rousseau scouted with scorn; the English people,
he declared, are free only at election time. Yet, upon
the scale of modern life, the alternative of direct government is unthinkable. What we can do is to insure
that those who wield the sovereign power derive from a
wider circle than at any previous time. We can be
tolerably secure that the influences which guide them, the
interests they will weigh, are less simple than before the
events of 1789. The sense of responsibility, the penalty
for perversion, go deeper than at any previous time.
The wills, that is to say, to which respect is due are more
numerous than in the past. The subconscious limitations
with which the governing power is surrounded are more
complex than when politics was the privileged possession
of a leisured class. That, at bottom, is the debt we owe
to Rousseau's teaching. The purpose he had in view

was, at least ultimately, as inescapable as its proposed
mechanism was fruitless. What he made impossible was
any final maintenance of those legal privileges by which
the existence of a decaying system is prolonged.

v

The foundations of sovereignty are, after Rousseau's
time, most largely conceived in terms of the synthesis
he envisaged. Bentham and Austin, at bottom, did little
more than translate the purpose he desired into the special
legal institutions adapted to their time. The state, with
them as with him, differs from every other form of
organization in that it defines a common ground upon
which the interests of men may be held identical. The
lawyers present us with a state whose sovereign organ
has unlimited and irresistible power. The philosophers
have reinforced the legal concept by drawing attention
to the greatness of the purpose by which the state has
been informed. They express, so to speak, the unexplored teleology of the legal system. The lawyer merely
describes the ultimate source of rights; the philosopher
justifies that source by an analysis of the mission it
implies. In either case, the hypothesis is one of unity.
In any conflict, the state is, *a priori,* bound to triumph
because the aspect of man that it expresses is common
to us all. For the state as a philosophic conception,
there is neither Jew nor Greek, neither bond nor free.
We meet there upon the common ground of identical
citizenship. That is why the state is held to be the
ultimate expression of the social bond. All other forms
of organization have a certain partial character about
them. The state embraces all men by its territorial na-

ture. It is universal because it is the one compulsory
form of association.

Yet, in such an outlook, the implied historic background of this assertion can hardly be said to have
been thoroughly explored. The national state made use
of unity as a weapon against the aggression of Rome.
It used unity as an instrument in an international controversy; to survive against the furious tides of Reformation and Counter-Reformation the national state
was driven to be one and indivisible. For such a conflict, the hypothesis of unity, with the structure it implies, has a meaning too valuable to admit denial.

But to move from that unified sovereignty which is a
protective against external attack to the more complex
problems of internal arrangement has no necessary validity. Internal change is movement against the interests
of an existing order which the sovereignty of the state
is, as a matter of history, used always to preserve. Its
legal right to be merges without the necessary inquiry
into ethical justification. Some, as Hobbes, may argue
that the price of resistance is always greater than the
value it obtains. Others, as T. H. Green, may urge that
we confront the state in fear and awe because the pre-
sumption in resistance is always against us. Others
again, as Bosanquet, may give the state unquestioned
right upon the ground that, ultimately, it will come to
summarize the best of ourselves. Yet the simple fact is
that from the standpoint of internal relations the true
heart of a state is its government; and the unity it represents is not so much the interest of its subjects as a
whole as of that part which dominates the economic life
of its members. England, France, America, mean on
domestic issues a complex of interests which struggle

among themselves for survival.   In any realistic analysis
there is no necessary unity of purpose between the groups
we there discover.   The wills we meet are aiming at
achievement which often involves the destruction of the
legal order maintained by government.   There is no
relevant unity between the England conceived by Ireton
and the England of the Levellers.   There is no common
ground upon which Cobden and Lord George Bentinck
could meet.   The Anglican Church of the seventeenth
century did not seek to confer the means of the good life
upon the Nonconformists.   The noblesse of the Ancien
Régime did not seek to share the means of happiness with
the common people.   Those who possessed political power
on the eve of the Reform Bill in 1832 did not understand
by the good life what it meant to Robert Owen or Francis
Place.   The will that secures expression seems always to
be a partial will seeking not so much a general benefit
as to use the vital organ of the state for its private purpose.   That is not, of course, to say that general benefit
may not be conferred.   That is not even to argue that
there may not be an objective common good transcen-
dentally better than the private goods secured.   But in
actual political conflict the sovereignty of the state means
the sovereignty of government.   The weapons at its
disposal consistently register a good not merely in fact
but in purpose also more narrow than the teleology of
the state would seem to warrant.

The fact is that the state as an external unit seeking
survival in a world of states is never the same to its
members as that same state in the ebb and flow of its
internal daily life.   The relations of its parts are, in
this latter aspect, unified neither in aim nor method.
What the orthodox theory of sovereignty has done is

to coerce them into an unity and thereby to place itself at the disposal of the social group which, at any given historic moment, happens to dominate the life of the state. It is not necessary to believe with Gibbon that history is an unrelieved record of crime to urge that it is full of instances where private well-being is consistently victorious not merely over public need but also over public right. That is why the legal theory of sovereignty can never offer a basis for a working philosophy of the state. For a legal theory of sovereignty takes its stand upon the beatification of order; and it does not inquire — it is not its business to inquire — into the purposes for which order is maintained. The foundations of sovereignty must strike deeper roots if they are to give us a true philosophy. Above all we shall need inquiry into the psychological impulses it is the business of social organization to satisfy. The instruments with which we work bear upon their face the marks of a crisis in which men sought at all costs release from the misery of religious difference. They do not suit a temper in which the development of initiative in the humble man is the main effort of the time. The liberty they gained was specialized to the epoch in which the recognition of difference was possible without material consequence to individual personality. Since at least the Industrial Revolution that day has passed. The main effort is in a direction which challenges the legal rights established by prescription in the name of an equality for which our institutions are unsuited. The implied corollary of our purpose is the widespread distribution of power. It will need a new philosophy of the state to satisfy the institutions that purpose will demand.

THE PROBLEM OF ADMINISTRA-
TIVE AREAS *

I

IT has become almost a commonplace that we have reached a critical epoch in the history of representative government. Certainly no man would now claim that the large aspirations of those who, with Bentham and the radicals, fought the great battle of parliamentary reform in the early part of the nineteenth century have been to any adequate degree fulfilled.[1] They are, indeed, different; for the direction taken by political activities in the last fifty years has been almost antithetic to that which he would have approved. The English state has become a positive state; by which is meant that instead of trusting to the interplay of possibly conflicting self-interests for the realization of good, it has embarked upon an effort, for some time at least to come, definitive, to control the national life by governmental regulation. We have reached the end of that period in which the influence of *laissez-faire* could, in any full sense, be detected.[2] Measures today seem politically and economically axiomatic which, to the age of Bentham, would have seemed the

* Reprinted from the *Smith College Studies*, Vol. IV, No. 1.
[1] Cf. Wallas, *Human Nature in Politics;* Introduction.
[2] Cf. Dicey, *Law and Public Opinion* (2nd. ed.); Introduction.

very nadir of statesmanship. It may be said without much fear of exaggeration that no single figure in the first half of the nineteenth century, with the doubtful exception of Disraeli, had any accurate prevision of the trend that has been taken by modern legislation. They were too near the intellectual dogmas of the Industrial Revolution to view state-action with any confidence; and Lord Morley, albeit unconsciously, has vividly illustrated the failure both of Cobden and Gladstone to understand the basic social questions. Nor is it yet certain that the effort made by the state towards the relief of social distress has behind it the dominant sympathy of experienced thinkers in our day. The new theory of the state limps far behind its practice.[3]

This is true not merely of England alone. In France and Germany the period of *laissez-faire* has long passed its apogee; and, whatever its origins, the social insurance of modern Germany has been a remarkable example of administrative ability. Even the United States has emerged from the uncritical individualism of a pioneer civilization to give demonstration of the social experiment made possible by a federal system. Australian democracy is a special study in itself; but, in things like the Court of Industrial Arbitration which has been made so significant by the wise administration of Mr. Justice Higgins,[4] its connection with this stream of thought has been obvious. Canada is less typical of this attitude; but the dominance of collectivist legislation is even here beyond dispute.

[3] Though it lies implicit in the writings of men like Green and Bosanquet in one school of thought and in the new liberalism of men like Mr. J. A. Hobson and Professor L. T. Hobhouse in another.

[4] See his article in the *Harvard Law Review* for November, 1916.

The change, particularly in England, bears witness to a striking reversal of emphasis; nor is it unfair to suggest that it implies a very real increase in humanitarian sentiment. A statesman, indeed, who endeavored to discuss the problems of poverty in a modern House of Commons with the underlying implications even of such radicals as Hume in one age or Bright in the next, would hardly be assured of an attentive hearing. The whole basis of our social philosophy has altered in a sense that can only be appreciated by a close comparison of a series of years in the parliamentary debates.

What has happened is the emergence of what Mr. Graham Wallas has happily termed The Great Society.[5] It was only in the forty years after 1870 that the full force of the Industrial Revolution began to be felt; it was only after the Reform Bills of 1867 and 1884 that the influence of a working-class electorate could be perceived in the tendencies of legislation. It is not, in truth, unfair to suggest that the measures which were concessions before 1867 were necessities afterwards. The attitude of a government to the Taff Vale decision could not help being influenced by the solid array of hundreds of thousands of voters opposed to it; and it is possible that even Mr. Balfour's immovability would have been different had not a general election given him, just previously, a new lease of power. It is no exaggeration to suggest that the measure produced in answer to the demands of labor would have been perhaps unintelligible, and certainly provocative of indignation to Mr. Gladstone and his colleagues some twenty years before. Even to the Royal Commission on Labour, in 1894, standing as it did on the

5 The first chapter of his book, *The Great Society*, seems to me the type-chart which every investigator must follow.

threshold of *Temperton* v. *Russell*[6] and *Allen* v. *Flood*,[7] it would have seemed reprehensibly audacious.

If there is thus a shift in perspective, it has not produced a greater degree of contentment. Rather may it be urged that with the growth of popular education — and it is well to remember that the first generation educated in the public elementary schools has barely passed the threshold of middle age — there has come an increasing desire for the amelioration of the disparities of social life.[8] In broad terms, there has been added to the characteristic English belief in certain practical and definite liberties a new confidence in the value of certain practical and definite equalities. The decline, for example, of the individualistic attitude to wealth in the last generation has been wholly remarkable. It is possible that the historian of the future will find the securest traces of this change in the study of the successive budgets of the last thirty years.[9] He will compare the ideals of Mr. Gladstone as Chancellor of the Exchequer with the ideals of Mr. Lloyd-George. He will note the attitude of Mr. Sidney Webb to grants-in-aid,[10] in our own day and that of Lord Avebury a generation before.[11] He will be compelled to conclude that the State, through the agency of government, has directly undertaken the control of the

6 [1893] I. Q. B. (C. A.) 715.

7 [1898] A. C. I.

8 See, for instance, the remarkable speech of Mr. J. McTavish reprinted in the appendix to Mr. Albert Manstridge's *University Tutorial Classes*. The same note is apparent in the more recent volume of Mr. Henderson: *The Aims of Labor*.

9 As revealed, for example, in Mr. Bernard Mallet's useful volume: *British Budgets*.

10 See his *Grants in Aid*, especially the last chapter.

11 Cf. his remark quoted by Mr. Graham Wallas in his preface to Mr. R. G. Bannington's *Public Health Administration*.

national life; but he will be at least equally compelled to
doubt whether it has thereby solved any of the really
basic problems that confront us.

It may be admitted that we have had, as yet, no such
period of marked disturbance as characterized the lean
and hungry years after Waterloo; but there has been no
comparable epoch, until our own day, of similar economic
dislocation.   Even as it is, the period after the advent of
socialized liberalism in 1906 has been marked by a rest-
lessness on the part of organized labor of which the
dangerous proportions have again and again been noted.[12]
Observers, indeed, have not been wanting to suggest that
we have reached the point where a transference of economic power from the middle class to the workers will
take place;[13] exactly as, in the half-century after the
Napoleonic wars, the squirearchy was replaced by the
manufacturers of the North of England.

The truth surely is that we have evolved the great
society without any safeguards that our political institutions would keep pace with the changes in social and
economic structure.   No one who examines the large outlines of the English governmental system can point to
any vast discoveries.   Differences, of course, there are,
and some of them are fundamental.   The emergence of
a labor party, the transference of the centre of political
power from the House of Commons to the Cabinet, the
consolidation of that pre-eminence given by Mr. Gladstone's long career to the office of Prime Minister, a
superb improvement in the quality of the civil service,

---

12 Cf. Cole, *The World of Labor,* Chs. 1, 2.
13 Cf. especially Leroy's *Les transformations de la Puissance
Publique,* and Duguit, *Les transformations du Droit Public.* A
translation of this book has been published by B. W. Huebsch.

these, and things like these, have an importance no
man may deny. But no small part of these changes
has been due to the breakdown of the main hypothesis
upon which the democracy of the nineteenth century was
founded.

Here, once more, it was the influence of Bentham and
his followers that was decisive.[14] They believed that all
men were more or less equal in their original endowments,
and that differences were the product of environment.
The more training was equalized, the more power would
be distributed in just proportions throughout the State.
Universal suffrage and the breakdown of social privilege
thus assumed a very vital significance. Once the factors
of depression were removed the natural equalities of men
would manifest themselves, and the reason of their enlightened self-interest would effect the improvement
desired. Bentham expected the average citizen to take
an interest in politics which would be based upon a
considered judgment of the questions at issue. That
may have been more possible than it is now in the negative
period before 1870;[15] but, certainly, since that time it
has been purely idle as a valid expectation. Conditions
have become so complex that no one can follow any problem in its different bearings without an unremitting attention. The average voter could not afford to give the
time to the consideration of affairs that their actual
understanding demanded; nor had his education been, on
any large scale, adapted to the needs of citizenship.

Mr. Croly has explained in an incisive work [16] how the

[14] Cf. Mr. Wallas' remarks in *Human Nature in Politics, passim,*
and especially pp. 199 seq.

[15] Certainly, I think, the quality of parliamentary debate was
higher.

[16] *The Promise of American Life,* pp. 117–126.

same conditions held in the United States. The founders of the Jacksonian democracy had exactly the same expectations as the Benthamite radicals of the possibilities of the "average man"; and it was for precisely similar reasons that they were falsified. But whereas in America the result was, on the one hand, the divorce of industry and politics, save by indirect relation, and, on the other, the growth of what is termed the "boss-system," in England that was only partly the case. There did, indeed, continue that not unbenevolent connection between politics and society which has given to English official life no small part of its charm. But it made less for the emergence of a special political class than for the increasing importance of the lawyer in politics and the need for a larger and more highly-trained civil service. Both these conditions have been fulfilled; and the English civil service before the war was probably the sole example in history of an efficient bureaucracy capable of liberalism.

But, as the State thrust more and ever wider functions upon government, even these provisions became inadequate to the burden. The fundamental hypothesis of government in a representative system is that it is government by discussion. The private member of Parliament was supposed, as in Burke's magnificent conception, to use his best judgment upon the bills presented by government, and to vote as the dictates of his instructed mind would seem to warrant. There has never, of course, been a time in which such an ideal could have been even approximately realized; and, certainly, anyone who reads the history of the first forty years of George III's reign will have cause to deny that any degeneration has taken place. But parliamentary government in the twentieth century is still essentially different from parliamentary government in the nineteenth. The change seems to date from the emergence of Mr. Parnell; but the impetus he gave to that change is no more than its beginning.

No one, in fact, who considers, however superficially, the working of the English parliamentary system can doubt that some of its defects are fundamental. The independence of the private member has, for practical purposes, disappeared.[17] The rigidity of party ties has notably been increased.[18] The reality of debate has been largely impaired by the simple necessity of getting business done. It is a commonplace to note the apathy of those not actively engaged in working the machinery of party. The unreality of party distinctions is at least as obvious as in the days when George III deliberately aimed at their obliteration.[19] Before such issues as Home Rule and Woman Suffrage that party government which Bagehot declared the vital principal of representative government was simply bankrupt. The books are everywhere full of lamentation upon these inadequacies. Mr. Graham Wallas, Sir Sidney Low, Mr. Ostrogorski, are equally emphatic that any unlimited satisfaction with the workings of democratic government is impossible. A large section of English labor even denies any real validity to the processes of the political state.[20]

Not, be it noted, that this sentiment is confined to England alone. The problem of representative government in France is perhaps even more passionately debated

---

[17] Cf. Low, *Governance of England*, Chs. 4, 5.

[18] Lowell, *Government of England*, II, 70 ff.

[19] Cf. Low, *op. cit.*, 126 f.

[20] Cf. *The Miner's Next Step* for the best English discussion of this attitude.

than in England; and what is significantly called *"la malaise de la démocratie"* is there even more distressingly apparent.[21] The conference of universal suffrage upon the Italian electorate has not brought results of any striking character. The principles of democracy secure almost universal acceptance in the United States; but there is nowhere any profound content with its workings.[22] The case of Germany is different since there it has been only an approximation to responsible government that was established; and Russia, until our own day, was the only surviving example in Western civilization, of an unlimited autocracy. It should perhaps be added that the working of the Russian system was calculated to promote a confidence as unlimited in the rightness of the democratic faith.

In whatever analysis is made of the conditions of the modern representative system, two facts stand out with striking clarity. On the one hand, it is obvious that there is no deliberative assembly that is not utterly overwhelmed by the multiplicity of its business; on the other hand, it is at least equally clear that the average elector, except in times of crisis or abnormal excitement, is but partially interested in the political process. Nor have the attempts to cure the latter evil, which have mainly, as in Switzerland and the United States, taken the form of experiments in direct government, been at all remarkable for their success. The statistics make it evident that the voter is more interested in persons than in events, and the very size of the modern state makes direct

21 Cf. Guy-Grand, *Le Procès de la Démocratie* for a good summary of the controversy.

22 Mr. Croly's *Progressive Democracy* admirably analyzes the problem.

government, at the best, but a partial aid.[23] Much more
is to be said for the possibilities of an adequate educational system on the one hand, and an increased leisure
on the other. Certainly we too little realize how piti-
fully small is the relation between the problems of modern
politics and the curriculum of that elementary school
which is alone compulsory for the next decade. Modern
studies in the problem of industrial fatigue [24] explain how
little of intellectual value can usefully, or even rightly,
be expected from a population whose energy is so largely
consumed in the simple task of earning its own living.
Something, too, might here be said of the relation of
work to that energy of the soul which Aristotle pro-
claimed the secret of happiness.[25] Certainly such evidence as we have tends to suggest that the increasing
subordination of the worker to the machine does not
improve the intellectual quality of our civilization. Indeed, it is not impossible that, in the future, democracy,
if it is to become an effective instrument, will be compelled
to transfer the centre of importance for at least a large
part of its manual workers from the hours of labor to
the hours of leisure. But that day is not yet.

Nearly a century ago, the profoundest French observer
of the last age analyzed the potentialities of that democracy which, as he predicted, was destined to become the
universal type of government. An aristocrat both by
birth and by nature, but little capable of that enthusiasm
for the multitude with which men so diverse as Gambetta

23 Cf. Lowell, *Public Opinion and Popular Government*, Chs.
11–15.

24 Cf. Goldmark, *Industrial Fatigue*, for a convenient summary of
recent research.

25 Cf. Wallas, *The Great Society*, Ch. 13, where the whole question
is brilliantly analyzed.

and Gladstone were so signally endowed, de Tocqueville could not regard its advent with unmixed gladness.[26] He found himself depressed by the prospect of certain dangerous contingencies. It was possible, he thought,[27] that a people might barter its responsibility for its own government in exchange for material comfort. Democratic rule might degenerate into simple majority rule without any safeguard that the majority would include the best opinion of which the society was capable. A jealous level of dull uniformity might depress the use by each citizen of his utmost talents for the common good. The richness and variety of the national life might well be drawn into the vortex of a governmental omniscience which would emulate a theological authority. The real object of a state, he thought,[28] was the emancipation of individuality; and he did not believe in the possibility of its attainment where the character of its government was a centralized and mercantile parliamentarism. He feared the influence of money upon its politics. He saw with distress the decline of religious faith without any accompanying compensation in the form of social sanctions. He perceived the novelty of the change effected by the Revolution; "a new political science," he said,[29] "is necessary to this new world."

It is difficult to deny the truth of his general attitude. Certainly the best approach to the defence of democracy is through the analysis of previous social systems. For the real justification of a democratic state is, after all, the fact that under its aegis a larger number of men share

[26] On de Tocqueville's democracy, the reader can consult the useful, if laborious, volume of Pierre Marcel, *Essai Politique sur Alexis de Tocqueville.*

[27] See the vital Ch. 5 of the fourth part of *Democracy in America.*

[28] *Ibid*, Part II, Ch. 5.   [29] *Ibid,* preface.

in the riches life can offer than under any alternative.
Nevertheless the evils predicted by de Tocqueville remain,
and it is difficult to see any immediate prospect of their
amelioration. Certainly in relation to the actual quality
of life, the things for which the interest of men can be
obtained, it is only to the slow influence of education
that we can look for change. Nothing would be more
fatal to the working of democratic government than a
permanent divorce between the process of politics and
the life that is led by the mass of men. The professional
politician is clearly necessary in the task of administration; but it would result in the negation of the democratic
hypothesis, if the making of policy were not conducted
with the active coöperation of the body of citizens. That
does not, indeed, imply that rotation of office in which
the Greek states placed so large a confidence and for
which the American commonwealth still cherishes so
singular and so dangerous an affection. Rather does it
imply the perpetual and widespread discussion of men
and measures, the ceaseless instruction of the public
mind, at which Harrington aimed in the clubs that formed
so attractive an element in his Utopia.[30] It means the
continuous existence of an urgent public opinion.

That is, as Mr. Wallas has recently shown,[31] no easy
matter. There are problems — the nature of electricity,
for example — upon which a public opinion cannot, in
the nature of things, be formed. There are others in
which a public opinion seems possible upon matters of
principle but, to say the least, extremely difficult on
matters of detail. Thus far, it must be admitted we
have done but little to utilize, in any full degree, the

[30] *Oceana* (ed. Toland), pp. 157–60.
[31] *Human Nature in Politics*, Part I.

material we have. The elements that go to the making of a political decision are rarely considered enough, on the one hand, or widespread enough, on the other, to make an external and detached observer convinced that the process by which that decision is reached is at all satisfactory. We have not, indeed, descended so low as that "man of superhuman mental activity managing the affairs of a mentally passive people," which Mill thought [32] the "most pernicious misconception of good government"; but, still, the number of people upon whom a decision depends, the number whose thoughts have to be weighed and consulted, is curiously small.

Nor, save in one regard, is the tendency to its increase. That exception is important. It is an obvious fact that the increase of governmental activity has implied a vast extension of the civil service. In France it is said that, in normal times, one-fortieth of the population is so employed.[33] While in Great Britain the proportion is far less, measures like the Insurance Act have notably extended it; and it remains true, as Mr. Graham Wallas has significantly remarked,[34] that every scheme of improvement upon which the state embarks entails an increase in the number of public officials. It may, indeed, be admitted that such increase is not necessarily a defect; but its magnitude, in recent years, raises grave questions of which those connected with the public revenue are only the smallest.[35] What remains vital is the fact that the growth of bureaucracy in every civilized country does not seem, on the evidence, compatible with the maintenance of a liberal spirit. It is difficult not to view with

[32] *Representative Government.* (Everyman's edition), p. 202.
[33] Lefas, *L'Etat et les Fonctionnaires.*
[34] *The Great Society,* p. 7.
[35] Cf. my *Authority in The Modern State,* Ch. 5

suspicion the growth of an administrative law which escapes the purview of the ordinary courts.[36] The revolt of the French civil service itself, on exactly those grounds of an incompatibility with liberalism is, to say the least, remarkable.[37] The attitude of the English working-class to government has, in recent years, undergone a significant change towards active distrust, and the general dislike of the public to the Insurance Act of 1911 is, in this connection, noteworthy.[38] However beneficial may be the consequence of social legislation — and that a large part of it does confer benefit is unquestionable — it does not compensate for improvements wrought out with their own minds by those upon whom the benefit is conferred. Social legislation has the incurable habit of tending towards paternalism; and paternalism, however wide be the basis of consent upon which it is erected, is the subtlest form of poison to the democratic state.

It may mitigate, but it does not solve, the essential problem: which is to interest the largest possible number of persons in the study of, and judgment upon, political questions. A far wider political enterprise is needed from the mass of men to make durable the gains of the last fifty years. It may even be urged that only in this fashion can we hope to make possible the emergence of that practical and speculative leadership of which the world has need; for a people of which the alternative interests are either half-whimsical contemplation or mere amusement will never produce a great civilization.

[36] Cf. Dicey in the *Law Quarterly Review,* 1915, on "The Growth of Administrative Law."

[37] The best discussion of this whole subject is by Georges Cahen, *Les Fonctionnaires.*

[38] Cf. Mr. Lloyd-George's remarkable admission, London *Times,* Nov. 24, 1913.

It is possible that, in this regard, we too greatly de-
preciate the significance of political mechanisms. It is,
of course, true that the main questions of democracy are
what may be termed moral questions, depending far more
upon the possession of mind and character than upon
any other factors. But mind and character are everywhere useless without the full opportunity of application.
It is here that the mechanisms of modern democracy seem
most inadequate. For we have not sufficiently related
the areas they traverse to the occupations of the average
man. We have generally left unconnected the life he
leads with the construction of those rules of conduct by
which that life is governed. We are suffering, in fact,
from an over-centralization which results from placing
too great an emphasis upon the geographical factor in
government. We have collected so much power at a single
point in the body politic, we have so much emphasized the
distribution of functions in terms of that point, that the
only systems of government of which we can conceive is
one which takes its orientation from that direction. Yet
it is at least uncertain whether new possibilities do not
exist.

II

England is what is termed a unitary state. The King
in Parliament is there the sole and final source of existent
powers. Every species of local authority derives those
powers it can exercise directly or indirectly from some
parliamentary enactment. It is generally admitted that
the result of this system has been to cast an overwhelming
burden of business upon the House of Commons, and
schemes for the relief of such pressure have taken, ever
since the famous "Radical Programme" of 1885, the form

of some measure of decentralization.[39]   To Mr. Chamberlain's enthusiastic vision what seemed desirable was the institution of national councils for the constituent parts of the United Kingdom; whereby he hoped not only to confine the House of Commons to functions of a general, and not a local nature, but, also, to find a way out of the labyrinth of the Irish question.[40]   More frequently and mainly through the immense financial complications such federalism would involve, what has been regarded with favor is the conference of far wider powers upon the local authorities.

The incoherent anarchy of the period before the Municipal Reform Act led, in the course of the nineteenth century, to a complete and necessary reconstruction of local government.   Until that time, and ever since the rigid centralization of the Tudor period, practically no administrative connection had existed between the local authorities and Whitehall.   The scandals of municipal corruption, coupled with the obvious limitations of government by county justices confined to a particular class, led the more rigid reformers, such as Chadwick, to attempt a complete administrative centralization; but the traditional opinion in favor of some active and quasi-independent local powers was sufficient to prevent the adoption of the rigorous bureaucratic methods which prevail so largely upon the continent of Europe.   As it is, the course of development has led to the emergence of a type of authority at once different from the centralized rigor of France, on the one hand, and the loose dispersion of

[39] *The Radical Programme,* Ch. 9.   Another instance of the same tendency is Henry C. Stevens, *Provincial Self-government,* which passed through several editions in the nineties.

[40] *The Radical Programme,* p. 247 f.

powers in the United States on the other.   There has, very happily, been no attempt, as in France and Germany, to adopt a classification which distinguished between "national" or "obligatory" duties, and "local" or "optional" duties; for it has been wisely seen that what Mr. Webb has happily termed the tyranny of categories does not, in any real sense, fit the facts it is intended to summarize.[41]

What has been done is, in the first place, to lay down the functions it is the business of the local authority to fulfil and, as a later and growing development, to assist and stimulate their performance either by a grant in aid or the conference of an assigned revenue.   It does not seem that the latter method, the invention of Lord Goschen, has any other advantage than the simplification of national bookkeeping; [42] but the former, the grant in aid, may well be claimed as a capital discovery in the technique of administration.   John Stuart Mill long ago insisted on the necessarily greater width of knowledge and experience that is available in the central depositary of government; and it is the unique value of the grant in aid that it enables the central authority to oversee performance without that detailed interference which a jealous localism might well consider excessive.   It has thus maintained, at least in part, the virtues of a decentralized administration, without suffering it to fall into the vices of negligent parochialism.   It makes efficiency in certain directions profitable, and thus stimulates at least a minimum of exertion.   Wherever the local authority desires to step outside the actual province of its powers, as in

41 See his remarkable article in the *Clare Market Review*, Vol. III, No. 3.

42 Grice, *National and Local Finance*, p. 95 f.

the case of the great Thirlmere scheme of Manchester, it must either acquire the privilege directly from Parliament or indirectly from a department delegated by Parliament to perform that office.

It cannot, on the whole, be denied that the workings of this scheme have justified its inception. Unquestionably, there is much to be desired. The county councils, mainly for reasons of distance, have remained like the old Quarter Sessions, aristocratic or, at least, propertied in character and, to some extent, conservative as a result, in outlook. The parish councils of Mr. Ritchie's famous act, from which the early Fabians hoped so much,[43] have been, indisputably, a failure. They have been too rarely instituted and, where instituted, financial weakness has prevented them, other causes apart, from doing much of an effective character.[44] The administration of the poor law has been recently condemned by the ablest Royal Commission since that which reformed it nearly ninety years ago; and it is now proposed by no one to retain it along its present lines.[45] The municipal councils have been, as was naturally to be expected, by far the most satisfactory in operation; and the opportunities that lie open to those who will work this fertile field the single, but classic, instance of Mr. Chamberlain has strikingly shown. More anonymous, but hardly less important, have been certain of the municipal enterprises, particularly the tramway systems, of a few cities like Manchester and Glasgow.

Yet the fact remains that over English life certain

[43] *Fabian Essays,* p. 152.

[44] Lowell, *Government of England,* II, 281.

[45] The Ministry of Reconstruction seems now to be in favor of its immediate abolition. Cf. the recent circular of the department on the subject.

shadows have in its local aspect fallen. It is not merely that the lines of central authority are drawn too uniform to admit the emergence of the needed spirit and enterprise; the distribution of toys to workhouse children, for example, need not, of necessity, be regarded as a heinous offense.[46] In things like education, public health, transportation, the supply of books, local authorities display a lack of creative energy which is not merely consequent upon the degree of control which is exercised from outside; for in this, as in parliamentary business, authority is always ultimately in its acts the translation of a dominant public opinion. They earn their grants, but they do little more than earn their grants. This is, perhaps naturally, even more true of the rural than of the urban districts; an improvement in the methods of government seems always to depend upon the presence of large populations. When Mr. Graham Wallas discovers volumes of the "Home University Library" and the "Cambridge Manuals" in his village shop,[47] one can only feel that a curve of their distribution would suggest that he was fortunate in his village.

It is idle to suggest that this is due to the substitution of a democratic for an oligarchic system.[48] It is true that the ablest men do not occupy themselves with local life. If they are politically-minded they try to drift towards London; and the local council becomes, with the local bench, what Mr. Wells has happily termed a Knighthood of the Underlings. The competition for place is small and the number of active voters compares unfavorably with the proportion in parliamentary elec-

46 Gwynn and Tuckwell, *Life of Dilke*, II, p. 23.
47 *The Great Society*, p. 302.
48 Lowell, *Government of England*, II, p. 199.

tions.[49] A few cities will be fortunate in their town-clerks as Nottingham was fortunate in Sir Samuel Johnson. Occasionally, a theory of political method will persuade a unique genius like Mr. Sidney Webb to fertilize the London County Council. But no one who has attended meetings of guardians or council committees can derive much enthusiasm from them. In the rural districts there are the types where the squire prevails, or where a vicarious representative pompously vindicates the Anglican inheritance against the resented intrusion of a chapel-going Nonconformist; more rarely, there is the type where some faded memory of Joseph Arch has left a leaven of finer and broader aspiration. In the towns, it is mostly upon the education committees that it is usual to discover a really intelligent grasp of the problems involved — a grasp, it should be added, which is usually due to the presence of the coöpted members. That the ideal mayor should be a rich peer, is, as Mr. Redlich drily observes,[50] a sufficient commentary upon that institution. Yet no one who reads the monumental history of aristocratic control collected by Mr. and Mrs. Webb can doubt the improvement in the quality of local government when its popular aspect is comparatively estimated. There is more width of outlook, more generosity, a vast technical advance. The source of dissatisfaction must be found in other directions.

The mood of the people is significant in this connection. Broadly, of course, it is a specialized reflection of the apathy about politics in general. There is so much that is technical in local affairs that it is difficult for interest to be aroused except where one is actually and actively

[49] *Ibid*, 153 f.   [50] *Local Government in England*, I, p. 263.

immersed in its details; an inadequate pavement will arouse criticism only amongst those who use the road. A scandal about contracts, of course, arouses the interest that must always come where the fierce light of angry publicity is concentrated upon a particular individual. But, for the most part, the tendency is for popular attention to relate itself only to the single and fundamental question of rates. No more popular election cry can be found than the promise of their reduction. Nothing — as witness the programs of ratepayers' associations — is more fiercely resented than increased municipal expenditure. The maxims of Mr. Gladstone upon that local government he never fully understood,[51] are here still paramount, with the result that far too few authorities are encouraged to the experiments that are essential. The spirit that led Mr. Lansbury to establish the great poor law school at Shenfield is the exception and not the rule; and it has been fiercely resented as wanton extravagance or a dole to the improvident. All this, it should be added, is very intelligible. Rates fall not upon landlord but upon the occupier, and to relieve them is only the prelude to an increase in taxation.[52] The average ratepayer is in any case hard pressed to make both ends meet on his income. He tends to see, in things like municipal housing, and school medical officers, and recreation centers, a movement towards that socialism of which he still stands in so much dread. It is only by urgent effort that he can start his sons at his own level, and prevent his daughters from knowing how to earn their own living. To him such expenditure, for which he pays, is like giving

51 Webb, *Grants in Aid*, p. 9.
52 Cannan, *History of Local Rates* (2nd ed.), Ch. 8.

freely to the poor the opportunity to outstrip him in the race.[53]

The limitations of such an outlook are, in this regard, most urgently manifest in things of the mind. Manchester, for example, has a single adequately-equipped library for a population of over three-quarters of a million; and its dramatic and musical pre-eminence are both of them due to the fortunate accident of a few rich patrons. Outside the technological sciences, for which commercial needs demand a somewhat fuller equipment than elsewhere, its university owes its main distinction, that in historical scholarship, not in any sense to a proper municipal endowment, but to the earnest zeal of two distinguished scholars who might equally well have been in Leeds or London or Oxford, for the municipal encouragement they have received; and it is noteworthy that little or no provision is made for the study or teaching of government. The citizen of Manchester may nobly hate the citizen of Liverpool; but his care for the rates makes him spend his dislike less in achievement than in vituperation; and, esthetically, anyone who walks down the mean and crowded streets of what is so singularly termed Angel Meadow, or examines the sordid and crowded narrowness of Cheetham, will realize how little Housing Acts interfere with the sacred rights of property; and his sense of this apathy will be sharpened when he compares it with the solid, if mahogany, magnificence of districts like the Palatine Road and its environs.

In the rural places, even this achievement is not emulated. The influence of the church and the land is still dominating and narrowing, and even so unexpected an

[53] See all this well put in Mr. Masterman's *Condition of England* in the chapter entitled "The Suburbans."

enthusiasm as that of Mr. Fisher could hardly extend
itself to the rural schools. The newspapers rarely penetrate into their recesses; and volumes on the domestic
life of the royal family seem the staple article, apart from
fiction, of library consumption. The country, indeed,
becomes mainly apparent to the nation at large when
some sporadic outbreak of anthrax is reported. Even
the paternal influence of the squire is rapidly ceasing,
since the motor car made London accessible, and, as
often as not, that hereditary influence is being supplanted
by the financial magnate who regards the village as an
accidental appurtenance to the estate to which he can
retire for the week-end. Men like Thomas Hodgkin will,
doubtless, still believe affectionately in the duties entailed
by property;[54] but rural statesmanship is either, like
his, benevolently paternal, or else non-existent. Yet it
is nowhere so greatly needed.[55]

It is, to some extent, accidental that this absence of
creativeness should be associated with a unified state. It
is doubtless true that the division of powers which is
characteristic of federalism, whatever it fails to do, does
create a spirit of experiment. It is, indeed, worthy of
note that the poverty of local powers should be mainly
connected with unified states like England and France
and Belgium, where too little attempt has been made to
create a coöperative sovereignty. Certainly, in municipal life, the historic localism of Germany has marvel-
ously survived the depressing effects of imperial centralization; and, with all their weakness, the municipal
systems there afford more outlet for an able mind than

[54] Creighton, *Life of Hodgkin*, 217–8.
[55] See all this finely put in Mr. F. E. Green's stimulating volume,
The Awakening of England.

is the case in Great Britain. In the United States, it
is true, the quality of enterprise has been far inferior
to the amount undertaken;[56] but the career of a man
who there engages in the politics of state or of city offers
more solid advantages in the possibilities of constructive
effort than in any country in the world. But, after all,
the fortunate accidents of history and geography are at
least partially responsible for this difference. The unified governance of America is a physical and economic
impossibility; and the roots of the federal tradition were
already laid there.

That is not the case with England; and though it is
not necessary to accept Mr. Freeman's dictum[57] that
what is now united ought not again to suffer division,
it is possible to doubt whether England has the institutional, economic, or territorial basis, upon which a federal
state could be founded. It is important to remember
that federalism has not, in general, resulted in lessening
the pressure of business upon the central authority; indeed
in America exactly the same complaints of overburdening
as in England are made.[58] Government by discussion
is there even more a euphemism than in the countries
centrally organized. The division of powers has certainly the result of lessening the number of subjects upon
which the federal government must concentrate its attention; but the difference in extent of purview seems more
than compensated by the increase of intensity; and England is so much an economic unity that, in the largest

---

[56] Though to say, as Mr. Webb says (*Grants in Aid*, p. 5), that it
is the "worst government of any country claiming to be civilized"
is simple nonsense.

[57] *History of Federal Government*, p. 70.

[58] Bryce, *American Commonwealth*, Ch. 13.

subjects, it is less a federal than a decentralized structure
to which attention ought to be given. Clearly, for
instance, a separate educational policy is, an agreed
minimum apart, possible and even desirable for the constituent parts of the United Kingdom; but a separate
policy in taxation would raise so vehement an opposition,
and create such vast difficulties in adjustment, as to
make it more than doubtful whether it would be worth the
cost. In questions that are obviously local in nature the
advantage, for example, of leaving the Welsh church to
Wales and the Scottish crofters to Scotland and the
Congested Districts to a Chief Secretary permanently
located in Dublin, is unquestionable. But all this would
still leave untouched the vital questions within each
group. Even supposing that it relieved the burden upon
the House of Commons it would do little more than create
an intermediate set of institutions which would in nowise
lessen the present administrative problems, on the one
hand, or associate with itself any new sources of public
opinion, upon the other. It is within the local group
that the real stimulus to action must come.

What clearly is needed, is something that affords the
advantages of a territorial federal system without the
destruction of parliamentary sovereignty, at any rate in
the sense of final control. It is worth while here to
insist that there is really no rigid line between federal
and unified governments; the only real difference, as Seeley
long ago pointed out,[59] is in the degree of power retained
by, or conferred upon, the localities. The United States
may, in theory, ascribe definite functions to the federal
government, and the indefinite residue of powers to the
states; but no one who watches the interpretation of

[59] *Introduction to Political Science*, p. 95.

the Constitution by the Supreme Court will question the impossibility of final classification. The flexibility of a federal system in this aspect will be obvious to anyone who compares *Haskell* v. *Noble State Bank* [60] with *McCray* v. *United States.*[61] Federalism, undoubtedly, results from the coalescence of what were before separate groups, and it is thus distinct from that decentralization which makes a partial separateness where, before, there was complete unity. Yet either system is, in reality, no more than an attempt at finding the most convenient areas of administration. Federalism, as Professor Dicey has insisted,[62] results in the creation of a national state, and, whatever the original powers, it will ultimtaely become true, as Mr. Justice Holmes has pointed out,[63] "that the national welfare, as understood by Congress, may require a different attitude within its sphere from that of some self-keeping state." Certainly the result of that wider need is a degree of local subordination which will change as the needs of the nation change. Yet it is the singular merit of a federal system that the creation of a national allegiance does not destroy the special interest of the citizen in the province to which he belongs. The Bavarian does not the less believe in Munich because of the predominance of Berlin; nor is it here without significance that the ablest disciple of Calhoun was a Bavarian professor.[64] Eager citizens of Chicago will explain its manifest superiority to Boston or New York; and the claims of size are resisted by the patriotism which

[60] 219, U. S., 104.

[61] 195, U. S., 27.

[62] *Law of the Constitution* (8th ed.), p. 81.

[63] See his dissent in the Child Labor Case, U. S. *v.* Degenhart, decided in 1917–18.

[64] Max Seydel.

the tiny cities of the Middle West can call into being.
It is that internal diversity of allegiance which makes
possible the creation of active governmental centers distinct from Washington.   There is no evidence to prove,
as the classic authority suggests,[65] that federal government is either weak or conservative.   The weakness is the
purely theoretical fact that a division of powers opens
up legal contingencies of conflict which are avoided in a
unified state; though it should be noted that England
also has had its civil war.   And where powers are needed
recent experience has vividly shown that they are present;
for no public official in the world has ever disposed of
such authority as the President of the United States in
1917.[66]   Nor, moreover, has the unified state escaped the
possibility of such danger.   Experience [67] seems to suggest that its avoidance is a matter not of law but of
policy.   The actual study of state and municipal effort
in America, moreover, traverses with completeness the
charge of conservatism; rather is the observer confronted
with a plethora of experiment through which he is only
able with difficulty to thread his way.   It is not asserted
that the administrative areas or the division of powers in
the United States are ideal.   On the contrary, it is all too
evident that they stand in grave need of change.[68]   That
only means, however, that the frame of government
adapted to the ideas of 1787 is inadequate a century and
a half later; which, after all, is no cause for complaint
in a period which has seen greater material changes than

[65] *Law of the Constitution* (8th. ed.), pp. 167, 169.
[66] Cf. especially the power to raise an army of unlimited size.
[67] Cf. my *Problem of Sovereignty, passim.*
[68] Cf. Mr. Croly's comment, "The Failure of the States," in *The New Republic,* Vol. IX, p. 170.

any previous age. It does not invalidate the underlying assumptions of federalism.

Lord Bryce has pointed out [69] that no argument relative to local government which can be urged in favor of federalism does not also hold for a decentralized system. Either will, if adequate, provide a means of experiment which is difficult, if not impossible, if applied to the area of a whole country. Either relieves the pressure of national business by the entrustment of its final charge, where it is merely local in nature, to local authorities. Either provides a substantial check, in these years a greatly needed benefit, against the fears of bureaucracy. And, within England, fiscal reasons seem to make decentralization the preferable method. Whitechapel, for instance, has a proportionately less ratable value than Hampstead, though its governmental needs are greater. Inevitably, therefore, improvements in Whitechapel must lean more upon central assistance than improvements in Hampstead. So long as the system of grants-in-aid is continued, and its cessation would be matter for deep regret, every local authority must rely upon the national exchequer for subventions. Anything in the nature of fiscal decentralization would at once deeply injure the prestige of the House of Commons — a more serious matter in its remoter ramifications than is lightly to be supposed — and raise every problem the central departments now confront in several places instead of one. Clearly, again, that subvention ought to be made dependent upon an adequate fulfilment of functions. That ought to involve in the central power — whether there are intermediate authorities or no — the retention of some inspective control. So long as local government

[69] *American Commonwealth*, I, Ch. 30.

is at least partially conducted out of national funds there
is no room for any final separateness.

It is not meant here to assert that the central control
of localities has been strikingly successful.[70]   On the contrary, no one would deny the need of widespread reforms
in this direction.   It is clear, for example, that the Local
Government Board, in its audit of local accounts, ought
to be compelled to employ professional auditors.[71]   Nor
is it doubtful that much of the so-called inspection is a
perfunctory examination to which little value in reality
attaches.[71a]   The right of entry is doubtless a reserve
power that does not fail of effect in dealing with ab-
normally backward localities; but it seems to have been
far less useful where the bare minimum standard has been
attained.   Much, too, remains to be done in the way of
central reports on local performance.   That form of
inquiry could be used with far more result than it in fact
is by the sheer influence of constant publicity, a fact
which is borne out by the interest which seems to be
locally taken in the inspector's inquiries into local
schemes.   But, when the last criticism has been made,
it is impossible to examine the relation between central
and local authorities without the conviction that it is
instrumental in the production of an efficiency that might
otherwise be absent.   It lacks the rigor of the French
deconcentration, which seems to act as a governmental
anaesthesia in local affairs; but it has enough flexibility
of presence to make it a weapon of real value.

The real need is for a far greater performance of duties
by local authorities than at present exists; nor are signs

---

[70] Lowell, *Government of England*, II, Ch. 46.
[71] *Ibid*, p. 292.
[71a] Cannan, *History of Local Rates* (2nd ed.), p. 12.

wanting that the need of such performance is properly appreciated. Mr. Herbert Fisher, for example, has emphasized the desire of the Board of Education that local authorities should go beyond the minimum of central compulsion.[72] That desire, indeed, strikes the real keynote of what is here needed. Local authorities are less in need of actual new powers than of the requirement from them of a far higher standard of minimum attainment by the central authority. In health and education, particularly, it is in the power of central authorities to lay down a basis of expenditure the attainment of which should be the basis of any grant-in-aid.[73] Achievement could easily be stimulated by a higher scale of grant-increases proportionately as the local expenditure passes beyond that required minimum. The system of assigned revenues ought forthwith to be abolished. It acts at present simply as the safeguard of inertia. A check should be placed upon all innovation where, in the considered opinion of the central inspectorate, the required services are not satisfactorily performed, and it is obvious that such a power would have the advantage of publicly ventilating the grievances the central authority is prepared to formulate. Much too, could be done by placing far greater restraints than at present upon the promotion of private bills. The procedure is, in any case, unduly expensive. It is rarely resorted to except where it is felt that the central authority would not be prepared to endorse the local scheme. Procedure by provisional order has proved itself in the working;[74] and a safeguard could be had against the danger of officialism by pro-

---

72 *Educational Speeches*, p. 35.
73 Cf. Webb, *Grants in Aid*, p. 106.
4 Cf. Redlich, I, 237 f.

viding for an endorsement or rejection of the central authority's order by the local electorate. But no one who has watched the private bill system in its operation can avoid being convinced of its wastefulness and dilatoriness on the one hand, and the undue consumption of national time that it entails on the other. It is little less than pathetic to see the House of Commons turn from the discussion of the largest issues to the problem of the Gravesend gas works or the tramways of Camberwell.[75] In another direction it may be useful to point out that no one can really judge the adequacy of local government until some attempt is made at equalizing the present system of valuation and providing for reassessment at more frequent intervals.[76] The whole subject is at present in so complete a chaos that it is difficult without a complex examination, which the local authority does not, and the central authority has no reason to, undertake, to tell whether the amount of money raised in any area at all equitably represents the contribution it should be making to the performance of its functions.

It is obvious in any such perspective that certain underlying assumptions have been made. Any attempt at a higher standard of local government will demand a higher expenditure and a more enlightened public opinion. Certainly it is the former of these that is the less difficult problem. We have realized in the last four years how many are the sources of wealth, at least in part derived from the mere fact of community — that we have left untouched. Much can here be effected when we cease to bestow upon the landed interest that tenderness by which Sir Robert Peel sought to convert them to an

75 Low, *Governance of England*, p. 292.
76 Webb, *Grants in Aid*, p. 110.

acceptance of the last and greatest of his unexpected revolutions.[77] Even more can be done when the emphasis placed upon local taxation by the influence of Sir Massey Lopes is removed.[78] We have to approach the problem of rating more in the spirit in which we approach the problem of taxation. We have got to decide less that so much is to be raised than that so much is needed.[79] Certainly in the matter of housing we do far too little to make plain to the owner of slum property the fact that our dissatisfaction must have financial consequence. The fundamental principle of taxation, that cost should be proportionate to the benefit received and fixed upon the recipient is too little used.[80] There would, moreover, be real benefit in allowing to local authorities, the basic rates apart, a larger variety of choice in the matter of taxation for local purposes. The taxation, for example, of amusements is a source of income to which the locality could refer with advantage; not all local authorities are as fortunate as Doncaster, but anyone who has stood outside the great football grounds of Manchester must have felt that the crowds are a heaven-sent boon to the theorist in search of an unfelt source of revenue.

Yet the greater problem of an adequate opinion remains; and it is purely idle to deny its complexity. The very fact that the possibilities of the Local Government Acts have not been used is testimony to the deeps it touches. Legislation may help to make public opinion, but it does not seem able to command it. Something of this, doubtless, is due to the habit of looking timidly

[77] See his great speech in *Hansard*, 3rd Series, Vol. LXXXIII, January 27, 1846.

[78] Cf. Grice, *National and Local Finance*, pp. 54 f.

[79] Cf. Cannan, *op. cit.*, pp. 3-5.

[80] Cf. Chapman, *Local Government and State Aid*, pp. 49 f.

to the central authority. More may be traced to a sheer ignorance of the power and influence that a strong local government can exert. But much of it is due to deeper and more urgent causes.

III

The problem of local government in this aspect is only in smaller perspective the problem of the modern state. It raises exactly the same issues as are raised by the general question of the modern representative system. The mere announcement of a plentitude of power in any authority will solve nothing; the essential business is to get that power to work. We are, in fact, beyond the sphere of law. We are dealing not with the conference of rights, but with their realization, which is a very different matter. It is, of course, important to consider the purpose by which such power is informed. But that purpose can never be, except for law, a mere matter of declaration; [81] the Supreme Court of the United States may well declare a statute constitutional which announces civil war. Purpose, in fact, must be discovered in pragmatic fashion, from the actual processes in their joint operation. It is today a commonplace that the real source of authority in any state is with the holders of economic power. The will that is effective is their will; the commands that are obeyed are their commands. Nor is this less true of local than of central government. The city council of Manchester, for example, will, on the whole, represent the normal purposes of a group of middle-class business men; their decisions will be imbued with that "intuition more subtle than any articulate major premise," which, as Mr. Justice Holmes

81 Cf. my *Authority in the Modern State*, Ch. 1.

has observed,[82] is the true origin of the convictions expressed by the Supreme Court of the United States. There is herein no suggestion of sinister motive. It is no more than the simple assertion that we cannot escape our environment. Those who hold power will inevitably feel that the definition of good is the maintenance, in some fashion, of the *status quo;* exactly as the landowners could find economic ruin in the repeal of the corn laws and the manufacturers commercial disaster in the factory acts. It is a general rule that we identify our private good with the common good and write the result out large in the election returns.[83]

Legislation, then, reflects the minds that make it, whether its makers be members of parliament or of the bench or the civil service; and it is only human that this should be so. Once it is perceived, what becomes of importance in the processes of politics is the character of those minds if that legislation is in any broad sense to represent general needs and general desires. The constituency from which its makers are drawn must cast its limits far; but the makers themselves must be not less representative in character. Here, surely, is a source of many of the difficulties by which modern government is faced. In England, at least, we have avoided that bare-faced travesty of the representative system that is embodied in the Prussian franchise; but property, in more subtle and indirect fashion, still securely finds the emphasis it desires. The business of government has, for the most part, been confided to the middle class; and the results have largely reflected the aptitudes and purposes of that class. In local government, for ex-

[82] 198, U. S., 45, 76.
[83] Cf. Wallas, *Human Nature in Politics,* p. 98 f.

ample, we have a wise insistence on adequate sewage systems, a proper supply of good drinking water, reasonable secondary education for those who can, in a wider sense than simple fees, afford it, technical instruction that the middle ranks of the industrial hierarchy may be adequately filled,[84] proper lighting systems — these are the characteristics by which it has been distinguished. They all of them represent common needs; and the local government has been successful in securing those common needs exactly as parliamentary government has been successful in securing the common freedoms. A sewage service can hardly be confined to a single class, any more than a modern university can be (outside of Ireland) confined to a single faith; and the flavor of generality that is implied in such service the present system has been able to secure.

But it has proved inadequate exactly at the point where the larger system has proved inadequate. Once, that is to say, we pass the frontier of middle-class needs, we enter the debatable land. English local and English parliamentary government has proved a satisfactory thing for the man whose income is secure and reasonably comfortable; it has accomplished little for the ranks below him. It was the perception of this truth in national politics which led, after 1906, to the revival of the idea of industrial democracy as the paramount issue; labor in politics had discovered to how large an extent theories of government reflect prevailing economic systems. The local government of England is a government for ratepayers, and that largely, under the present system, must mean a government according

[84] Though it should in honesty be added that thus far most of our technical schools have been half-starved.

to the ideas of those who feel the burden of the rates. But it is exactly the needs of the working-class which lie outside the realm of subjects to which the will of the rate-payer can be fruitfully directed. Immense housing extension, a large development of the public library system, schemes of education of which even that of Mr. Fisher is but a faint beginning, do not interest those who are already satisfactorily provided for in these regards. The result is that the workers' interest, pale enough, in any case, in the details of national government, is but the shadow of a shadow in local concerns.

It is doubtless a good rhetorical answer to urge that the larger part of the working-class has the franchise and that if it does not choose to exert its power it must take the consequences. But that is to mistake the superficial appearance of a political system for its inner reality; it is no more a real expression of the "general" will of the state than the election of Tweed to a state senatorship of New York expressed contentment with the vices of Tammany.[85] The King of England does not rule in practice because he rules in theory. England has developed a system of governmental institutions which provide an admirable opportunity for the workings of democracy; but it is at least equally clear that the institutions only partially work. Surely the real source of this disharmony is to be found in the way in which any political system must necessarily reflect its economic environment. The local institutions of England, for example, do not reflect the mind or desires of the working-class because they are in substance adjusted to a situation which, economically, at any rate, is far from demo-

[85] Cf. Bryce, *American Commonwealth* (ed. of 1910), II, p. 379, for Tweed episode.

cratic. They are representative in theory but not in practice. The problem then becomes the permeation of them with the ideas of the working-class. Nor is that a simple matter. It does not merely imply the running of working-class candidates at local elections. The question of expense apart,[86] there is not sufficient likelihood of their getting elected to make the experiment worth while on any large scale. It is not a sufficient answer that if they cannot get elected the state does not want them. We know too much and too little about the problems connected with the group will to make warrantable such *ex cathedra* pronouncements. The question is whether things like Whitechapel and Angel Meadow are to remain. They will remain so long as the poor endure them; and the poor will endure them until their economic power is so organized as to secure political expression. It was that kind of public opinion which produced the Trade Union Act of 1875–6; which secured the statutory reversal of the Taff-Vale decision; which cut at the root of the fatal clause in the House of Lords judgment in the Osborne case.[87] The problems of labor are, of course, so vast, that it is in general difficult to do more than focus its attention on national questions. But more than that is needed.

It is in some such fashion that we are driven back to that decentralization which, as has been suggested, is in reality a method of securing the results of federalism without the juristic basis upon which the latter, as

[86] A useful note upon this will be found in a letter of Mr. Sidney Webb in *The New Republic* for June 29, 1918.

[87] There is room for much speculation as to the validity of purely political action in the contrast between the complete victory of a small party in the Taff-Vale case, and the partial defeat of a proportionately more numerous party in the Osborne decision.

classically conceived, rests. Here, it is probable, our thinking has been conceived in terms too narrowly spatial in character. What we have mostly done is to think of the average factor in the formation of opinion as a single individual equipped to understand the arguments on either side; with the corollary belief that one vote is in the process the moral equivalent and influence of another. That is, of course, absurdly untrue. Much opinion there undoubtedly is; man is not less a solitary than a social creature. But, for the most part, it is as a member of a special fellowship that the average man is accustomed both to think and act. He is, maybe, a citizen of Manchester; but his desire, say in 1908, to assist his constituency to be represented by a cabinet minister in the person of Mr. Winston Churchill is checked, as a churchman, by the memory of Mr. Birrell's Education Bill, and as a holder of brewery shares, by a dim feeling that Mr. Asquith's licensing proposals have been condemned by the proper authorities who protect those widows and orphans who, in England, so curiously limit their investments to brewery shares. The average elector, in fact, is instinct with that spirit of the herd which he cannot escape by simple virtue of his humanity.[88] All such relationships create what, for want of a better word, we call a personality. That does not necessarily imply that a new physical person has come into being.[89] It simply means that we encounter a unified activity which comes from the coalescence of the thoughts and wills of divers men. That personality, as so defined,

[88] Though I do not accept all its implications, I think that Mr. Bradley's famous essay, "My Station and its Duties," in his *Ethical Studies*, still best expresses this truth even for political purposes.

[89] The best general view of this controversy is in the first volume of L. Michoud's *Theorie de la Personnalité Morale*.

gives rise to interests; and, in the modern state, it is largely by the interplay of interests that policy is determined.

No one can watch the evolution of politics without seeing that this is the case. Burke has made the necessity of parties politically axiomatic; but we have to admit that only a small part of us is exhausted by that connection. English education, for instance, has been largely determined by a church "interest." Agricultural policy has at every stage been dominantly influenced by the "interest" of the landowners; and even when, as in 1846, the landowning "interest" has suffered defeat, it was a victory for the temporarily antagonistic "interest" of the manufacturers. Every country in the world is honeycombed with associations which represent the activity of those "interests." No man, for example, is ignorant of the vital part played in English politics by the Licensed Victuallers' Association. What is perhaps more singular is the indirect way in which the power of these associations has had to be exerted. There has not, indeed, been anything in English politics which avowedly corresponds with the unclean selfishness of an American lobby. The representatives of these associations have at least secured their influence through the open door of the party system.[90] But even Bagehot could admit the existence of a railway "interest" in the House of Commons, at the same time that he viewed with suspicious dislike the growth of a labor "interest." The organization of political life has been so predominantly geographical in character that these functions have found no direct place in the structure of government.

[90] For a suggestion of the power they can exert cf. the *Memoir of Lord Hobhouse*, by L. T. Hobhouse and J. L. Hammond, p. 237.

It need not be argued that representation by function is more real than representation by area to make it evident that it has solid advantages to offer. Such an argument would be, in any case, untrue; for the interest of men as neighbors has a very solid and urgent reality about it. Yet there can be little or no doubt that the political opinions of men are largely determined by their industrial situation. Disraeli's theory of Tory Democracy was largely based on that perception. He hoped that a proper receptiveness to working-class needs, as in his Trade Union Act of 1875, would bring its votes to the right party. To give that industrial situation a domicile in politics is to give permanent expression to much which now escapes the immediate purview of political structure. Professional representation is not, at least in idea, a new device; and it has a particular fascination at a time when it is assuming a new importance in industrial government. Anyone who has watched the development, particularly in the last few years, of a labor theory of politics will have noted the tendency of trade-unionism to connect itself, nationally and locally, with that system of ideas and needs which has least opportunity for self-expression at the present time. If it is possible to relate that theory to the problems of government, a new and valuable stream of thought can be directed into channels where it is badly needed.

But what is wanted in professional representation is not either an addition, on that basis, to the House of Commons, or a similar reconstruction of the House of Lords.[91] The geographical basis has a real value for certain types of problems, particularly with those in which the interest of consumers is dominantly concerned;

[91] As Mr. Graham Wallas has desired, *The Great Society*, p. 339.

and it would result in mere confusion to connect it with
a producers' interest which is concerned with different
problems. Nor does the suggested second chamber assist
much. Its value as an institution seems, in any case,
rather a foible of the political scientists than an expression of real need; and it looks as though the second
chamber of the future would be less a deliberative assembly
than a body of administrative experts seeing to it that
the bill as passed, really represented the will of the lower
chamber, and holding constant inquiries, not necessarily
at London, into the process of administration. The
real way, surely, in which to organize the interests of
producers is by working out a delimitation of industry
and confiding the care of its problems to those most concerned with them. This is, in fact, a kind of federalism
in which the powers represented are not areas, but functions. Anyone can see that the railways are as real
as Lancashire; and exactly as the specifically local problems of Lancashire are dealt with by it, so could the
specifically functional problems of the railways be dealt
with by a governing body of its own. The necessary
relation to the state is not a difficult matter of adjustment. It would be necessary, in the first place, to see
to it that such a governing body did not pass beyond
its powers; that would be in part a matter for the courts
and in part, on the permissive side, a matter for some
such department as the Board of Trade. Where the
interest of the public outside defiantly entered in, as,
for instance, in such a matter as railway fares, the Railway Commissioners could render invaluable service by
performing the functions today so admirably performed
by the Interstate Commerce Commission of the United
States. In such a fashion, it should not be necessary to

go to Parliament at all; though it would, of course, still be possible to use it as a court of last instance and a depository of grievances. It is worth while noting that the attempt to govern industry by joint representative councils, as recommended in the Whitley Report, is in reality an attempt at such administrative devolution which, while it as yet retains the theory of parliamentary sovereignty, is, in fact, by handing over the making of rules to the trade unions and the employers, creating, within certain functions, what is little less than a federal state. The Whitley Report is based, in the first place, upon a division of powers. It divorces the business of production from the business of consumption and leaves the former the control of the processes upon which it is engaged. It is, of course, true that Parliament remains outside and omnipotent; but no one can for a moment doubt that if such a delegated power proves workable, parliamentary control will, whatever theory may say, be as real in practise as it is over the internal legislation of Canada and Australia, both of which are, in strict juristic fact, simply immense instances of decentralization. It is based, in the second place, upon an attempt to discover separate and national units of industrial government which, while they may at first work in independence, will be compelled later to discover some means of connection. The railways, for example, cannot possibly regard with indifference what is happening in the coal mines, and, sooner or later, they will be compelled to work out a basis of relationship for the hinterland of their mutual interests. Neither will, of course, surrender it to the other; and in the debate over terms they will discover the value of its cession to a body representative of both, exactly as has happened in the general history of political federations.

But to confine our speculation to the case of two industries alone is, of course, to obscure the vista that here reveals itself. For if there is one thing that can be predicted with certainty it is the ultimate interpendence of all forms of industry, and though we may, for purposes of convenience, attempt a system of delimitation, the units so formed are bound to look to federation as the means of settling their common differences and realizing their common aims. In the trade-union world, indeed, this movement towards federalism has been the real measure of progress. Trade unions grew up by chance in all times and places; but it has only been in the degree to which they have recognized the unity of interest in the working-class that they have been saved from the moral and economic quagmire of particularism. Indeed the real weakness of trade-unionism has been an internal competition of units; and the immense accession of strength that such things as the Triple Alliance can bring is known to every observer.[92] Of the larger process of production this is not less the case. If we omit, for the moment, any consideration of internal antagonisms within each industry, it is clear that we are facing an industrial future in which the joint interests of all producers must be matters of joint debate. For no state could permit the anarchy that would result if separate bargains of a particularistic kind could be made with every producer of raw materials by the industrial council of each trade. They involve not less than a federal council of producers in which minimum common standards can be erected, with an executive organization to enforce them. There are questions, for instance, of output, wages, hours, training, in which the old criteria of

[92] Cf. Cole, *The World of Labour,* pp. 205-84.

supply and demand are no longer applicable. The only way in which they can even be approached, much less solved, is by agreement through debate. And the more this ideal is approached the more will it tend to create an economic sovereignty either outside the legal sovereignty of Parliament, or using the latter merely as an organ of registration. Nor is it difficult to doubt that the immense decentralization that is implied in such effort will be better managed by the producers themselves. They at any rate know the conditions. Their interest is in the making of real solutions rather than in the acceptance of those partial and unsatisfactory compromises to which governmental interference has in recent years accustomed us. Here it is notable that experience of government intervention on a large scale seems, in those industries most closely related to the business of war, to have produced a healthy desire, both in masters and men, for self-determination of conditions under which work is to be carried on.[93] The reaction against officialism has been everywhere intense; and part, at least, of the welcome accorded to the Whitley Report, may be traced to a desire to free the processes of industry from the direct control of government.

The real significance of that welcome lies, however, much deeper. During the nineteenth century there has been growing around us an inchoate but vital economic federalism to which far too little attention has been paid.[94] The rules and standards of things like the legal and medical professions, the trade-unions and, in a less

[93] See the Reports of Mr. Lloyd-George's Commissions on Industrial Unrest, *passim.*

[94] The best discussion of this subject is still J. Paul Boncour, *Le Fédéralisme Economique.*

degree, the teachers, constitute expressions of group-solidarity of which the state has been compelled to take account. There has been inherent in them ideals of law and of justice. They have implied a decentralization of industrial control which has grown ever wider in its ramifications. The influence of trade-union standards, for example, has been obvious in the way in which government has been compelled to insert them in large regions of its own contractual relations. The power was again seen in the attitude assumed by the medical profession to the Insurance Act of 1911 and the concessions it was able to exact. It is a solidarity which the essentially political conception of democracy, as exemplified in the *Loi le Chapelier* in France,[95] and the attitude to trade-unions of Francis Place,[96] was compelled to deny; but it is a solidarity which the Trade Union Act of 1875 and the *Lois des Associations* of 1884 and 1901 tacitly admitted. They are, in reality, the abolition, for political purposes, of the economic abstraction called man as set up by the individualistic thinkers of the nineteenth century. The object of these groups was to safeguard professional interests. Each profession and industry had questions and standards peculiar to itself, upon which its own determination was the most competent. No real benefit was derived from state intervention, after a certain level had been reached,[97] because the external character of government in relation to these groups clothed its action with a mechanical uniformity and a rigorous permanence unsuited to such questions as arise

95 Cf. Faget de Casteljau, *Droit d'Association*, Chs. 1-4.
96 Wallas, *Life of Place*, pp. 217-8.
97 I do not deny, that is to say, the value of government interference in sweated trades.

in so delicate and complex a structure as that of modern industry. No state, for example, could possibly enter into the minute ingenuities by which a modern trade-union secures the observance of the standard rate. The process by which an agreement is reached between masters and men is left to the interests concerned. The result is a rule of conduct which, if it lacks the binding force of parliamentary enactment, has yet the force of law to the consenting powers. And it is probable, as M. Paul-Bancour has pointed out,[98] that this removal of the settlement from the province of the state has this especial value that it prevents the use of the public power from being perverted to the use of one or other of the parties in presence. So to do would, as he has noted, transform every political conflict into a naked class-struggle of the most disastrous kind.

The existence of this accidental decentralization, valuable as it is, should not blind us to its imperfections. It has had little or no force behind it save that of strict compulsion in regard to standards. No one imagines, for instance, that the miners won their right to the checkweighman or the eight-hour day, other than by the extent to which they had unionized their trade.[99] Industrially, at least, the existence of standards has been less the result of a realization of right than an acceptance of necessity. That is the consequence of the unreal relation in which the state has stood to industry. It has never pretended, for example, to enforce that national minimum of civilized life which ought, at the very least, to be the price of capitalistic existence. Apart from the few cases, like the labor of women and children,

[98] *Op. cit.*, p. 382.
[99] Webb, *Industrial Democracy*, p. 309.

in which a very obvious humanitarianism has intervened,
every conquest of a fraction of that minimum has been
the work of organized labor.   There has been, thus far,
nothing that could with truth be called, in Rousseau's
sense, a "general will" of the state.   What, rather, we
have had, has been a series of conflicts between particular
wills in which now one and now another has prevailed.
The attitude in which labor and capital and the state
approach each industrial situation is so different that
any ultimate harmony between them seems impossible.
The real demand of labor is for the democratization of
industrial processes, by which is meant that the truths
of popular political government are applicable to industrial government as well.   That, obviously enough, cannot be the attitude of capital, since it is at the destruction of capitalism that it is aimed.   Nor, broadly,
is it the attitude of those who operate the machinery of the modern state; for the latter are dominantly influenced by the prevailing economic system and
they cannot, in the nature of things, aim at fundamental
disturbance of the economic status quo.   The concessions they seek to secure are not founded upon any theory
of abstract justice but upon the minimum that must be
given to maintain social peace.   The object of labor
is the foundation of a new social order which is incompatible with the fragmentary concessions of the last
hundred years.

Here, in reality, is the seat of the modern democratic
discontent.   The liberty and equality implied in the
modern state are purely theoretic in character.   The
industrial worker has the suffrage; but he is caught in
the ramifications of a system which deprives its use of
any fundamental meaning.   He finds that he cannot se-

cure from the operations of politics either that say in the
determination of his life or the opportunity to conquer the
riches it can offer, that a democratic civilization is supposed to afford. He sees that democracy in politics does
not in the least imply democracy in industry and, since the
better portion of his life is spent in earning his daily
bread, it is to the latter that he has turned. He has
found the state useless for the purpose he has in view,
and that is why he must refuse to accept it as in any
fundamental sense the representative of the community.
The economic federalism that exists largely results from
his effort to conquer through industrial action what he
has failed to gain from political. The labor movement
has been his real training-ground in politics. It has,
of course, thus far been largely confined to material
questions of hours and wages but it has come, in more
recent years, to turn more and more its attention to
questions of policy, such as discipline and the like. It
is refusing, for instance, to allow labor to be extracted
from the laborer and to be regarded as a commodity
which can be bought and sold at will. Nothing is more
significant in recent trade-union history than things like
the famous Knox strike; for if the employers are driven
to make the question of the right to dismissal something
in which other criteria than their arbitrary will may
enter, obviously a serious inroad has been made upon the
autocracy of their present control.

The Whitley Report has emphasized the need for a
share in that control on the part of the workers. Not
less important, it has insisted that this control must
receive its expression through the trade-unions. The
solutions that such joint-effort as the councils it estab-
lishes may propose will, of course, be merely interim

solutions; for, in the fundamental sense, there cannot be better relations between two groups one of which is aiming at the abolition of the other. The very admission, indeed, of joint-control may well presage the advent of that transition period from capitalism to industrial democracy which will doubtless be characterized by labor's taking a greater share in industrial government. The experiment, however its result, is bound to involve far-reaching change. If it fails, an organized labor will confront an organized capital with the knowledge that the immense sacrifices it has made in the last four years were made for a lie; for if the result of the war is not an improvement in the internal conditions of the western democracies, the unrest of the period before 1914 is bound to go further; for no experiment in democratization that is successful can stop short of completeness.

And the immediate implications of its induction are important. The systematic consideration of industrial questions, locally as well as nationally, is a training in self-government of which the significance is not to be minimized. For it is vital to bear in mind that the consideration of industrial questions cannot stop short at industry. Inevitably they will tend more and more to emphasize the connection between industry and the general background of social life. Labor, for example, is already well aware of the importance to itself of education;[100] and in the cotton trade, to take only the most notable instance, an extension of the educational system will have the most far reaching effect on wages. Wages, again, are so intimately connected with rent that the housing-system of each wage district is immediately

[100] Cf. *Labour and the New Social Order, passim,* and Fisher, *Educational Speeches,* p. 9.

brought into perspective. The Industrial Council, in fact, will find itself taking up attitudes on social questions in exactly the same way that the trade-unionist has been driven to consider the general theory of the state, to have an attitude to life, in addition to his specific, immediate economic demands. Indeed it is permissible to suggest that the Industrial Councils will be successful in proportion as they consider profoundly the ramifications of the immediate issue they confront. That does not, of course, mean that they will pass resolutions on secular education or the disestablishment of the church; though it may well lead them locally to insist on the neglect of things like the provision of technical instruction and nationally to influence profoundly such things as fiscal policy and international relations.

It is obvious, in fact, that immediately production is given the opportunity of organized speech, its utterance must profoundly affect political programs in nation and locality. The light it throws upon the process of production throws light upon the needs of the consumer as well. It in fact acts in such fashion as to orientate the consumer in the realities of the situation. An industrial council that asked for better education in Manchester, for example, could hardly meet with a light refusal from the municipal council. Nor ought one to minimize the value of giving to the employers the opportunity of systematic meetings with labor. That will not produce the abdication of the capitalist. But it will teach him how esentially human are at once the demands of labor and the labor "agitator" himself. Nothing, surely, is ever lost by the rational consideration of difficulties. The rate of progress towards the realization of labor's program itself depends upon the degree in which knowledge of its character and implications is spread abroad. The industrial council is a vehicle towards that end. The employer who meets the trade-unionist round a table talks of his ideas at his club. The way in which Mr. Webb has permeated the liberal party by conversation, by published writings, by lectures, is only different from the kind of permeation these councils afford in that he is one and the councils are many. They are an element in making the needs and desires of labor public such as it has rarely before enjoyed. We ought to be optimistic enough to believe that labor will be fortunate in that publicity.

IV

It has already been suggested that the Whitley Report accepts the chaotic federalism of the modern industrial system and brings into it something like ordered connection. It does not, indeed, suggest, as yet, any relationship between the national industrial councils. That however, as has been pointed out, must logically result from the very fact of industrial interdependence. Such a hierarchical structure, from works to district, from district to national industry, from the national unit to the whole system of production is, in reality, little less than the creation of a state. It brings the whole process of production face to face with the whole process of consumption; for the latter, dominantly an interest of territorial juxtaposition, is the underlying implication of our parliamentary structure. This division of function necessarily throws its shadow far across our usual concepts of the state. We have, indeed, so naturally regarded the latter as the representative of society as a whole that our own erection of an authority which is in a position to challenge

the uniqueness of that claim comes with something of a
shock. Yet it is nothing less that is involved in the
logical outcome of our present tendencies.

Nothing less, at least, on a single supposition. If it is
at all true that the center of power is passing more and
more to the working-class then this division of control by
function has a peculiar significance that demands a close
analysis. No one, indeed, who examined the condition of
labor as it is organized in the trade-unions today could
seriously urge that it was fitted to take charge of the
state. But it is at least equally true that so long as
the state is built upon a class structure of which capitalism is the main characteristic the interest of the working
class is not dominantly regarded. Possibly, of course,
the outcome of the next few years may be a new kind of
industrial feudalism in which the workers will exchange
liberty for comfort. Certainly as Dean Pound has
shown,[101] there have been important ways in which the last
fifty years have seen a remarkable transition from contract to status. Were that to be the case it is probable
that the industrial councils contemplated by the Whitley
Report would either serve no useful purpose at all, or
act merely as a means towards lulling the creative tenets
of trade unionism into somnolence. It is in any event
true that they predicate a trade unionism far more virile
and intelligent than in the past. What it secures is going
to depend in part upon the ability with which its case
is presented and in part upon the way in which it organ-
izes each special industry. A trade-union defeated at
the council table will get even less than it now gets by an
appeal to Parliament. But there is no special occasion
for such pessimism. Even when the last fears of a guar-

101 See his article in the *Harvard Law Review* for January, 1917.

antee of capitalist existence by the state [102] have been taken into account, it remains true that the forces of education are on the side of labor. It remains not less true that the appeal it can make is to the name of freedom and, however curiously, that appeal has its roots deep in every human soul. If it can be shown that capitalism is incompatible with freedom and that the modern state must necessarily assume a capitalistic complexion, there is every reason to suppose that the movement of events will be in the direction of more democracy rather than less. In that aspect the future of the state becomes an inquiry of special significance. If there is a necessary permanence about the sovereignty of the King in Parliament what, clearly, we must expect is a gradual replacement of a capitalist state by a form of organization in which a vast series of government departments control modern industries as they now control the telephone and postal services. Parliament would represent producer not less than consumer and the business of production would be carried on by officials in something like the fashion in which local government is now organized relative to central control.

Yet it is surely difficult to believe that a simple nationalization has anything of final value to contribute to the general problem before us. Nationalization might well solve the basic problem of property in the sense that expropriation of the capitalist would leave a surplus of wealth for the increase of wages. But that is in no real sense the root of the matter. What our general experience of nationalization suggests is its invariable tendency to the bureaucratic government of the industries con-

102 Cole, *Self-government in Industry*, Appendix B.

cerned. The Post Office provides, on the whole, a service which compares more than favorably with that of any other country; but no one can examine the Holt Report without the feeling that it has not gone to the root of industrial freedom. The same is true, in an even greater degree, of municipal ownership. There is a slightly better average rate of wages, and a slight decrease in the average rate of hours of labor. But no real attempt is anywhere made at the democratization of any industry owned, or operated, by the agencies of the state. It is a fact of the highest import that in France the most revolutionary hypotheses of social reorganization should have come from the employees of the state.[103] That has not been true of England; but the two definite demands for a share in industrial control have come from a section of the postal workers, on the one hand, and the employees of the monopolistically-organized and state-protected railways, on the other. Any government which charges itself with industrial control will be bound, first of all, to look to continuity of service. In that aspect the officials will be tempted to keep control in their own hands. That, as they believe, is necessary in the interests of standards of efficiency and of uniformity of regulation. But that is also, in sober fact, to state a final case against any systematic national control in the sense of the control exercised by government over the telephones. It implies a centralization which, while it may improve the material condition of the worker, does nothing to offer him a definite spiritual interest in his work. It is not enough, as a recent and remarkable government report has pointed out,[104] to put up a suggestion box in the office and urge

[103] Cf. my *Authority in the Modern State*, Ch. 5.
[104] *Report on Works Committees*, p. 35.

that the worker's experience and inventiveness ought to find adequate satisfaction there. That is not and cannot be the case. The only real satisfaction comes from an actual share in deliberation and in the determination of its results. That has been the value of much of the success of the Works Committees so recently instituted by the war; the opportunity organically to state a case satisfies the hunger for self-determination which cannot be subverted in any system which accepts the criteria of democracy. We cannot, of course, govern industry by public meeting; but we cannot govern industry well until the thoughts and aspirations of its workers find a full place in its institutions.

That is why the organization of industry must necessarily relate itself to federalism. The worker must be given the opportunity of a real voice in the choosing of industrial management. It must be understood that there is a politics of industry not less real than the politics of the House of Commons. A workshop that elects its own foreman, a clerical staff that chooses its own chief, heads of departments who choose their own manager, have a far more real interest in the firm for which they work than if the bond between them and their employers is the merely nominal bond of wages. Nothing, indeed, would be more fatal than such an industrial organization as led to the state being regarded simply as an employer. Trade-unions would then, as Mr. Webb has insisted,[105] be necessary; but would be necessary for purposes fatal to the underlying conception of the state. They would be organizations of which the purpose would be simply to drive as hard a bargain as possible with the government department which controlled them; and their success

105 *Industrial Democracy*, last chapter.

would be in proportion to the size and communal importance of the industry concerned. In such a conception there is nothing of that idealism it is so necessary to introduce into political processes. Mr. Wallas has noted the mystic effect [106] upon the youthful porter of identification with the Great Northern Railway. But the influence lasts only for the first few months of labor. Once it has become a daily routine what he notes is not the splendor of service, the pride of self-support, but the technical drudgery it involves. The real problem of industrial organization is to enable the porter to retain through his working life the enthusiasm of its inception.

It is the main problem of the state as well; and that is why we cannot divorce the problem of industry therefrom. What, in reality, is involved is the meaning of freedom, the way in which we translate our definition of its content into the stuff of which the state is made. We perhaps too little remember that the theory of freedom has a history in the light of which its immediate significance must be read. Lord Morley has somewhere said that the definitions of liberty are innumerable, but they have been, for the most part, conceived in narrowly political terms.[107] What we need is rather such a conception as applies to those impulses of men that are mainly at work in political society. It is herein that the value of T. H. Green's definition of liberty is to be found.[108] For our main business is to get the creative impulses of men to work and it is herein that modern organization has

[106] *The Great Society*, p. 7.

[107] This is eminently true, for instance, of the criterion suggested by Acton in his *History of Freedom*, p. 3. It fails because it has no relevance to the problem of industrial organization.

[108] *Works*, II, p. 309.

so signally failed. Concentration of power has been, in general, the only known source of efficiency, nor has it been seen that it implies the negation of democracy. For, after all, where power is concentrated in a few hands there is lacking that spirit of responsibility without which no man can attain the full expression of his faculties. There is more than a negative danger in such concentration. It is not only, as Acton scathingly said,[109] that it "corrodes the conscience, hardens the heart, and confounds the understanding" of those who hold power; it deadens in any state the impulses which make for the greatness of a civilization. That is why any state in which the political office is united to the religious will sooner or later tread the path of despotism. That is why, also, any state in which a single class is predominant sooner or later must disregard the public interest in order to retain their power. That disregard, indeed, will cause the destruction of their government; for the belief of Plato that a state ought not to secure obedience if it fails to secure respect is no more than the summary of historic experience. The real truth is that the members of a state are powerless against an efficient centralization wielded in the interest of any social fragment, however large. It prevents the balance of associations which is the safeguard of liberty. It secures uniformity of which, from the very constitution of human nature, liberty is the direct antithesis. For where the creative impulses of men are given full play, there is bound to be diversity, and diversity provokes, in its presence, a decentralized organization to support it. That is why the secret of liberty is the division of power. But that political system in which a division of power is most

109 *History of Freedom*, p. 11.

securely maintained is a federal system; and, indeed, there is a close connection between the idea of federalism and the idea of liberty.

In Europe, at least this is too little understood, for the sufficient reason that liberty and equality are understood as separate instead of as different facets of the same ideal. Nor can we preserve equality in any state without a measure of federal structure; for the distribution of power is the real check upon its usurpation. It is more than that. It is the only way in which sufficient centres can be created of deliberation and enterprise to enlist the abilities of men in the public service. It is clear, for example, that the real barrier to creative opinion in the Roman Catholic Church is its excessive centralization. So long as ideas radiate outwards from a single point in the circle they will not adequately radiate inwards from the circumference. The concentration of power in the papal hands will mean that thought is inactive everywhere save at the point of responsibility; or, at least, that thought will strive less to master the facts than to distort them to the service of power. A system that cannot contain Lamennais and Döllinger and Tyrrell stands, governmentally, self-condemned.[110] But what is here true of Rome is true also of the political state. We need to federalize the organization of England simply in order to give play to the mass of creative opinion which remains today untouched by political forces. It is here urged that the secret of its revivification is to associate in the exercise of power those who have thus far been too merely its subjects. The principle of tacit consent upon which we work in government

[110] See this worked out in detail in Chapter III of my *Authority in the Modern State.*

is too theoretical in character. It results in the virtual annihilation of every individuality that is not either at the center of things, or finding its compensation for exclusion in some such activity as art. We have to provide that political consent be no longer passive, but active in character, that it come from free and instructed minds widespread among the mass of men.

v

What, in fact, does this involve? No system of politics is firmly grounded that is not securely built upon the past. We cannot attempt anything like the revolution in spiritual form of which we have need in a day. We cannot, even in our remotest dreams, give every man some actual share in the business of administration. Not, indeed, that Aristotle's definition of citizenship has not enshrined a truth we too easily forget; but the size of the modern state makes the hope of anything other than a representative system not merely inadmissable but, in the nature of things, undesirable. We have to work with the materials we are given, and that involves the acceptance of their limited capacity.

We start from the theoretic purpose we admit in the state. It aims at the development of the fullest capacity for good possessed by its members. That implies at once liberty and equality; and it implies a federal structure that they may be given their due expression. It does not matter whether the federalism be a division of the unified purpose from above, rather than from below, whether it take, that is to say, the form of decentralization rather than the type of division with which the government of the United States has made us familiar. What is important is that too great power should at no place be concentrated in a few hands lest the individuality of man be repressed by the very institutions he has created to preserve it.

The problem is not merely one of area. Primarily, it is a problem of functions simply because the institutions of areas are, in England at least, reasonably adequate to their purpose, and because it is in the aspect of function that the possibilities of decentralization are most strikingly manifest. Unless we make power a process of democracy we withdraw energy from the consideration of social questions that could with value be directed into its channels. A single illustration will perhaps throw the process at issue into a clear perspective. It is doubtful whether any civil service in the world has so noble a record as the Civil Service of England. Yet no one can examine its workings without being struck at a certain curious intellectual inertia which suggests a too rigid stratification. The reason is not far to seek. Its system of promotion is determined from above. Little or no attempt is made to associate any personnel save that of heads of departments in the determination of any advance other than that of automatic increase of pay. The result is that the ideal of work chiefly inculcated is that of "correctness." Too great an activity outside the department is to be deprecated because it leads the heads to believe that one's full energy is not concentrated upon the labor in hand. It is best simply to follow the lines they lay down and establish a reputation for zeal and punctuality.[111] Inventions should be confined to new filing systems or a better method of keeping accounts. Things like this surely explain the abyss that exists

111 Cf. The amusing comments of Mr. F. G. Heath, *The British Civil Service*, Chs. 11–14.

between the divisions of the service. If promotion were, within each office, determined by a council in which each section had elected representatives, the heads of departments would learn much and call forth more. No system ought to be considered satisfactory in which the motives to originality are not emphasized. If Sir Henry Taylor does his work thoroughly, *"The Statesman"* ought to be an element in his promotion. Ways and means should be provided whereby the tragedy of Balzac's *"Les Employés"* can be avoided. But that can only be effected by the most thorough-going democratization.

If this is true of the Civil Service, it is far more true of business enterprises; for there the exigencies of a capitalistically-organized industrial system have necessitated the retention of oligarchic institutions. That does not mean to say that ability meets no recognition. It implies rather that the only interest organized by capitalistic industry is the material interest. The spiritual factors which self-government calls into play are too widely ignored. It is the error which is made in a military system which fails to emphasize the individual initiative of the private soldier; without it, the army may be a magnificent machine, but with it there comes into activity a spirit which, other factors being equal, is indomitable. For that initiative can feed itself upon the ideals at stake and it fights against overwhelming odds with a fire unquenchable. If such an effort is necessary in the army of war, it is surely far more vital in the army of peace. The brain of an army may be in its general staff; but that oligarchy is dependent upon that sum of qualities we call morale for the success of its efforts.

The same holds true in the industrial sphere; and,

so far, we have made no effort of any kind to apply it.
Everyone knows that profit-sharing and labor co-part-
nership are no more than *magni nominis umbrae*. Inevitably, therefore, we have suffered from political inertia
and economic discontent. We have suffered from political inertia because the reaction of economic upon political structure is so profound. We have suffered from
economic discontent because the structure of industry
does not provide an adequate expression for the impulses
of men. That is why it is rather upon industry than
upon politics, upon function rather than upon area, that
the consideration of a revival of political interest must
centre. We are presented with a quasi-federal system:
that is to say that large functions are left by the state
to settle their own problems. But, on the one hand, no
real effort has been made to relate that economic federalism to the categories of the political structure, and, on
the other, within each function there is no adequate
representative system.

The Whitley Report, in substance, though not in form,
answers the first need. It gives state-recognition to
those industrial units sufficiently organized to warrant
it, and provides the means for unorganized units to pass
into the stage of organization and recognition. Sooner
or later, it has here been suggested, that recognition of
control of productive effort, of functions, will tend to
influence the control of geographical areas, and so to
fructify the normal life of politics. From the purely
internal point of view, far less is done. An intermediate
economic sovereignty is recognized in the industrial
councils in the sense that the solutions they propose for
the problems of industry will, for working purposes,
become law. But no attempt is made as, in the nature

of things, it hardly could be made, to determine in what direction the balance of forces is to rest.

Yet that balance of forces is the crux of the whole question and the significance of this new structure is not completely understood until the direction of political evolution is, however summarily, examined. It is generally admitted that the outbreak of the present war heralded the end of an age; but so far, we have too little examined the meaning of what has gone before. Briefly, the nineteenth century was the period of middle-class supremacy. Those, that is to say, who were possessed of mobile economic power supplanted in the state those whose holdings were so largely confined to real property. It is inaccurate to say that the dominant characteristic of this middle class was the pursuit of money; Harpagon apart, money was for the city alderman who traded with the East Indies no more a final object than it was the final object of an English squire to increase his family acres by a lucky marriage for his eldest son; [112] both valued their possessions as the symbol of a power which could manifest itself in the most varied ways. Both secured a share in the political supremacy of their class as an expression of its economic supremacy.

But there is a fundamental difference between the character of middle-class dominance and that of the landowner. Not only does the former cast its net far more widely. It was a dominance which came in the name of freedom. That is, perhaps, more immediately obvious in the case of France and England, though no one who examines the arguments for the repeal of the Test and Corporation Acts and for political reform, can mis-

---

[112] This is, I think, the main error of Mr. R. H. Gretton's interesting study, *The Middle Class*. It mistakes means for ends.

take the strength of that sentiment of freedom in England also. It was merely because the privileges of the *ancien régime* were so much less obvious in England than in France, so much less narrowly conceived and firmly buttressed, that the French Revolution took a form so much more violent and dramatic. But, both in England and France, the content of social structure failed to adjust itself to older forms. Private good had become identified with public good to an extent no longer to be borne. It is unnecessary to attribute that disharmony to careful selfishness; rather is it due simply to an inability of adjustment to conditions which had changed so slowly as to leave their extent unrealized by any save the acutest minds.

It is that slowness of change which distinguishes in England the control of the squirearchy from the control of the middle-class. An agricultural civilization is necessarily less progressive than an industrial. Its wants are fewer and it has, accordingly, fewer and less disturbing ideas. The attainment to power of the middle class expressed the replacement of agriculture by industry as the type of English civilization. Not only did the wants of men grow vastly greater, but the means of supplying them, mostly through the application of science to industrial enterprise, grew vastly greater also. The result was to create an environment which changes with a rapidity that goes unnoticed unless we view it in historical perspective. Change, of course, produces its penalties, and a class which proves incapable of sufficient adaptation is bound to suffer loss of its power. It is in France, again, that such incapacity is most clearly visible; but in every country, at some period, the same phenomenon is visible. The Southern cotton-planter of America, for instance, who held sway until 1860, was unable to comprehend the industrial revolution caused by the immense development in the means of transportation, and the consequence was his rebellion against, and defeat at the hands of, the new social order that came into being. What is not less noticeable than the change in personnel is the redistribution in property that almost invariably accompanies it. The readjustment of wealth is, indeed, the inevitable mark of change in social relations; for we have as yet no historic instance of a poor class exercising power but subsidizing the wealthy whom it has supplanted. These changes have come more rapidly since 1760 simply because the environmental changes have been more rapid. Almost always it is a broadening of the base of power that results. Almost always, in addition, that growth in base is symptomatic of an increase of freedom.

This new federalism which, as we have seen, is slowly reaching the stage of articulate utterance is perhaps the herald of a similar change of this kind. It is at least noteworthy that the emphasis of its advocates is laid upon the additional freedom it can confer. Nor can one mistake the fact that the accusations levelled by it at the middle-class partake in general character of the typical counts of accusation against a class of which the domination is beginning to disintegrate. It is pointed out that the worker is unfree in his factory exactly as it was in 1832 pointed out that the manufacturing of Manchester lacks the essential symbol of freedom; and if we sought to explain the reason why the insistence is industrial rather than political it would be necessary to trace the history of a political thought which goes back on one side, to the failure of chartism, and, on the other, to the doctrines of Hodgskin and his allies which Marx made the common possession of the labor movement.[113] That sense of cramped impulses which seek the channels of larger movement is seen, almost equally, in the shift in the burden of taxation. The graduated income-tax, the taxation of land-values, the enormous increase in death-duties, the vague but vital sense that the cost of social improvement must be borne by those who can afford to purchase luxuries — all these have a significance no man may mistake. Even the general direction of social policy contributes its quotum to such an interpretation. To make freely accessible to all what was before a matter of hard effort and careful purchase is a denial of the fundamental axiom of the capitalist state. The idea that poverty was the expression of sin, probably inherited from the Non-conformist relation to trade,[114] is an idea to which only a few of the more ardent and ancient individualists now cling. Measures like Workmen's Compensation, the new interpretation put upon vicarious liability,[115] all point in the same direction. They mean, at bottom, that if the business man has the profits of industry, he must pay the cost of the state-life in part return. And the cost is of a state-life that grows ever wider and more complex.

It may be said that there are men in the business world who realize all this and that they are for nothing more anxious than to work out an amicable basis of relation-

[113] Cf. Prof. Foxwell's well-known introduction to the translation of Menger's *Right to the Whole Produce of Labour.*

[114] As is pointed out by Professor Levy in his *Economic Liberalism.* Cf. my *Political Thought from Locke to Bentham,* Ch. 8.

[115] Cf. my paper in the *Yale Law Journal* for November, 1916.

ship with labor.[116] There is undoubtedly some truth in such assertions; but of the business world in general it is not even remotely accurate. Capital shows nowhere, on any large scale, a desire to abdicate from its control; rather is its effort, by the highway of compensated nationalization to escape the tragedy that might result from any widespread industrial disruption. It is still widely true, as Mr. and Mrs. Webb wrote twenty years ago,[117] that "to the brain-working captain of industry, maintaining himself on thousands a year, the manual-working wage-earner seems to belong to another species, having mental faculties and bodily needs altogether different from his own." The familiar plea of the business man that he will manage his factory in his own way is the expression of that sense. But there has everywhere grown up the belief that the full fruition of the democratic state demands that the conditions of production be determined by the democratic coöperation of its agents. In the long run that is fatal to capitalism in its present form. We shall not continue forever to leave industry in that bureaucratic tradition where, as has been admirably said,[118] its habits of mind are "nourished upon a belief that everybody in an office except the head of it is so stupid that the only way to get business done is to reduce every problem to a few simple formulae and insist that every case is brought under them." It is coming to be seen quite clearly that the traditions of capitalism are historic categories like any other; and no

116 As Mr. W. L. Hichens, for example, in his *Some Problems of Modern Industry,* the Watt lecture for 1917.

117 *Industrial Democracy* (ed. of 1902), p. 821.

118 See an admirable article, "Thoughts on Bureaucracy," in the *London Times Educational Supplement* for June 20, 1918.

one can read the debates on the tenth clause of the Education Bill of 1918 [119] without realizing that they are outworn. A business that insists on child labor as the condition of its existence is simply parasitic upon the national life. No one denies that, however we construct the state, some form of organizing power will be necessary. What is coming more and more to be denied is the belief that, as in modern industry, that power must be clothed in oligarchic garb. The modern business man, amid many high qualities, has thought so much in terms of money, that the numerous and interlacing social interests, upon which the equilibrium which supports him so largely depends, have in great part escaped his notice.

What, largely, has escaped his notice is the political significance of trade-union structure. In a rudimentary way it is coming more and more to assume all the typical characteristics of a state. It is developing organs of reasoned government. It is becoming expert in the processes of which special knowledge was originally supposed to be the prerogative of the man of business. It has worked out a view of life which achieves an ever-greater political influence. It has passed, as has been pointed out, the stage where its influence was confined to hours and wages and more and more becomes concerned for the spiritual freedom of its constituents. It would, of course, be absurd to claim that there is any widespread consciousness of the details of this process in the trade-union world; like every great movement, what we see at work is the leaven of an eager minority. But as it becomes every day more obvious that the hold of the business

[119] Cf. The report of the debate on this — the Child-Labor clause —and the concessions extracted from Mr. Fisher in the *Times Educational Supplement* for June 13, 1918.

theory of life upon the state is weakening, so does it also
become more clear that the trade-unions are becoming
the categories into which the structure of capitalism may
be absorbed. We do not, of course, know the time such
evolution will take. We can, also, be very certain that
the prophecies of its character will all, in some degree,
be mistaken. What we do know is that a capitalist
state has failed to specialize in certain final human impulses, and that the trade-unions are organizing a means
to their satisfaction. We can see, too, how the effort
of a government which is not predominantly trade-
unionist in sympathy unconsciously hastens that evolution by its attempt, however small in scope, to find a
representative government for industry. For that is
clearly the admission that the oligarchical control of
industry has failed. It is the provision of a mechanism
which, wisely used, may well serve as the vehicle of transition to self-government in industry. The whole point
seems to be that the complexity of the structure of an
industrial state is beyond the grasp of a mind, like the
capitalist mind, which mainly is specialized in the direction of money-making. For that direction is becoming
not merely less important, but, within the framework of
capitalism there has developed another type of mind
which has specialized in the directions in which its fore-
runner was most notably a failure.

It is difficult, in such an aspect, not to believe that
trade-unionism is destined to absorb the directive ability
that, undoubtedly, capitalism can furnish, and turn it
to its own purposes. That prospect has become the
more likely as a result of the experience of the last four
years. The democratic forces of civilization have been
put to the test of conflict against an autocratic system;

and it is now indubitable that they will survive. But they have not withstood the shock without serious and searching confusion. Few things have been more obvious than the inability of the capitalist structure, in its pre-war form, to meet the national need. It has had to receive assistance from the state. It has had to be controlled by the state in the interests of national safety. It has had to ask trade-unionism for the surrender of those safeguards by which, in the past, an adequate minimum of civilized life could alone be preserved for the workers. The only institutions which, in the course of war, have worked at all well have been those, at least in industry, of democratic tendency. Governmental control has been an unsatisfactory expedient. The abdication of Parliament has made obvious the utter insufficiency, for human needs, of a bureaucratic system. The restoration of industrial conditions, at the close of war, can only be made upon the basis of returning within their basic trades, a large measure of popular supervision. Everything, in fact, has tended to emphasize the human factor in industry at the expense of the money-making factor. The sole condition of industrial peace was the acceptance of this fact as a starting point. Labor was led, from this, to the formulation of a policy which goes down to the foundations of the state. What, at the moment, has clearly emerged, is a two-fold novelty of outlook. On the one hand it has become evident that the state must dictate to industry certain minimum terms upon which alone it can be conducted. Business, on the other, is to be transformed from a chaotic autocracy into, at least in certain aspects, a federal and representative system.

Such, at least, seems the alternative to revolution, but

it is to be noted that it is the minimum alternative. The
war has to be paid for, and it is already becoming obvious that whatever forms the payment takes, it is bound
to strike at the roots of the economic barrier which
separates class from class. The debt, certainly, cannot
be repudiated. If its payment take the form of a capital
levy the industrial power in the hands of government
will at least vie with that of capitalism itself; and it
will be equal at a time when the electorate has been
transformed beyond all past recognition. This latter
factor, like all such factors, is one upon which few hopes
and only the rarest certainties can be builded. But it is
universally agreed that the last four years have made
a return to the economic status before the war impossible; and that, in itself, will change the political system.
Political institutions, indeed, are themselves in grave need
of change. The one institutional benefit derived by government from the war is the prime minister's secretariat,
which can hardly be called fundamental.[120] The attempted
division between policy and administration has proved
as barren in practice as is every such attempt at a
separation of powers.[121] The abdication of parties has
in nowise cleansed the atmosphere; and ministries of all
the talents have only borne witness to the truth of
Disraeli's famous dictum that England does not love
coalitions. A glimpse of the possibilities of education,
indeed, we have caught. We shall no longer, in Mr.
Fisher's admirable phrase,[122] send out the generations
chartless upon an unending ocean. We have seen, too,

---

[120] It was suggested by Mr. Graham Wallas before the war; see
The Great Society, p. 290.

[121] Cf. my note in *The New Republic*, August 25, 1917.

[122] *Educational Speeches*, p. 13.

the real need for plan in the state, the folly of attempting to go forward by waiting upon the crises that may occur; Ireland, at least, will not have sacrificed herself in vain if she has given point to that stupidity. We have learned, also, that there is, in any public service, a point in official staffs beyond which mere increase is incompatible with liberalism. Government may be strong, but if it is to be human it cannot have the tentacles of an octopus. The value, also, of publicity has been demonstrated by the very danger of its opposite. A democracy, as we know by hard experience, cannot hope to prosper unless its fundamental fights are contested in the House of Commons.

So much, at least, is gain even though we have paid a heavy price for it. Yet, as our knowledge and the facts we encounter converge, they bring out the first question of all questions in political life. We have to decide what we mean the state to do before we pronounce that what it does is good. If its object is the preservation of individuality, in so far as its specialism contributes to the public good, our present system stands largely self-condemned by the mere description of it. Nor is there any reason in the world why we should expect it to be otherwise. The path of history is strewn with the wreck of social systems; there is no cause why our own should be the sole exception. There is perhaps cause rather for congratulation than regret in the vision of its disappearance. It passes because it fails to fulfil the more generous aspirations of a new time. We seek today the ways and means whereby we can renew in men their interest in the state which so greatly weaves itself into the stuff of their lives. "War," said Burke in one of his flashes of incomparable wisdom,[123] "war is a situation which sets in its full light the value of the hearts of the people." What it has revealed to us is the riches that have gone unused. What it has most strikingly shown is the importance of the people. And with its realization there must be, as he said, the end of that "interior ministry" of which he skilfully portrayed the danger. That, above all, at which we aim is the representation in the structure of the state of all that makes for its enrichment. But we do not believe in the adequacy of a representation without power. We do not believe that a power can be other than futile which is not directly related to the immediate business of men. We believe, as Burke believed, that the "heart of the citizen is a perennial spring of energy to the state." But energy is impossible when it is deprived of liberty and liberty is impossible save where there is a division of power. So long as the offices of men do not make their souls erect and their minds intelligent we cannot assert that they have been given the credit of their humanity. That has been, in the past, our failure; it is to its repair we must bend our effort.

[123] Thoughts on the Present Discontents (*Works,* World's Classics ed., Vol. II, p. 39).

THE RESPONSIBILITY OF THE STATE IN ENGLAND *

I

THE British Crown covers a multitude of sins. "The King," says Blackstone in a famous sentence,[1] "is not only incapable of doing wrong, but even of thinking wrong, he can never mean to do an improper thing; in him is no folly or weakness." A long history lies behind those amazing words; and if, as to Newman,[2] they seem rather the occasion for irony than for serious political speculation, that is perhaps because their legal substance would have destroyed the argument he was anxious to make. In England, that vast abstraction we call the state has, at least in theory, no shadow even of existence; government, in the strictness of law, is a complex system of royal acts based, for the most part, upon the advice and consent of the Houses of Parliament. We technically state our theory of politics in terms of an entity which has dignified influence without executive power. The King can do no wrong partly because, at a remote period of history, the place where alone the doing of wrong could best be righted was his place, and had won

* Reprinted from the *Harvard Law Review*, Vol. XXXII, No. 5.
[1] 1 *Com.*, 1813 ed., 254.
[2] *The Present Position of Catholics in England*, 27 f.

103

preëminence only after a long struggle with the courts
of lesser lords. The King's courts became the supreme
resort of justice simply because, in his hands, that commodity was more purely wrought and finely fashioned
than elsewhere; and since it is clearly unintelligent to
make a man judge in his own cause, since, moreover, the
royal judges do not, in legal fact, conceal the royal
presence, there seems to have been no period of history
in which the King could be sued in the courts of the
realm.

It is difficult to say at what precise period this non-
suability of the Crown passed into infallibility. The
Tudor despotism seems to have been that critical period
of transition when learned lawyers like Plowden will talk
what Maitland has aptly termed "metaphysiological
nonsense;" [3] and the aggressive Coke will dispatch the
Crown into a corporation sole of a kind but rarely
known to previous English history.[4] Not, indeed, that
men are not troubled by the consequences of that dual
personality the Tudor lawyers called into being. Thomas
Smith did not write aimlessly of an English commonwealth;[5] and that public which the royal burglary of
1672 forced into responsibility for the National Debt
shows, clearly enough, that the fusion of Crown and state
is not yet complete.[6] Even in the nineteenth century
Acts of Parliament will be necessary to show that behind
the robes of a queen can be discerned the desires of a
woman.[7]

---

3 3 *Collected Papers,* 249.

4 *Ibid.,* 244–45.

5 *Ibid.,* 253.

6 1 Macaulay, *History of England,* Everyman's edition, 170.

7 25 & 26 Vict. c. 37 (1862); 36 & 37 Vict. c. 61 (1873).

It is probable that the reëmergence of the dogma of divine right exercised a potent influence on this development. Certainly men could not have encountered the speech of James and his eager adherents, or the logic of that continental absolutism which is merely summarized in Bossuet, without being affected by them. Even when the Revolution of 1688 destroys its factual basis, it has become capable of transmutation into a working hypothesis of government; and anyone can see that Blackstone, who best sums up the political evolution of this creative period, writes "Crown" where the modern political philosopher would use the term "State." The vague hinterland of ancient prerogative went also, doubtless, to show that the Crown is a thing apart. The privilege of the King's household leaped to the eyes.[8] His freedom from unpleasant proximity to arrest declared the sacred character with which he was invested.[9] "The most high and absolute power of the realme of England," says Sir Thomas Smith, not less learned, be it remembered, in the mysteries of law than of politics,[10] "consisteth in the Parliament"; but even so noteworthy an assembly cannot bind the Crown by its statutes.[11] Indeed, its position is even more privileged since the Crown, by prerogative, takes advantage of statute.[12] Fictions [13] and estoppel [14] pale into insignificance before the overmastering power of

[8] 2 Co. Inst. 631, 4 *ibid.*, 24; Rex *v.* Foster, 2 Taunt. 166–67 (1809); Rex *v.* Moulton, 2 Keb. 3.

[9] 3 Bl. Com. 289.

[10] *De Republica Anglorum*, ed. Alston, 48.

[11] Magdalen College Case, 11 Co. Rep. 66; Sheffield *v.* Ratcliffe, Hob. 334.

[12] Rex *v.* Cruise, 21 Ch. 65 (1852).

[13] Anon., Jenk. 287 (1613).

[14] Coke's Case, Godb. 289.

its presence. Laches [15] and prescription [16] lose their meaning when the Crown has become desirous of action. It chooses its own court; [17] it may, save where, of its own grace, it has otherwise determined,[18] avoid the payment of costs.[19] Here, assuredly, is a power that does not need the sanction of collective terminology that men may recognize its strength.

Prerogative such as this would be intolerable did the Crown act as in theory it has warrant. But the English have a genius for illogical mitigation; and the history of ministerial responsibility enshrines not the least splendid contribution we made to the theory of representative government. The seventeenth century in England makes definite a practice which, if irregular in its operation, can yet trace its pedigree back to the dismissal of Longchamp in 1190; [20] the execution of Strafford and the impeachment of Danby are only the two culminating peaks of its development. What ministerial responsibility has come to mean is that the King's ministers shall make answer for the advice they proffer and the acts which flow therefrom; and in the period in which the royal power is delegated, for practical purposes, to the Cabinet we have herein a valuable safeguard against its arbitrary abuse.

Yet ministers are not the Crown. What they urge and do does not, however politically unwise or legally erroneous, involve a stain upon the perfection of its character. It may be true that when they order action, the Crown

15 Co. Litt., 57 b.
16 Wheaton v. Maple [1893], 3 Ch. 48.
17 4 Co. Inst. 17; Bl. Com. 257.
18 23 & 24 Vict. c. 34.
19 Johnson v. Rex [1904], A. C. 817.
20 Stubbs, *Constit. Hist.*, 6 ed., I, 539.

has, in substance, been brought into play; but the responsibility for their acts remains their own since the King can do no wrong. The law knows no such thing as the government. When the King's ministers find their way into the courts it is still a personal responsibility which they bear. Statutory exceptions apart, no such action need cause a moment's qualms to the grim guardians of the royal treasury; the courts' decision does not involve a raid upon the exchequer.

In such an aspect, state-responsibility, in the sense in which continental theorists use that term, remains unknown. The state cannot be sued, because there is no state to sue. There is still no more than a Crown, which hides its imperfections beneath the cloak of an assumed infallibility. The Crown is irresponsible save where, of grace, it relaxes so stringent an attitude. Foreign writers of distinction have thus found it easy to doubt whether the protection the English constitutional system affords to its citizens is in fact as great as the formal claims of the "rule of law" would suggest.[21] For while it is clear enough that the broad meaning of this principle is the subjection of every official to definite and certain rules, in the nature of things that which gives the official his meaning and is equivalent in fact to the incorporation of the people as a whole, escapes the categories of law.

Nor is this all. Careful analysis of the responsibility of a public servant suggests that the rule of law means less than may at first sight appear. There has been unconsciously evolved a doctrine of capacities which is in its substance hardly less mystical than Plowden's speculations about the kingly person. Certain protec-

[21] M. Leroy in *Libres Entretiens*, 4me series, 368.

tions are offered to the King's servants which go far to placing them in a position more privileged than the theory underlying the rule of law would seem to warrant. The growth, moreover, of administrative law in the special evolution characteristic of the last few years is putting the official in a position where it becomes always difficult and often impossible for the courts to examine his acts. We have nothing like the *droit administratif* of the Continent of Europe; but we are nevertheless weaving its obvious implications into the general system of our law.

It is easy to understand that in the days when the functions of government were negative rather than positive in character, the consequences of its irresponsibility should hardly have pressed themselves upon the minds of men. For it is important to have constantly before us the fact that the essential problem is the responsibility of government. Our English state finds its working embodiment in the Crown; but if we choose to look beneath that noble ornament we shall see vast government offices full of human, and, therefore, fallible men. We choose to ignore them; or rather we know them only to make them pay for errors they have not committed on their own behalf. So do we offer vicarious victims for a state that hides itself beneath an obsolete prerogative.

Public money is, of course, a trust; and it is perhaps this that has involved the retention, in relation to the modern state, of a notion the antiquarian character of which is obvious the moment the real machinery of government is substituted for the clumsy fiction of the Crown. Public money is a trust; and thus it was that until the nineteenth century things less than the state, like charitable institutions, were beyond liability for the acts of

their servants. But *Mersey Docks Trustees* v. *Gibbs* [22]
emphasized, half a century ago, that defective administration in any enterprise not conducted by the Crown
must entail its just and natural consequence. It is but
obvious justice that if the public seek benefit, due care
must be taken in the process not to harm the lesser interests therein encountered. It is a matter not less of
political than of economic experience that the enforcement of liability for fault, often, indeed, without it,[23] is
the only effective means to this end. Where we refuse
to take the state for what it in fact is, all we do is to
make it superior to justice. Responsibility on the part
of the Crown does not involve its degradation; it is
nothing more than the obvious principle that in a human
society acts involve consequences and consequences involve obligations. We are invested with a network of
antiquarianism because the conceptions of our public law
have not so far developed that they meet the new facts
they encounter. We, in a word, avoid the payment of
our due debts by a shamefaced shrinking behind the kingly
robe we have abstracted from the living ruler.

It is well to analyze the meaning of responsibility
before we examnie our remoteness from it. The modern
state is, in the American phrase, nothing so much as a
great public-service corporation. It undertakes a vast
number of functions — education, police, poor-law, defense, insurance against ill-health and unemployment —
many of which, it is worth while to note, were, in the
past, provided for by private endeavor. State acts are
performed by individuals, even though the act is invested
with the majesty of the Crown; for an abstract entity

[22] L. R. 1 H. L. 93 (1866).
[23] Cf. Laski, 26 Yale L. J. 105 f.

must work through agents and servants. To-day such acts are protected from the normal consequence of law. Often enough, indeed, the individual agent is not so protected; if he drives a mail van recklessly down the street he can be sued as a private person. But we cannot penetrate through him to the master by whom he is employed. The resources of the Postmaster-General are not at our disposal for the accidents that may be caused by the acts of his servants.[24] Yet, in real and literal fact, these acts are not a whit different from those of other men. The Postmaster-General may be the depositary of special powers; but that should surely cast upon him rather a greater obligation than a freedom from responsibility for their exercise.

The theory of responsibility is, in this regard, no more than a plea that realism be substituted in the place of fiction. It urges that when the action of the state entails a special burden upon some individual or class of men, the public funds should normally compensate for the damage suffered. Everyone can see that if the state took over the railways it would be unfair to refuse the continuance of actions by those who had on some account previously commenced them; nor is it less clear that if a postal van runs over Miss Bainbridge she has, in precisely similar fashion, a claim that should not go unanswered. There must, in short, be payment for wrongful acts; and the source of those acts is unimportant. We can, indeed, see that there are reasonable grounds for certain exceptions. Complete freedom of judicial expression, without any penalization of utterance, is too clear a need to demand defense. In a less degree, a member of Parliament needs protection from the normal

[24] Bainbridge v. Postmaster-General [1906], 1 K. B. 178.

consequence of law, if he is at all fully to perform his function; though, even here, experience suggests the value of some extra-parliamentary means whereby the member can be made to weigh his words.[25]   Still, in general, the principle is clear. Government must pay where it wrongs. There are no arguments against it save, on the one hand, the dangerous thesis that the state-organs are above the law, on the other, the tendency to believe that ancient dogma must, from its mere antiquity, coincide with modern need. Dogmas, no less than species, have their natural evolution; and it may well result in serious injustice if they linger on in a condition of decay.

II

The personal liability of the Crown to-day is, broadly speaking, not merely non-existent in law, but unimportant also in political fact. No king is likely, as in Bagehot's classic illustration, to shoot his own Prime Minister through the head; though the servants of Elizabeth and her boisterous father must not seldom have stood in fear of personal violence. The real problem here concerns itself with government departments. They are the constitutional organs of the Crown, and their acts are binding upon it. But how are they to be reached if an injured person deem that he has suffered injustice? The law is clear upon this point beyond all question. The subject cannot bring action against the Crown because the Crown can do no wrong. A government department lives beneath the widespread cloak of that infallibility, and it cannot, unless statute has otherwise provided, be

25 This will be clear to anyone who follows the questions and speeches of Mr. Pemberton Billing through the Parliamentary Debates for 1917 and 1918.

sued in the courts. The law, indeed, is thick with all manner of survivals. For practical purposes, the Elder Brethren of Trinity House are under the jurisdiction of the Admiralty and the Board of Trade; but they are, in origin, a private body, and their acts thus render them liable to answer to the law.[26] So, too, for certain purposes, the Secretary of State for India in Council is the successor of the East India Company, and where those purposes are concerned the courts will take cognizance of his acts;[27] but if the reader of Macaulay is tempted to think that Clive and Warren Hastings did not hesitate, on occasion, to perform sovereign functions, he yet must legally remember that the company was not technically a sovereign body.[28] There is thus a definite environment which surrounds each seeming exception to the general rule. If there is limitation, it is that act of grace which continental theorists have taught us to deduce from the inherent wisdom of the sovereign power.[29] But the exceptions are relatively few in number, and, for the most part, they cautiously reside within the narrow field of contract.

The broad result is, to say the least, suggestive. Until 1907, and then only as a result of statute, no government department could be sued for violation of the very patent of which the Crown itself is grantor.[30] The acts of the Lord-Lieutenant of Ireland, even when they involve the seemingly purposeless breaking of heads at a public meet-

26 Gilbert v. Trinity House, 17 Q. B. D. 795 (1886); Cairn Line v. Trinity House [1908], 1 K. B. 528.

27 Jehanger M. Cursetji v. Secretary of State for India in Council, 1 L. R. 27 Bomb. 189 (1902).

28 Moodaly v. Moreton, 2 Dick. 652 (1785).

29 Cf. my Authority in the Modern State, Ch. 1.

30 Feather v. Regina, 6 B. & S. 257 (1865).

ing, are acts of state, and so outside the purview of the courts.[31] The servants of the Crown owe no duty to the public except as statute may have otherwise provided;[32] so that even where a royal warrant regulates the pensions and pay of the army, the Secretary of State for War cannot be compelled to obey it.[33] He is the agent of the Crown; and only the Crown can pass upon the degree to which he has fulfilled the terms of his agency. Yet, in sober fact, that is to make his acts material for the decision of his colleagues, and, in an age of collective cabinet responsibility, thus to make him judge in his own cause. Sir Claude Macdonald may, as Commissioner for the Nigerian Protectorate, engage Mr. Dunn as consul for a period of three years; but if he chooses to dismiss Mr. Dunn within the specified limit, even the question of justification is beyond the competence of the courts.[34] Nor will the law inquire whether adequate examination has been made before the refusal of a petition of right; the Home Secretary's discretion is here so absolute that the judge will even hint to him that the oath of official secrecy is jeopardized when he remarks that he considered and refused the petition.[35] A captain of the Royal Navy may burn the schooner of a private citizen in the mistaken belief that she is engaged in the slave trade, and even if the vessel so destroyed were its owner's sole means of livelihood, he is left without remedy so far as the Crown is concerned.[36] Neither Mr. Beck nor Mr. Edalji had rights against the

[31] Sullivan v. Earl Spencer, Ir. Rep. 6 C. L. 173 (1872).
[32] Gidley v. Palmerston, 3 B. & B. 275 (1822).
[33] Ibid.
[34] Dunn v. Macdonald [1897], 1 Q. B. 555.
[35] Irwin v. Gray, 3 F. & F. 635 (1862).
[36] Tobin v. Regina, 14 C. B. (n. s.) 505 (1863).

Crown for long years of mistaken imprisonment.[37] So, too, it did not assist Miss Bainbridge when a duly accredited agent of the Crown injured her in his progress; what was left her was a worthless remedy against a humble wage earner from whom no recovery was possible.[38]

It is the realm of high prerogative that we have entered; and it would be perhaps less arid if it but possessed the further merit of logical arrangement. The truth is that in its strictest rigor the system is unworkable; and from ancient times an effort has been made to mitigate the severities it involves. The origin of the Petition of Right is wrapped in no small obscurity;[39] but its clear meaning is an ungracious effort to do justice without the admission of a legal claim. Nor is the remedy at all broad in character, for the Crown is avaricious where to show itself generous is to compromise the Exchequer. The Petition of Right is limited to a definite class of cases. Until 1874 it could be used for the recovery of some chattel or hereditament to which the suppliant laid claim; and it was only in that year that the genius of commercial understanding by which Lord Blackburn was distinguished secured its extension to the general field of contract.[40] Even when judgment has been obtained no execution can issue against the Crown. The petitioner remains dependent upon a combination of goodwill and the moral pressure he may hope to secure from public opinion.

The matter is worth stating in some little detail. "The

---

37 For a French attempt to remedy this defect, see *infra*.
38 Bainbridge *v.* Postmaster-General, *supra*.
39 Clode, *Petition of Right*, Ch. 1.
40 Thomas *v.* Regina, L. R. 10 Q. B. 31 (1874).

proceeding by petition of right," said Cottenham, L. C.,[41] "exists only for the purpose of reconciling the dignity of the Crown and the rights of the subject, and to protect the latter against any injury arising from the acts of the former; but it is no part of its object to enlarge or alter those rights." A later definition is even more precise in its limitations. "The only cases," said Cockburn, C. J.,[42] "in which the petition of right is open to the subject are, where the land or goods or money of a subject have found their way into the possession of the Crown, and the purpose of the petition is to obtain restitution; or, if restitution cannot be given, compensation in money; or where the claim arises out of contract as for goods supplied to the Crown, or to the public service. It is only in such cases that instances of petitions of right having been entertained are to be found in our books." The remedy is thus the obvious expression of the needs of a commercial age. The Crown must do business, and it must obey the rules that business men have laid down for their governance if it desire effective dealings with them. So leasehold property,[43] demurrage under a charter-party,[44] duties of all kinds paid by mistake,[45] property extended by the Crown to answer a Crown debt,[46] are all cases in which it is clear enough that the petition will lie; and, in various cognate direc-

---

[41] Monckton v. Attorney-General, 2 Mac. & G. 402 (1850).

[42] Feather v. Regina, 6 B. & S. 257, 293 (1865).

[43] In re Gosman, 15 Ch. D. 67 (1880), confirmed in part 17 Ch. D. 771 (1881).

[44] Yeoman v. Rex [1904], 2 K. B. 429.

[45] Percival v. Regina, 3 H. & C. 217 (1864) (probate); Dickson v. Regina, 11 H. L. C. 175 (1865) (excise); Winans v. Rex, 23 T. L. R. 705 (1907) (estate duties), are sufficient instances of the kind.

[46] In re English Joint Stock Bank W. N. 199 (1886).

tions, the privilege has been developed by statute.[47] In
mixed cases of tort and contract the issue seems largely
to depend upon the skill and subtlety of opposing
counsel.[48]

Once the realm of contract is overpassed the remedy
of petition ceases to be effective. Tort lies completely
outside the region of responsibility. The negligence of
Crown servants may destroy the Speaker's property,[49] as
the zeal of a naval captain may destroy Mr. Tobin's
schooner; the Crown may, without authorization, infringe
Mr. Feather's patent,[50] or see its officers act wrongfully
at a court-martial;[51] in none of these cases will a petition
lie. The Crown may ask for volunteers and form them
into regiments; but the regimental funds are Crown funds
and the colonel's errors do not render them liable.[52] Nor
are these the hardest cases. Arrears of pay due to naval
and military officers cannot be recovered;[53] an alteration
in the establishment may place an army surgeon upon the
half-pay list without claim of compensation;[54] both here
and in the unreported case of *Ryan* v. *R.*[55] no inability in
the petitioner was suggested. They are servants of the
Crown, and the Crown has the general right to dismiss

[47] *E. g.*, under the Telegraph Acts. Great Western Railway *v.*
Regina, 4 T. L. R. 383 (C. A.) (1889).

[48] *E. g.*, Clarke *v.* Army and Navy Coöperative Society [1903],
1. K. B. 155–56.

[49] Canterbury *v.* Attorney-General, 1 Ph. 306 (1843).

[50] Feather *v.* Regina, 6 B. & S. 257 (1865).

[51] Smith *v.* L. A. 25 R. 112 (1897).

[52] Wilson *v.* 1st Edinburgh City Royal Garrison Artillery [1904],
7 F. 168.

[53] Gibson *v.* East India Co., 5 Bing. (N. C.) 262 (1839); Gidley *v.*
Palmerston, 3 Ba. & B. 275 (1822).

[54] *In re* Tufnell, 3 Ch. D. 164 (1876).

[55] Robertson, *Civil Proceedings against the Crown*, 357.

any member of the military establishment without compensation of any kind.[56]   Not, indeed, that this power is limited to a field where a special case for expediency might perhaps be made out.   The Superannuation Act [57] expressly reserves to the Treasury and the various government departments their power to dismiss any public servant without liability of any kind.   Except where ancient office is concerned,[58] there is no such thing as wrongful dismissal from the service of the Crown,[59] and even where there is statutory provision against dismissal, the royal prerogative to abolish the office remains.[60]   It is, clearly, impossible to make a contract that will bind the Crown against its will; [61] and as in the case of the French *fonctionnaires*, the Civil Service is left to its collective strength if it is to protect itself against the spider's web of public policy.[62]

III

The protection taken to the Crown has not, in general, been extended to public officers.   "With us," says Professor Dicey,[63] "every official, from the Prime Minister down to a constable or a collector of taxes, is under the same responsibility for every act done without legal justification as any other citizen."   No one can doubt the value of this rule, for it constitutes the fundamental safe-

[56] Grant *v.* Secretary of State for India in Council, 2 C. P. D. 445 (1877).

[57] 4 & 5 Will. IV, c. 24, § 30.

[58] On which see Slingsby's Case, 3 Swanst. 178 (1680).

[59] Shenton *v.* Smith [1895], A. C. 229.

[60] Young *v.* Waller [1898], A. C. 661.

[61] Dunn *v.* Regina, 1 Q. B. 116.

[62] Cf. my *Authority in the Modern State*, Ch. 5.

[63] *Law of the Constitution*, 8 ed., 189.

guard against the evils of bureaucracy. Nor have its results been of little value. A colonial governor [64] and a secretary of state [65] have been taught its salutary lesson; and it is, as a learned commentator has pointed out,[66] that which makes for the distinction between the policemen of London and the policemen of Berlin. It has the merit of enforcing a far more strict adherence to law than is possible within the limits of any other system. It restrains those notions of state prerogative which have an uncomfortable habit of making their appearance in the courts of the Continent. Nothing, at least on the surface of things, is more liable to make an official careful than the rule that he cannot make his superior liable for the act of which he has been guilty.[67]

Yet there are obvious difficulties about this system which must make us cautious about its too enthusiastic acceptance. Not only do immunities exist, but there is a broad field of discretion within which the courts do not venture interference. The plea of act of state is, of course, a final bar against all action; though when it operates so as to prevent government from paying to certain persons money received under treaty for that specific purpose,[68] it is not clear that the result is all gain. It is justifiable enough that an official should not be made liable for a contract he has made on behalf of the Crown;[69] nor, on a similar ground, for money erro-

[64] Mostyn v. Fabrigas, Cowp. 161 (1774); Musgrave v. Pulido, 5 A. C. 102 (1879).

[65] Entick v. Carrington, 19 St. Tr. 1030 (1765).

[66] 1 Hatschek, *Englische Staatsrecht,* 93.

[67] Raleigh v. Goschen, 1 Ch. 73 (1898).

[68] Barclay v. Russell, 3 Ves. 424, 431 (1797).

[69] See Palmer v. Hutchinson, 6 A. C. 619 (1881), where the cases are reviewed.

neously paid to him as its agent.[70]   Here the real onus
of our grievance lies against that principal whose *a priori*
infallibility is in law assumed.   The problem of irresponsibility for advice given to the Crown is more difficult; [71]
for the actual organization of political life makes it well-
nigh impossible to separate the particular facts involved
from the general policy of the government.   Nor is there
liability for a tort done in the exercise of a discretion
conferred by law, so long as there is an absence of malice
or improper motive.[72]   The courts are unwilling, and
with obvious reason, to substitute their own view of policy
for that of the recognized agents of administration.
So, too, protection must be afforded to the police or the
proper execution of a warrant;[73] it would be intolerable
if a mere defect of technical procedure brought with it
liability to an unconscious agent who was also the hum-
blest minister of the law.

Far more questionable is the refusal to enforce liability
against an officer for the torts of his subordinate.   Problems of public policy apart, the negligence of a postman
ought not less to affect the Postmaster-General [74] than
the stupidity of a teacher may affect her employers.[75]
If there is to be equality before the law in any fundamental sense, there must be equality in the persons affected
by its application; and the irresponsibility of a government official in this aspect is, at bottom, excused only
by introducing exactly that notion of state which it is

70 Whitbread *v.* Brooksbank, 1 Cowp. 66 (1774); Sadler *v.* Evans,
4 Burr. 1984 (1766).

71 West *v.* West, 27 T. L. R. 476 (1911).

72 Tozer *v.* Child, 7 E. & B. 377 (1857).

73 24 Geo. II, Ch. 44 (1751).

74 Lane *v.* Cotton, 1 Ld. Raym. 646 (1701).

75 Smith. *v.* Martin [1911], 2 K. B. D. 775.

the purpose of the rule of law to avoid. Nor, save on similar grounds, can the Public Authorities Protection Act be defended;[76] for what, essentially, it does is to put certain officials on a different footing from other men. Both these categories of protection raise here the general question that is involved. The obvious aim of the system is to prevent the individual official from violating the law. It does not, as on the Continent, look to the sufferer's loss. It simply insists that if an official has made a legal mistake he must pay for it. But it is, to say the least, far from clear whether the rule results in justice. To throw upon a humble man the burden of a mistake he commits to the profit of another is surely hard measure. There will, for the most part, be no adequate opportunity for the complainant to have adequate remedy. Broadly speaking, it must be enough for him that he has vindicated a principle otherwise left empty. Nor does the protection come, damages apart, where it is most needed. For the main business of the ordinary citizen who wreaks his vengeance upon an unconscious offender is to reach those superiors whom the law does not permit him to touch. No protection is offered against the negligence or stupidity of an official so long as he keeps within the strict letter of his statute. His order may be wanton or arbitrary, but it is law. The burden of its error will fall upon the humble official who acts rather than upon the man in office who issues a valid order. The system may, as Mr. Lowell has aptly said,[77] make liberty depend upon law, but it is a liberty which denies regard to that equality fundamental to its operation.

[76] 56 & 57 Vict. Ch. 61.
[77] 2 Lowell, *Government of England*, 503.

It intensifies, moreover, the tendency of the state to escape the categories of law. For, by emphasizing a remedy that is in no real sense substantial, it conceals the real defects involved in the system. It is true, of course, that the number of officials to whom the system applies is smaller than on the Continent; for the English state does not throw the cloak of its sovereignty about its local constituents. But the number of officials is growing;[78] and the real problem is simply the maxim of whether a principal should be responsible for the acts of his agent. In private law, that is obvious enough; yet the state, by a subterfuge, escapes its operation. The protection of individual rights is not maintained except at the expense of other individuals; where the real point at issue is to maintain them at the expense of the illegally assumed rights of the state. For, theory apart, the Crown has not less acted when a colonel mistakenly orders his men to fire upon a mob than when the King by his signature turns a bill into an Act of Parliament.

The lack, again, of any control over acts that are technically legal is thrown into clearer relief by the recent development of administrative law. Indeed, it may be here suggested that what that development essentially reveals is the limitation of the rule of law where the rule operates in the presence of an irresponsible state. If, under the Second Empire, the Napoleonic police arbitrarily suppress a newspaper,[79] or destroy the proof-sheets of a work by the Duc d'Aumale,[80] it is not difficult to perceive that the invasion of individual liberty,

[78] Cf. Wallas, *The Great Society*, 7.
[79] Dalloz, 1856 III, 57.
[80] *Ibid.*, 1867, III, 49.

where no cause save the will of government is shown, is, in fact, most serious. A state, in brief, the officials of which can act without the proof of reasonableness inherent in the methods of their policy, has gone far to destroy the notion which lies at the basis of law.

This recent development has, indeed, a history that goes back to the tendency of the official to show deep dissatisfaction with the slow-moving methods of the law. The technicalities of the Merchant Shipping Act, for instance, actually operate, so we are told,[81] to make its provisions for detaining unseaworthy ships substantially null and void. Effort has in recent years been made to free the administrative process from the hampering influence of the rule of law. Where, a generation ago, Parliament laid down with strict minuteness the conditions of taxation, to-day the Board of Customs and Excise has practically legislative powers.[82] "Wise men," said Sir Henry Taylor in a remarkable sentence,[83] "have always perceived that the execution of political measures is in reality the essence of them"; and it is this which makes so urgent the rigorous regard of executive practice. In the stress of conflict, perhaps, cases like *R*. v. *Halliday*[84] may be pardoned; though it is well even there to consider whether the end the means is to serve may not be lost sight of in the means a narrow expediency seems to dictate. But a far wider problem is set in the Arlidge case.[86] For here, in fact, not only is the

---

[81] *Dicey, Law of the Constitution*, 8 ed., 393.

[82] Fourth Report of the Royal Commission on the Civil Service (1914), Cd. 7338, 28.

[83] *The Statesman*, 89.

[84] [1917] A. C. 260.

[85] Cf. Lord Shaw's dissent in Rex v. Halliday, *supra*.

[86] [1915] A. C. 120.

court excluded from the consideration of an administrative decision, but the tests of judicial procedure which have been proved by experience are excluded without means at hand to force their entrance. What, broadly, the Arlidge case means is that a handful of officials will, without hindrance from the courts, decide in their own fashion what method of application an Act of Parliament is to have. And where the state that is acting through their agency is an irresponsible state, we have in fact a return to those primitive methods of justice traditionally associated with the rough efficiency of the Tudor age.[87]

This is not to say that administrative law represents a mistaken evolution. The most striking change in the political organization of the last half century is the rapidity with which, by the sheer pressure of events, the state has been driven to assume a positive character. We talk less and less in the terms of nineteenth-century individualism. The absence of governmental restraint has ceased to seem the ultimate ideal. There is everywhere almost anxiety for the extension of governmental functions. It was inevitable that such an evolution should involve a change in the judicial process. Where, for example, great problems like those involved in government insurance are concerned, there is a great convenience in leaving their interpretation to the officials who administer the Act. They have gained in its application an expert character to which no purely judicial body can pretend; and their opinion has a weight which no community can afford to neglect. The business of the state, in fact, has here become so much like private

[87] Cf. Pound, Address to the New Hampshire Bar Association, June 30, 1917.

business that, as Professor Dicey has emphasized,[88] its officials need "that freedom of action necessarily possessed by every private person in the management of his own personal concerns." So much is tolerably clear. But history suggests that the relation of such executive justice to the slow infiltration of a bureaucratic régime is at each stage more perilously close; and the development of administrative law needs to be closely scrutinized in the interests of public liberty. If a government department may make regulations of any kind without any judicial tests of fairness or reasonableness being involved, it is clear that a fundamental safeguard upon English liberties has disappeared. If administrative action can escape the review of the courts, there is no reality in official responsibility; and cases like *Entick* v. *Carrington*[89] become, in such a contest, of merely antiquarian interest. If the Secretary of State, under wide powers, issues a regulation prohibiting the publication of any book or pamphlet he does not like without previous submission to a censor, who may suppress it without assignment of cause, the merest and irresponsible caprice of a junior clerk may actually be the occasion for the suppression of vital knowledge;[90] nor will there be the means judicially at hand for controlling the exercise of such powers. The legislative control that misuse will eventually imply is so slow in coming that it arrives almost always too late. And the cabinet system, with its collective responsibility, virtually casts its enveloping network of protection about the offender. A member of

[88] 31 L. *Quart. Rev.* 148, 150.

[89] 19 St. Tr. 1030.

[90] Defence of the Realm Act, Order No. 51. Cf. The London *Nation*, § 8, 1917.

Parliament may resent the stupid imprisonment of a distinguished philosopher; but his resentment will rarely take the form of turning out the government as a protest.[91]

In such a situation, it is obvious that we must have safeguards. It is not adequate to give half-protection in the form of the rule of law, and then to destroy the utility of its application. What, in fact, is implied in a state which evades responsibility is, sooner or later, the irresponsibility of officials immediately the business of the state is complex enough to make judicial control a source of administrative irritation. Administrative law, in such an aspect, implies the absence of law; for the discretion of officials sitting, as in the Arlidge case, in secret, cannot be called law. What is needed is rather the frank admission that special administrative courts, as on the Continent, are needed, or the requirement of a procedure in which the rights of the private citizen have their due protection.[92] What, in any case, is clear is the fact that the official will not, in any other way, be substantially subject to the rule of law. In the vital case the avenue of escape is sufficiently broad to make legal attack of little use. It is hardly helpful to be able to bring a policeman into court if the real offender is the Home Secretary. It is utterly useless even to make protestation if the government is, by virtue of its growing business, to take its acts from the public view. Growing functions ought rather to mean growing responsibility than less; and if that should involve a new system of

[91] On the private member's protest, cf. Low, *Governance of England*, 5 ed., Ch. 4.

[92] As in the United States. New York *v.* Public Service Commission, 38 Sup. Ct. Rep. 122 (1917).

rights it makes thought about its content only the greater
need. The ordinary citizen of to-day is so much the
mere subject of administration that we cannot afford to
stifle the least opportunity of his active exertions. The
very scale, in fact, of the great society is giving new
substance to Aristotle's definition of citizenship.

IV

The America which a Revolution brought into being
did not relinquish the rights surrendered by George III
at Versailles. If the people is to be master in its own
house, it will not belittle itself and cease, in consequence, to
be sovereign. Rights here, as elsewhere, are to flow from
the fount of sovereign power; and its irresponsibility is
the natural consequence. That the state is not to be
sued, in truth, is taken, even by the greatest authority,
as a simple matter of logic. "A sovereign," says Mr.
Justice Holmes,[93] "is exempt from suit, not because of
any formal conception or obsolete theory, but on the
logical and practical ground that there can be no legal
right as against the authority that makes the law on
which the right depends." Nor did Mr. Justice Holmes
fail to draw the inevitable conclusion from that attitude.
The sovereignty of the people will mean, in actual terms
of daily business, the sovereignty of its government.[94]
"As the ground is thus logical and practical," he said,
"the doctrine is not confined to powers that are sovereign
in the full sense of juridical theory, but naturally is extended to those that, in actual administration, originate
and change at their will the law of contract and property

[93] Kawananakoa v. Polyblank, 205 U. S. 349 (1907).
[94] Cf. my paper on "The Theory of Popular Sovereignty" in the
Mich. L. Rev. for January, 1919.

from which persons within the jurisdiction derive their rights." Here is the Austinian theory of sovereignty in all its formidable completeness; though it is worth noting that its complications have elsewhere driven Mr. Justice Holmes to the enunciation of a doctrine of quasi-sovereignty that the hardness of the rule might suffer mitigation.[95] No such certainty, indeed, existed in the early days of the Republic; and Chief Justice Jay and Mr. Justice Wilson regarded the immunity of the state from suit as the typical doctrine of autocratic government.[96] But, from the time of *Cohens* v. *Virginia*,[97] the doctrine of non-suability has taken firm hold; and men such as Harlan, J., have urged it with almost religious fervor.[98]

The result is that, broadly speaking, the situation is hardly distinct in its general outlines from that of Great Britain. In eight of the states there is actual constitutional provision against suit; and in sixteen more special privileges are erected as a tribute to its sovereign character.[99] It is, in short, the general rule that a state will not be liable for acts which, were they not, directly or indirectly, acts of the government, would render the doer responsible before the courts.[100] The United States will abuse the patents of its citizens hardly less cheerfully than the British Admiralty.[101] State duties, like prison

[95] Georgia v. Tenn. Copper Co., 206 U. S. 230 (1907).

[96] Chisholm v. Georgia, 2 Dall. (U. S.) 419 (1793).

[97] 6 Wheat. (U. S.) 264, 382 (1821).

[98] Cf., for instance, United States v. Texas, 143 U. S. 621 (1892), and Fuller, C. J., in Kansas v. United States, 204 U. S. 331 (1907).

[99] Beard, *Index of State Constitutions*, 1360.

[100] Murdock Parlor Grate Co., v. Commonwealth, 152 Mass. 28, 24 N. E. 854 (1890).

[101] Belknap v. Schild, 161 U. S. 10 (1896).

maintenance [102] and the repair of roads,[103] may be done without reference to the neglect of private interests. The rule goes even further and protects a charitable institution like an agricultural society from the accidents that happen in the best-regulated fairs.[104] If the state leases an armory for athletic purposes and has failed, through sheer negligence, to repair a defective railing,[105] it does not, to say the least, seem logical to refuse compensation, especially when damages may be obtained in a similar case from a municipal body.[106] But a sovereign is perhaps unamenable to the more obvious rules of logic.

Nor has America made substantial departure from the British practice in regard to ministerial responsibility. Only one case against the head of an executive department seems to exist, and it was decided adversely to the plaintiff.[107] Nor are purely ministerial officials held responsible for actions following upon instructions legal upon their face;[108] and that although the officer may be convinced that the instruction in fact breaks the law.[109] The law, indeed, has many anomalies about it. A company which serves as a mail carrier is not responsible to the owner of a package for its loss;[110] it is here an agent

[102] Moody v. State Prison, 128 N. C. 12, 38 S. E. 131 (1901).

[103] Johnson v. State, 1 Court of Claims (Ill.), 208.

[104] Berman v. State Agricultural Society of Minnesota, 93 Minn. 125, 100 N. W. 732 (1904).

[105] Riddoch v. State, 68 Wash. 329, 123 Pac. 450 (1912).

[106] Little v. Holyoke, 177 Mass. 114, 58 N. E. 170 (1900). I owe my knowledge of this and the other state cases in America to the brilliant article of Mr. R. D. Maguire, 30 *Harv. L. Rev.*, 20 ff.

[107] Stokes v. Kendall, 3 How. (U. S.) 87 (1845).

[108] Erskine v. Bohnbach, 14 Wall. (U. S.) 613 (1871).

[109] Wall v. Trumbull, 16 Mich. 228 (1867); Underwood v. Robinson, 106 Mass. 296 (1871).

[110] Bankers' Mutual Casualty Co. v. Minneapolis, etc. Ry., 117 Fed. 434 (1902).

of government, and so, as it seems, protected from the consequences of its acts. But a mail contractor will be liable for the negligence of the carrier whom he employs.[111] Once an official engages a private servant to perform a task, the ordinary rules of principal and agent are said to apply.[112] Certain mystic words are here, as elsewhere, the vital point in the evasion of law.

Such facts converge towards an argument first stated in a distinct form by Paley. "Sovereignty," he says,[113] "may be termed absolute, omnipotent, uncontrollable, arbitrary, despotic, and is alike so in all countries." Certainly the forms of government could in no two countries remain more substantially distinct than those of England and the United States; yet, in each, the attributes of sovereign power admit no differentiation. What mitigation there is of a rule hard alike in intent and execution is the mitigation of the sovereign's generosity; that is to say, a mitigation which stops short where the Treasury becomes concerned. For this theory of an auto-limitation of the sovereign's power has in fact nothing of value to contribute to our problems. The real need is the enforcement of responsibility, and that cannot be effected if the test is to be our success in convincing the sovereign power of its delinquencies. The fact is that here, as elsewhere, the democratic state bears upon itself the marks of its imperial origin. The essence of American sovereignty hardly differs, under this aspect, from the attributes of sovereignty as Bodin distinguished them three centuries ago.[114] What emerges, whether in

[111] Sawyer v. Corse, 17 Gratt. (Va.) 230 (1867).

[112] Dunlop v. Munroe, 7 Cranch (U. S.) 242 (1812).

[113] *Moral and Political Philosophy*, Bk. VI, Ch. 6. Cf. my *Authority in the Modern State*, 29 f.

[114] *De La République*, I, 8, 9. Cf. Chauviré *Bodin*, 311 f.

England or in the United States, is the fact that an Austinian state is incompatible with the substance of democracy. For the latter implies responsibility by its very definition; and the Austinian system is, at bottom, simply a method by which the fallibility of men is concealed imposingly from the public view.

v

The Anglo-American system exists in isolation; and it is, in a sense, the only one which has remained true to the logical conditions of its origin. In France and Germany a régime exists which, while in no sense antithetic, may be usefully contrasted with the more logical effort here discussed.[115] No text, indeed, declares in France the responsibility of the state; such concession to the historic content of sovereign power is here, as elsewhere, deemed fundamental. But the courts have little by little been driven through circumstances to desert this rigidity, so that in the France of to-day the older notion of irresponsibility is no longer existent. The state, indeed, is in nowise liable for the consequence of its legislative acts; though the demand for compensation in cases where a state monopoly has been created are not without their interest. Nor must we miss the significance of ministerial protest against the easy thesis that the obligations of the state are liable to instant change by statute.[116]

115 The literature of the responsibility of the state in France and Germany is now enormous. The two best treatises on the former country are those of Tiessier and Tirard. On Germany the best general discussion is still that of Otto Mayer, *Deutsches Verwaltungsrecht*, Bk. III, § 17. Cf. also Loening, *Die Haftung des Staates*.

116 Duguit, *Les Transformations du Droit Public*, 235–39 (a translation of this work has been published as *Law in the Modern State*).

What is perhaps more significant than the substance of the decision is the manner in which this jurisprudence has been evolved. We start, as in England, with an irresponsible state. Little by little a distinction is made between the acts of the state in its sovereign capacity, where irresponsibility remains, and in its non-sovereign aspect, where liability is assumed. But it has been in the last decade seen that such distinction is in fact untenable and that the test of liability must be sought in different fashion. While, therefore, the sovereignty of the state finds its historic emphasis within the chamber,[117] it is less and less insistent before the Council of State. And even within the Chamber suggestions of a notable kind have been made. It was M. Clemenceau who proposed statutory compensation for unlawful arrest;[118] and a vote of credit for this purpose has been made in every budget since 1910. Here, at least, is a clear admission that the sovereign state is a fallible thing.

But a more notable change even than this may be observed. The administration has become responsible for faults in the exercise of its functions. There has been evolved, if the phrase may be permitted, a category of public torts where the state becomes liable for the acts of its agents. And this is, in fact, no more than the admission of that realism which, in the Anglo-American system, has no opportunity for expression. For every state act is, in literal truth, the act of some official; and the vital need is simply the recognition that the acts of an agent involve the responsibility of his superior. Where the service of the state, that is to say, is badly performed in the sense that its operation prejudices the

117 Cf. my *Authority in the Modern State*, Ch. 5.
118 Duguit, *op. cit.*, 252.

interest of a private citizen more especially than the interests of the mass of men, the exchequer should lie open for his relief. Obviously enough a responsibility stated in these terms becomes no more than equitable adjustment. If the state comes down into the market-place it must, as even American courts have observed,[119] put off its robe of sovereignty and act like a human being.

This modern development goes back to a distinguished jurist's criticism of the Lepreux case, in 1899.[120] Lepreaux was injured by the state-guard in the performance of its duties; and his plea for damages was rejected on the ground that it was an inadmissible attack on the sovereignty of the state. M. Hauriou argued that this was the coronation of injustice. He did not deny that there are cases where public policy demands irresponsibility; but he urged, in effect, that in the general business of daily administration negligence ought, as with the relations of private citizens, to have its due consequence. The result of his argument was seen in the next few years. In the Grecco case, for example, though the plaintiff was unsuccessful, the ground of his failure was not the irresponsibility of the state, but the fact that he had not proved his claim of negligence.[121] It was thus admitted that the state was not infallible, and the way lay open to a striking development. The Council of State was willing to insist upon damages for an unduly delayed appointment of a retired soldier to the civil service; it held the state responsible for the faulty construction of

119 Charleston v. Murray, 96 U. S. 432 (1877); United States Bank v. Planters' Bank, 9 Wheat. (U. S.) 904 (1824); The Royal Acceptances, 7 Wall. (U. S.) 666 (1868).
120 Sirey, 1900, III, 1.
121 Ibid., 113.

a canal.[122] Most remarkable of all was perhaps the Pluchard case in which a civilian obtained damages for a fall occasioned by an involuntary collision with a policeman in pursuit of a thief.[123] Nor has the evolution stopped there. It has become possible to overturn governmental ordinances — the analogue of the English provisional order; or, at least, to obtain special compensation where hardship in the application of the ordinance can be proved.[124] What practically has been established is governmental responsibility where the administrative act is in genuine relation to the official's duty. It is only where, as in the Morizot case,[125] the official goes clearly outside his functions that the state repudiates liability.

No one will claim for this French evolution that it has been the result of a conscious effort to overthrow the traditional theory of sovereignty; on the contrary, its slow and hesitating development suggests the difficulties that have been encountered.[126] But no French court will say again, as in the Blanco case,[127] that problems of state are to be ruled by special considerations alien to the categories of private law. The real advantage, indeed, of the system is its refusal to recognize, within, at least, the existing limits of this evolution, any special privilege to the state. It judges the acts of authority

122 Cf. Duguit, *op. cit.*, 261.

123 Recueil (1910), 1029.

124 Sirey, 1908, III, 1, and see the account of the Turpin case in Duguit, *op. cit.*, 266, for the application of responsibility to ministerial negligence of a special kind.

125 Sirey, 1908, III, 83.

126 The Ambrosini case, for example, Sirey, 1912, III, 161, suggests a revulsion of sentiment.

127 Hauriou, *Précis de Droit Administratif*, 8 ed., 503, note 1.

by the recognized rules of ordinary justice. It asks, as it is surely right to ask, the same standard of conduct from a public official as would be expected from a private citizen. The method may have its disadvantages. There is undoubtedly a real benefit in the Anglo-American method of bringing the consequences of each act rigidly to bear upon the official responsible for it. Yet, as has been shown, this theory is far different from the application of the rule in practice; it does not affect those upon whom the cloak of sovereignty is thrown; and it offers no prospect of any full relief to the person who has been prejudiced. These evils, at least, the French method avoids. It conceives of the state as ultimately no more than the greatest of public utilities, and it insists that, like a public utility in private hands, it shall act at its peril. In an age where government service has been so vastly extended, the merit of that concept is unquestionable.

It may, of course, be argued that such an attitude is only possible in the special environment of French administrative law. That system is as Professor Dicey has taught us in his classical analysis,[128] essentially a system of executive justice, basically incompatible with the ideals of Anglo-American law. Yet there are many answers possible to that attitude. French administrative law may be in the hands of executive officials; but no one who has watched its administration can urge a bias towards the administration on the part of the Council of State.[129] Nor, if the fear remain, need we insist upon the rigid

---

128 *Law of the Constitution*, 8 ed., 324–401.

129 Cf. E. M. Parker, 19 *Harv. Law Rev.*, 335. Mr. Parker gives good examples of this tendency; but I do not think he has altogether realized the substantial character of Professor Dicey's strictures,

outlines of the French inheritance. The Prussian system
of administrative law is administered by special courts,
and it has won high praise from distinguished authority.[130] If it be true that the pressure of executive business
makes continuous recourse to the ordinary courts impossible, the establishment of such may be the necessary and
concomitant safeguard of private liberty; and Mr. Barker
has pointed out that in the English umpires and referees
we have the foundation upon which an adequate system
can be erected.[131] Certain at least it is that in no other
way than some such development can we prevent the annihilation of that sturdy legalism which was the real condition of Anglo-Saxon freedom.

VI

"It is a wholesome sight," said Maitland in a famous
sentence,[132] "to see 'the Crown' sued and answering for
its torts." We perhaps too little realize how much of
historic fiction there is in the theory of the English state.
Certainly there have been moments in its early development when it almost seemed as though the great maxim
respondeat superior would apply to official persons; for
in documents no less substantial than statutes the germ
of official responsibility is to be found.[133] But the doctrine seems to climb no higher than the sheriff or
escheator, and it is in Council or Parliament that the
greater men make what answer they deem fit. And, as
Maitland said,[134] we should not expect to find the medieval

130 Cf. E. Barker, 2 *Political Quart.* 117.
131 *Ibid.*, 135 f.
132 3 *Collected Papers*, 263.
133 *Statute of Westminster* II, 13 Edw. I, St. I, Ch. 2, § 3 (1285);
Articuli Super Cartas, § 18.
134 3 *Collected Papers*, 247.

King a responsible officer simply because he was every
inch a man. When theory develops it was thus too late.
The wholesome sight is beyond our vision. The state is
still the King; and if an ocasional judge, more deeply
seeing or blunter than the rest, tells us that our cases
in fact concern not the state or the Crown but the government, a phrase used *obiter* is not strong enough to
point the obvious moral.[135]

Yet obvious it is; and if, for a moment, we move from
law to its philosophy the groundwork of our difficulties
will be clear enough. We are struggling to apply to a
situation that is at each moment changing conceptions
that have about them the special fragrance of the Counter-Reformation. It is then that the absolute and irresponsible state is born, and it is absolute and irresponsible from the basic necessity of safeguarding its
rights against the Roman challenge.[136] But the attributes are convenient, especially when they are in actual
fact exercised by government. For then, as now, in the
normal process of daily life what we in general fail to
see is that acts of state are governmental acts which
command the assent of the mass of men. The classic
theory of sovereignty is unfitted to such a situation. The
fundamental characteristic of political evolution is the
notion of responsibility. If our King fails to suit us we
behead or replace him; if our ministry loses its hold, the
result is registered in the ballot-boxes. But the categories of law have obstinately and needlessly resisted
such transformation. The government has for the most
part kept the realm of administration beclouded by high

[135] Mersey Docks *v.* Gibbs, L. R. 1 H. L. 93, 111, per Blackburn, J.

[136] Cf. my *Authority in the Modern State,* 22 f.

notions of prerogative.   What is here argued is the simple
thesis that this is legally unnecessary and morally inadequate.   It is legally unnecessary because, in fact, no
sovereignty, however conceived, is weakened by living
the life of the law.   It is morally inadequate because it
exalts authority over justice.

It would not persist but for the use of antiquarian
terminology.   The Crown is a noble hieroglyphic; and
it is not in the Law Courts that effort will be made to
penetrate the meaning of its patent symbolism.   Crown
in fact means government, and government means those
innumerable officials who collect our taxes and grant us
patents and inspect our drains.   They are human beings
with the money-bags of the state behind them.   They
are fallible beings because they are human, and if they
do wrong it is in truth no other derogation than the admission of their human fallibility to force responsibility
upon the treasury of their principal.   To avoid that
issue results not merely in injustice.   It makes of authority a category apart from the life that same authority insists the state itself must live.   By its sanctifi-
cation of authority it pays false tribute to an outworn
philosophy.   "Whatever the reasons for establishing
government," said James Mill,[137] "the very same are
reasons for establishing securities."   It is this absence
of safeguards that makes inadequate the legal theory our
courts to-day apply.   Nor has it even the merit of
consistency; for the needs of administration have necessitated governmental division into parts that may or may
not be sovereign or irresponsible without regard to logic.
The cause of this moral anachronism may be imbedded
in history; but we must not make the fatal error of con-

[137] Essays reprinted from the Encyclopedia Britannica, V.

founding antiquity with experience. We live in a new world, and a new theory of the state is necessary to its adequate operation. The head and center of practical, as of speculative effort, must be the translation of the facts of life into the theories of law. The effort to this end is slowly coming; but we have not yet taken to heart the burden of its teaching. The ghost of old Rome, as in Hobbes' masterpiece of phrase, still sits in triumph upon ruins we might fashion anew into an empire.

THE PERSONALITY OF ASSOCIATIONS *

THE state knows certain persons who are not men. What is the nature of their personality? Are they merely fictitious abstractions, collective names that hide from us the mass of individuals beneath? Is the name that gives them unity no more than a convenience, a means of substituting one action in the courts where, otherwise, there might be actions innumerable? Or is that personality real? Is Professor Dicey right when he urges [1] that "whenever men act in concert for a common purpose, they tend to create a body which, from no fiction of law but from the very nature of things, differs from the individuals of whom it is constituted"? Does our symbolism, in fact, point to some reality at the bottom of appearance? If we assume that reality, what consequences will flow therefrom?

Certainly no lawyer dare neglect the phenomena of group life, even if on occasion [2] he denies a little angrily the need for him to theorize about them. For man is so essentially an associative animal that his nature is largely determined by the relationships thus formed. The churches express his feeling that he has need of religion. His desire for conversation and the newspapers

* Reprinted from the *Harvard Law Review,* Vol. XXIX, No. 4.
[1] *Law and Public Opinion,* p. 165.
[2] See, for instance, H. A. Smith, *Law of Associations* (1914), p. 129.

results in the establishment of clubs. The necessity of social organization gave birth to the state. As his commercial enterprise began to annihilate distance, the trading company came into being. It would not, one urges, be over-emphasis to assert that in every sphere of human activity associations of some kind are to be found. They are the very life-breath of the community.[3]

And, somehow, we are compelled to personalize these associations. They demand their possessive pronouns; the church has "its" bishops. They govern a singular verb; the railway company "employs" servants. The United States of America is greater than all Americans; it becomes a single individual, and fraternizes, Jonathan-wise, with a John Bull in whom all Englishmen have their being. The Bank of England is — the phrase, surely, is remarkable — the "little old lady of Threadneedle Street"; but no one would speak of seven distinguished merchants as a little old lady. The House of Commons is distinct from "its" members, and, no less clearly, it is not the chamber in which they meet. We talk of "its" "spirit" and "complexion"; a general election, so we say, changes "its" "character." Eton, we know well enough, is not six hundred boys, nor a collection of ancient buildings. Clearly, there is compulsion in our personalizing. We do it because we must. We do it because we feel in these things the red blood of a living personality. Here are no mere abstractions of an over-exuberant imagination. The need is so apparent as to make plain the reality beneath.

---

[3] On the relation between individual personality and social groups the reader will find much of deep interest in Wilfred Richmond, *Personality as a Philosophical Principle* (1900). I personally owe much to this fascinating book.

II

Now lawyers are practical men dealing with the very practical affairs of everyday life, and they do not like, in Lord Lindley's phrase,[4] "to introduce metaphysical subtleties which are needless and fallacious." The law, so they will say, knows persons; by Act of Parliament[5] "persons" may include bodies corporate. Persons are the subjects of rights and duties which the courts will, at need, enforce. If a body corporate is a person, it will also be the subject of rights and duties. If it is a person, it is so because the state has conferred upon it the gift of personality; for only the state can exercise that power. And the terms of such conference are strictly defined. The corporation is given personality for certain purposes to be found in its history, in its charter, its constituting act, its articles of association. The courts will say whether certain acts come within those purposes; whether, to use technical terms, they are *intra* or *ultra vires*. This limitation is in the public interest. "The public," so the courts have held,[6] "is entitled to hold a registered company to its registered business." The company has a personality; but it has a personality capable only of very definitized development.

Why is it so limited? English lawyers, at any rate, have no doubt upon this question. The corporation is the creature of the state.[7] Its will is a delegated will;

4 Citizens' Life Assurance Co. *v.* Brown [1904], A. C. 423, 426.

5 52 & 53 Vict., Ch. 63, § 19.

6 Attorney-General *v.* Great Eastern Ry. Co., L. R. 11 Ch. D. 449, 503 (1879), per Lord Bramwell.

7 I. e., they accept the "concession" theory, so called. That they have accepted the "fiction theory" is denied by Sir F. Pollock in the *Law Quart. Rev.* for 1911.

its purpose exists only because it has secured recognition. And, so the lawyers will tend to imply, it is in truth a fictitious thing. Persons, they know well enough, are human beings; the corporation is invisible and *in abstracto*.[8] It has no human wants. "It cannot," so an American judge has said,[9] "eat or drink, or wear clothing, or live in houses"; though hereto a sceptic might retort that a theory of domicile has given some trouble, and ask if there is not a solid reality about the dinners of the Corporation of London. "It is," said Marshall, C. J.,[10] "an artificial being, invisible, intangible, and existing only in contemplation of law" . . . "it is precisely," he says again, "what the act of incorporation makes it." "Persons," said Best, C. J., in 1828,[11] "who, without the sanction of the legislature, presume to act as a corporation, are guilty of a contempt of the King, by usurping on his prerogative."

Nor are the textbook writers less definite. "They are legal persons," says Austin,[12] "by a figment, and for the sake of brevity in discourse." "To the existence of all corporations," wrote Kyd in 1793,[13] "it has long been an established maxim that the King's consent is absolutely necessary." "Ten men," notes Professor Salmond satirically,[14] "do not become in fact one person because they associate themselves together for one end any more

---

8 Sutton's Hospital Case, 10 Co. 13 (1612).

9 Darlington *v.* Mayor, etc., of New York, 31 N. Y. 164, 197 (1865).

10 Dartmouth College *v.* Woodward, 4 Wheat. (U. S.) 518, 636 (1819).

11 Duvergier *v.* Fellows, 5 Bing. 248, 268.

13 1 *Treatise on Corporations*, p. 41.

14 *Jurisprudence* (ed of 1902), p. 350.

than two horses become one animal when they draw
the same cart." "The most marked distinction," Mr.
Holland has written in a famous textbook,[15] "between
abnormal persons is that some are natural . . . while
others are artificial . . . which are treated by law
for certain purposes as if they were individual human
beings."

Here is clear doctrine enough — a vivid picture of an
all-absorptive state. But when this supposed limitation
has once been admitted, it is evident that the state is
compelled to do remarkable things with the bodies it has
called into being. It fails to regulate them with the
ease that might be desired. The definition of *ultra vires*,
for example, has become a formidable problem; there
seems not a little of accident in the formulation of its
principles. Corporations will have a curious habit of
attempting perpetually to escape from the rigid bonds
in which they have been encased. May we not say that,
like some Frankenstein, they show ingratitude to their
creators? Or, as artificial things, must we deem them
incapable of such thought? A corporation will possess
itself of an empire, and resent [16] interference with its
domain. An American colony will incorporate itself;
and when its creator shows signs of wanton interference,
will take the lead in rebellion against the state which,
in legal theory, at any rate, gave it birth. Truly the
supposed sovereignty of the state is not apparent in the
relations thus discovered. The orthodox doctrine needs
somewhat closer examination before we accept its truth.

15 *Jurisprudence,* 11 ed., p. 385.
16 J. S. Mill, *Autobiography,* p. 143,

III

But even when we have so examined, there are associations which technically at least are not corporations. That trust which Maitland taught us to understand as so typically English will embrace many of them under its all-protecting fold. Contract, as in the club, will account for much, and with the aid of a little fiction we need have no fear of theory. A mighty church will in Scotland be a trust and not a corporation. In America the operations of certain trusts which are not corporations will necessitate a famous Act of Congress. For otherwise they can hardly come into the courts. They have no name by which to be sued. To the law, they are not persons, have no personality; they are bodies unincorporate, bodies — the thought is charmingly English — which are bodiless. Yet, curiously, the technical formulæ do not by their absence reveal any essential lack of corporate character. The Stock Exchange has, in any real meaning of the term, a personality as assuredly effective as that of Lloyds. If, to the law, they are essentially distinct, to practical men and women it seems useless to insist on the distinction as other than an empty formalism. The Stock Exchange is simply a property vested in trustees for the benefit of a few proprietors. Is it? Dare those trustees use it as property in that unpublic sense? Dare they so claim it and retain the respect of men with eyes to see? The technical distinction only made Archbishop Laud impatient when a Puritan trust had ruffled his temper.[17] Sour Bishop Montague who avowed that he had "spent some time in

---

17 7 Gardiner, *History of England*, p. 258. Cf. Maitland's introduction to Gierke, *Political Theories of the Middle Age.*, p. 33.

reading bookes of the Lawe," was beside himself at the unincorporate character of Lincoln's Inn.[18] Certain words of condemnation died out on Lord Eldon's lips when he thought of the silver cup the Middle Temple treasured. Here, as it seemed, was virtual corporateness, without the state's blessing of incorporation. Wrong, may be, it was thus to presume on kingly right; yet, of a truth, it was also significant.

Significant in what sense? In the sense, we argue, that legal practice has improved on legal theory. The judges builded better than they knew; or, mayhap, they have added yet another to the pile of fictions so characteristic of English law. If corporations can alone come up the front stairs, then they will admit the unincorporate association at the back. For, they know well enough, the life of the state would be intolerable did we recognize only the association which has chosen to accept the forms of law.

Clearly there is much behind this fiction-making. A sovereignty that is but doubtfully sovereign, an unincorporate body of which the bodiliness may yet equitably be recognized — certainly our fictions have served to conceal much. What, as a fact, is their justification? Why do they still invite, as they receive, a lip-given, if a heart-denied, profession of faith?

IV

When the history of associations which have been technically incorporated comes to be written, one clear generalization as to its tenor during the nineteenth century will be admitted: the courts have been in practice increas-

[18] 2 *Black Book of Lincoln's Inn*, pp. 332-3.

ingly compelled to approximate their position to that of an ordinary individual. The history has not been without its hesitations. The clear and vigorous mind of Lord Bramwell, for instance, left the emphatic mark of his dissent from its tendency written deep on English law.[19] The evolution, dating, so far as one can see, from no earlier time than the forties of last century,[20] of the doctrine of *ultra vires*, has in many ways acted as a limiting factor. Certain philosophic difficulties, moreover, as the significance of the *mens rea* in criminal liability, have proved stumbling blocks of a serious kind. Yet, on the whole, the progress is clear. The corporation is an obvious unit. It has rights and duties. It acts and is acted upon. The fact that its actions are of a special kind is not to prevent the courts from getting behind the visible agents to the invisible reality. If it is civilly reprehensible, it must bear the burden of its blameworthiness. Should it be guilty of crime the courts will, indeed, be less confident, but, as we shall see, the thin edge of the wedge has already been inserted. It needs but a little courage, and the reality of corporate crime will pass the current coin of legally accepted doctrine.

Let us look at this tendency in some little more detail. Let us take, as a starting point, the corporate seal. It is but three quarters of a century since Rolfe, B., was laying down with emphasis that the seal was "the only authentic evidence of what the corporation has done or agreed to do." [21] Within thirty years that doctrine is

19 See especially his remarks in Abrath *v.* North Eastern Ry. Co., 247, 252 (1886).

20 Mr. Carr in his brilliant essay on the Law of Corporations dates its origin from Colman *v.* Eastern Counties Ry. Co., 16 L. J. (Ch.) 73 (1846). I have been unable to find an earlier case.

21 Mayor, etc., of Ludlow *v.* Charlton, 6 Mee. & W. 815 (1840).

obsolete. The seal, Cockburn, C. J., will declare,[22] as
it seems to us almost lightly, "is a relic of barbarous
antiquity," and will establish that the contracts of a
trading corporation, made in pursuit of trade purposes,
do not need that "only authentic evidence" of which
Rolfe, B., had spoken. Nor has Parliament been less
generous.[23] It is not now necessary, we know further, to
use the seal in contracts of daily occurrence.[24] Nor may
the absence of the seal be used to defeat the ends of
justice. Work performed for purposes incidental to the
corporate end must be paid for even when the contract
is unsealed and the corporation public in its nature.[25] If
Parliament lays it down that urban authorities in their
sanitary pursuits [26] must use the seal for all contracts
over £50 in value,[27] that is an exception sufficient in itself
to validate the general rule; nor do we feel aught save
harshness in Lord Bramwell's grim comment upon its
enforcement.[28]

The change is worth some little thought. We end the
century with a doctrine almost entirely antithetic to that
with which it began. The seal, once so lauded as alone
authentic, a Chief Justice dismisses as barbarously an-
tiquated. Why? The inference is clear. The seal
hinders the free play of corporate activity, just as the

[22] South of Ireland Colliery Co. v. Waddle, L. R. 4 C. P.
617 (1869)

[23] 30 & 31 Vict., c. 131, § 137.

[24] Wells v. Mayor, etc. of Kingston-upon-Hull, L. R. 10 C. P.
402 (1875).

[25] Clarke v. Cuckfield Union, 21 L. J. (Q. B.) 349 (1852); Law-
ford v. Billericay Rural District Council, L. R. [1903], 1 K. B. 772.

[26] The limitation is that of Joyce, J. Douglas v. Rhyl Urban
District Council, L. R. [1913] 2 Ch. 307.

[27] 38 & 39 Vict., c. 55, § 174.

[28] Young & Co. v. Mayor, etc., of Leamington, 8 A. C. 517 (1883).

robes of state hide beneath them the humanity of a king. And just as the latter will have his withdrawing-room, where, free from ceremonial, he may be himself, so will the corporation put off its seal that (if we may invoke a relic of barbarous anthropomorphism) its limbs may have free play. The corporation acts, seal or no seal. So it is right that the courts should look beneath the stiff encasement of formalism to the living reality which moves there.

We turn to contract. We approach it warily, for here is the head and center of fictional security. Here, we shall be told, it is finally made evident that the corporation exists nowhere save in legal contemplation. For what do we find? Take first the association incorporate by Act of Parliament. Beyond the four corners of its articles of association no movement is possible.[29] Even the corporation which the common-law prerogative has made will have limitations upon its capacity. It cannot do what it will. It has been created for a specific purpose. It must conform to that purpose, because it is the creature of those who called it into being.[30]

Now this theory of *ultra vires* is fundamental in the law of corporations. What is to be said for it? This, of a certainty, that it is in some wise needful to protect the corporators. A man who gives his money to a railway company does not expect it to engage in fishing; he ought to be protected against such activity. But an act incidental to the purposes of the company is not

[29] Ashbury Railway Carriage Co. *v.* Riche, L. R. 7 H. L. 653 (1875).

[30] But § 9 of the Companies Consolidation Act of 1908 allows the alteration of the memorandum by special resolution. This is a great advance.

ultra vires. What is so incidental? It is incidental to the business of the South Wales Railway Company to run steamboats from Milford Haven;[31] but that function was seemingly beyond the competence of the Great Eastern.[32] One steamship company may, without hindrance, sell all its vessels;[33] but another company makes the mistake of retaining two of its boats, and its act is without the law.[34] There were two railway companies within recent memory which agreed to pool their profits and divide them with judicial blessing;[35] but two other railway companies speedily discovered their powerlessness when they attempted partnership.[36] It is fitting, so the courts have held, that Wigan and Ashton should supply their citizens with water;[37] but there was, so we may suppose, something unfitting when Southampton and Sheffield attempted that enterprise.[38] But perhaps the nadir of such confusion is seen by anyone who contrasts *Stephens* v. *Mysore Reefs, etc. Co., Ltd.*[39] with *Pedlar* v. *Road Block Gold Mines of India, Ltd.*[40]

Logic here there certainly is not, though the basis of the distinction is easy to understand. "Where a cor-

[31] South Wales Ry. Co. *v.* Redmond, 10 C. B. n. s. 675 (1861).

[32] Colman *v.* Eastern Counties Ry. Co., 10 Beav. 1 (1846).

[33] Wilson *v.* Miers, 10 C. B. n. s. 348 (1861).

[34] Gregory *v.* Patchett, 33 Beav. 595 (1864).

[35] Hare *v.* London & N. W. Ry. Co., 2 J. & H. 80 (1861).

[36] Charlton *v.* Newcastle & Carlisle Ry. Co., 5 Jur. n. s. 1096 (1859).

[37] Bateman *v.* Mayor, etc. of Ashton-under-Lyne, 3 H. & N. 323 (1858), and Attorney-General *v.* Mayor, etc. of Wigan, 5 DeG. M. & G. 52 (1854).

[38] Attorney-General *v.* Andrews, 2 Mac. & G. 225 (1850); Sheffield Waterworks Co. *v.* Carter, 8 Q. B. 632 (1882).

[39] L. R. [1902] 1 Ch. 745.

[40] L. R. [1905] 2 Ch. 427. See especially the remarks of Warrington, J., at p. 437.

poration," said Coleridge, J.,[41] "has been created for the
purpose of carrying on a particular trade, or making
a railway from one place to another, and it attempts to
substitute another trade, or to make its railway to another place, the objection is to its entire want of power
for the new purpose; its life and functions are the creation of the legislature; and they do not exist for any
other than the specified purpose; for any other, the members are merely unincorporated individuals." But the
doctrine results in manifest injustice. A company has
by its charter the right to borrow not more than a
specified sum; it borrows more. It is held that the
lenders cannot sue for the surplus.[42] Yet it is obviously
unjust that a corporation should thus benefit by an
error of which it has been cognizant. It is surely an
unwise restriction of business enterprise so closely to
restrict the interpretation of powers as to refuse a company the legal benefit of its commercial capacity to
build a railway.[43] A corporation can be prevented from
contributing to a charity;[44] it may, on the other hand,
show gratitude to its servants.[45] It is clear enough that
we have no straight rule of construction to guide us.
It is held that a corporation "may" not do certain things.
Does that imply that it should not have done so, or that
it is legally incapable — "stricken with impotence" is

[41] Mayor, etc. of Norwich v. Norwich Ry. Co., 4 E. & B. 397,
432 (1855).

[42] Wenlock v. River Dee Co., 10 A. C. 354 (1885).

[43] As in the great Ashbury case.

[44] Tomkinson v. South Eastern Ry. Co., L. R. 35 Ch. D. 675
(1887).

[45] Hampson v. Price's Patent Candle Co. And yet an able writer
can argue that the existence of corporate gratitude does not come
within the lawyer's purview. Smith, *Law of Associations*, pp. 130-1.

a distinguished lawyer's forcible phrase [46] — of doing them? Is an *ultra vires* act not a corporate act? The courts would seem to uphold this view. "The question is not," said Lord Cairns in the Ashbury case,[47] "as to the legality of the contract; the question is as to the competency and power of the company to make the contract." But that is not a very helpful observation when it is borne in mind that *ultra vires* acts are performed every day. And if the courts hold such acts *a priori* illegal, why do they time and again enforce them in order to prevent harshness? Is not that a virtual admission of their corporateness? Such admission can only mean that in the great realm of contract, as in the case of the seal, we cannot confine the personality of a corporation within the four walls of a document. We are in fact compelled to abandon the doctrine of special capacity. We have to admit that a person, whether a group person or a human being, acts as his personality warrants. Legal theory may deny the fact of a contract which has obviously taken place; but in that event it is only so much the worse for legal theory.

For it results in the divorce of law and justice. A corporator, for instance, severs his connection with a corporation in a manner that is *ultra vires;* ten years later he is held responsible for its debts.[48] Of a surety, no man will claim justice or sweet reasonableness for such an attitude. The courts, again, in the case of a man who has made a contract and then feels it irksome, will not admit the plea that he was originally incapable

[46] Mr. E. Manson in 12 *Encyclopedia of the Laws of England,* 1 ed., p. 360.

[47] Ashbury Railway Carriage Co. *v.* Riche, L. R. 7 H. L. 653, 672 (1875).

[48] *In re* Stanhope, 3 DeG. & Sm. 198 (1850).

of making it. They will say with Wilmot, C. J., that "no polluted hand shall touch the pure fountain of justice." [49]   But if the hand be a corporate hand, as, for instance, in *Hall* v. *Mayor, etc. of Swansea*,[50] they would have no hesitation in admitting the pollution.

What are we to say? Only one thing surely, and that is that the doctrine of *ultra vires* breaks down when it is tested. It is not true because it fails to conform to the canon of scientific hypothesis: it does not fit the facts. We assume the artificiality of our corporation. We suppose that it is no more than we have made it, with the result that common sense must be thrown to the winds. What, in brief, the theory compels us to urge is this, that a class of acts may be performed by the corporation which are not corporate acts. Is it not better to risk a little for the sake of logic? Our fiction-theory may, indeed, break down; but we shall bring the law in closer harmony with the facts of life. We shall then say that the corporation, being a real entity, with a personality that is self-created, must bear the responsibility for its actions. Our state may, in the result, be a little less Hegelian, a little less sovereign in its right of delegation. Therein it will only the more certainly make a direct march upon the real.

v

The corporation has rights and liabilities in tort. Here, again, the tendency has been more and more to make it approximate in situation to the ordinary individual. So long ago as the reign of Henry VII the cor-

[49] Collins *v.* Blantern, 2 Wilson 341, 350 (1767).
[50] 5 Q. B. 526 (1844).

poration could bring an action for trespass.[51] When a
patron of a living it could bring an action of *quare
impedit*.[52] It can sue for libel where it can show that
its property is affected,[53] though it is not clear that it
could sue for words spoken in derogation of its honor
or dignity.[54] This is, so we are told, due to the physical
limitations to which it is subject. "It could not sue,"
said Pollock, C. B.,[55] "in respect of an imputation of
murder, or incest, or adultery, because it could not commit those crimes. Nor could it sue in respect of a charge
of corruption, for a corporation cannot be guilty of
corruption, although the individuals composing it may."
But is this, in fact, true? No one would think of charg-
ing an association with incest or adultery. But it can
be sued for malicious libel,[56] for assault and imprisonment,[57] for fraud and deceit,[58] and, after a long struggle
in which the formidable Lord Bramwell played a noteworthy part, for malicious prosecution.[59] Now when this
formidable list of torts is considered it seems curious
to say that the corporation cannot sue for libel that
touches its honor or dignity. The reason, so far as
one can see, is twofold. It is, in the first place, as-

[51] Y. B. 7 Hen. VII, pl. 9.

[52] Chancellor, etc. of Cambridge *v.* Norwich, 22 Viner's Abr. 5
(1617).

[53] Metropolitan Saloon Omnibus Co. *v.* Hawkins, 4 H. & N. 87
(1859); South Hetton Coal Co. *v.* North-Eastern News Ass'n, L. R.
[1894] 1 Q. B. 133.

[54] Mayor, etc., of Manchester *v.* Williams, L. R. [1891] 1 Q. B. 94.

[55] Metropolitan Saloon Omnibus Co. *v.* Hawkins, 4 H. & N. 87
(1859), at p. 90.

[56] Whitfield *v.* South-Eastern Ry. Co., 27 L. J., (Q. B.) 229 (1858).

[57] Eastern Counties Ry. Co. *v.* Broom, 6 Exch. 314 (1851).

[58] Barwick *v.* Eng. Joint Stock Bank, L. R. 2 Ex. 259 (1867).

[59] Citizens' Life Assurance Co. *v.* Brown [1904], A. C. 423, 426.
The story of the struggle is well told in Mr. Carr's book, pp. 78–87.

sumed *ipso facto* that the corporation has no mind to feel. It is no more than a way of dealing with certain rights in property in such a way that they can be conveniently protected by the courts. The doctrine of agency, moreover, is used as a means of avoiding the complex metaphysical problem of what is behind the agent. This was well shown in Lord Lindley's remarkable judgment in *Citizens' Life Assurance Co. v. Brown.* "If it is once granted," he said, "that corporations are for civil purposes to be regarded as persons, *i. e.*, as principals acting by agents and servants, it is difficult to see why the ordinary doctrines of agency and of master and servant are not to be applied to corporations as well as to ordinary individuals." In that case, clearly, the actual tort is the act of the agent and the principal is reduced to a mere fund from which adequate compensation may be obtained. But is that in truth a satisfactory method of procedure? Are the "metaphysical subtleties" of which Lord Lindley spoke so deprecatingly in truth "needless and fallacious?" Is it not in fact necessary to have some clear view of their nature if a true decision is to be reached?

In order to see this aspect in a clear light let us turn to the criminal liability of corporations. It is now well established that a corporation may be indicted for misfeasance,[60] for obstruction,[61] under the Lotteries Act[62] (though here the courts refused to admit an indictment of the corporation as a rogue and vagabond), for selling impure food[63] and for adulterating milk.[64]   But in all

---

[60] Queen *v.* Birmingham & Glouc. Ry. Co., 3 Q. B. 223 (1842).
[61] Queen *v.* Great North of England Ry. Co., 9 Q. B. 315 (1846).
[62] Hawke *v.* Hulton & Co., L. R. [1909] 2 K. B. 93.
[63] Pearks, etc. *v.* Ward, L. R. [1902] 2 K. B. 1.
[64] Chuter *v.* Freeth, etc., L. R. [1911] 2 K. B. 832.

these cases conviction has been obtained on the basis
of a supposed liability for an agent's act.   This is well
brought out in a remark of Alverstone, C. J., "I think
that we ought to hold that a corporation may be liable
. . . unless *mens rea* is necessary in order to constitute the offence." [65]   But that is the exact point.   Is a
corporation to be held guiltless where the presence of
mens rea is necessary to the crime?   A laundry company
fails adequately to protect its machinery in accordance
with law, and one of its employees is killed.   There was
clear criminal negligence; but on an indictment for manslaughter the judge, a little reluctantly, refused to allow
the action to proceed.[66]   In the next year a railway company caused the death of some of its passengers through
not keeping a bridge in proper repair; here again, though
with obvious difficulty, the court thought the demurrer
must be admitted.[67]   Clearly, the problem of whether a
corporation can have a *mens rea* has, if sometimes a little
doubtfully, been answered in the negative.[68]   Taken with
the cases in tort, we must collect the opinion that it
cannot have a mind at all.

VI

Yet we cannot, in fact, do without that mind.   Just
as we have been compelled by the stern exigencies of
events to recognize that the corporation is distinct from

[65] Cited in Pearks, etc. *v.* Ward, L. R. [1902] 2 K. B. 1, at p. 8.

[66] Queen *v.* Great West. Laundry Co., 13 Manitoba Rep. 66
(1900).

[67] Union Colliery Co. *v.* H. M. The Queen, 31 Can. Sup. Ct.
81 (1900).

[68] Perhaps Lord Bowen in Queen *v.* Tyler & International Commercial Co., Ltd., felt some difficulty also. L. R. [1891] 2 Q. B.
588. See especially pp. 592, 594, 596.

its members, so, too, we have to recognize that its mind
is distinct from their minds. A corporation votes an
annual pension to a servant; its gratitude is not merely
the gratitude of the individual members expressed in a
single term, for one of those members will endeavor to
restrain its generosity.[69] So it may well be urged in the
cases of manslaughter noted above a penalty ought to be
exacted in some wise commensurable with the offence.
When we talk of a company as a "bad master," there
is surely reality behind that phrase. Individually its
members are probably meek and kindly; but the company
is differently constituted. Where that "badness" passes
into the region in which it becomes criminally culpable,
the company ought to suffer the penalty for its blameworthiness. Certainly it does so suffer when it is morally
but not legally at fault. Its men work for it with less
zeal. It finds it difficult to retain their services. The
quality of its production suffers. It loses ground and
is outstripped in the industrial race. Why the courts
should refuse to take cognizance of that which is an
ordinary matter of daily life it is difficult indeed to understand. Take, for example, the charge of manslaughter. Any student of workmen's compensation cases
will not doubt that in a choice between the adoption of
a completely protective system and the possibility of
an occasional accident, there are not a few corporations
anti-social enough to select the latter alternative. Human life, they will argue, is cheap; the fencing, let us
say, of machinery is dear. But admit the existence of
the corporate mind and that mind can be a guilty mind.
It can be punished by way of fine; and if it be mulcted
with sufficient heaviness we may be certain that it will

69 Cyclists' Touring Club v. Hopkinson, L. R. [1910] 1 Ch. 179.

not offend again.   What is the alternative?   To attack
some miserable agent who has been acting in the interest
of a mindless principal, an agent, as Maitland said,[70]
who is the "servant of an unknowable Somewhat."   But
if that Somewhat be mindless, how can it have selected
an agent?   For selection implies the weighing of qualities, and that is a characteristic of mind.

VII

When, therefore, we look at the association which has
chosen to incorporate itself, we cannot but feel that less
than the admission of a real personality results in illogic
and injustice.   It is purely arbitrary to urge that personality must be so finite as to be distinctive only of the
living, single man.[71]   Law, of a certainty, is not the
result of one man's will, but of a complex fusion of
wills.   It distills the quintessence of an infinite number
of personalities.   It displays the character not of a
Many, but of a One — it becomes, in fact, unified and
coherent.   Ultimately pluralistic, the interactions of its
diversities make it essentially, within the sphere of its
operations, a single thing.   Men obey its commands.   It
acts.   It influences.   Surely it is but a limitation of
outlook not to extend the conception of personality into
this incorporeal sphere.

It is urged that to neglect this is to commit injustice
where the corporation is concerned.   Even less happy
shall we feel when we turn to the association that is, oddly
enough, termed voluntary; as if your unincorporate

[70] Introduction to Gierke, *Political Theories of the Middle
Age*, p. 40.

[71] Cf. F. H. Bradley, *Appearance and Reality*, p. 532.   "For me
a person is finite or is meaningless."

body were any less the result of self-will than its corporate analogue. We shall find no law of associations.
What we shall find is rather a series of references to the
great divisions, contract, tort, and the like, of ordinary
law. For here, in the legal view, we have no bodiliness,
nothing more than a number of men who have contracted
together to do certain things, who, having no corporate
life, can do no more than those things for which the
agreement has made stipulation. Legally they are no
unit, though to your ordinary man it is a strange notion
that a Roman Church, a Society of Jesus, a Standard
Oil Trust — the most fundamentally unified persons, so
he would say, in existence — should be thus devoid of
group will because, forsooth, certain mystic words have
not been pronounced over them by the state. Laugh-
able to most of us this may indeed be; yet none the less
certainly is it good law.

We take the voluntary society in contract. Its acts
are *ultra vires* unless they were clearly implied in the
original agreement. You join a club. An unwise draftsman has failed through inadvertence to make binding the
right to change the rules. When, therefore, the club
falls on evil days and changes its subscription you may
refuse to pay on the ground that you have not contracted
to do so.[72] It does not matter that the subscription
had been already raised several times; it does not matter
that you had assented to the previous changes; that
there was practical unanimity among the members as to
the need for the change; that without it the whole future
of the club was jeopardized. Of all this the courts made
entire abstraction. The contract is a fundamental agreement which cannot admit of change. A society clearly

[72] Harington *v.* Sendall, L. R. [1903] 1 Ch. 921.

living a life of its own will be denied the benefits of that life because it has failed to take advantage of a section in an Act of Parliament.

Nor is the full significance of this judgment clear until one places it side by side with the case of *Thellusson* v. *Valentia*.[73] The Hurlingham Club from its origin indulged in pigeon-shooting. It was decided to do so no longer, and the plaintiff sought to obtain an injunction preventing the change on the ground that he had contracted for this sport on joining the club. Yet it was held that the change came under the clause admitting the alteration of the rules and was not a fundamental change. It surely will not be argued that a change in a subscription rate is any more fundamental than this. As a plain matter of common sense it is surely obvious that if a society can do the one thing the other should be permitted. If the courts will not protect the prejudices of members whose sporting tastes verge on the antiquarian, why should it protect those whose social tastes verge on the sullen disagreeableness of the boor?

Nor are matters improved when the trust conceals the reality of this group life. The trust, says Maitland,[74] "has served to protect the unincorporated *Genossenschaft* against the attacks of inadequate and individualistic theories. We should all agree that if an *Anstalt* or a *Genossenschaft* is to live and thrive it must be efficiently protected by law against external enemies." If it is to live *and thrive* — let us repeat the words in the way in which we would wish the emphasis to lie. The association is to thrive. It is not to have its life cramped, its development impeded. It is to be sheltered against the attacks of men willing to take advantage of its

corporality. So, at least one would think, the trust
came into being. And yet it is in precisely the opposite
way that the courts have interpreted their purpose.
Men's minds may change. Their purposes may change.
Not so the purposes of men bound together in an association. The famous Free Church of Scotland case needs
no retelling; the House of Lords chose to regard its
life as fixed for it by the terms of a trust — not seeing
that the fact that the church has a life must necessarily
connote its right to develop the terms on which that
life is lived.[75] Certain eloquent words of Lord Macnagh-
ten, spoken in his dissenting judgment, serve to make
clear the opportunity the highest English tribunal chose
to neglect. "Was the Church," he asked, "thus puri-
fied — the Free Church — so bound and tied by the
tenets of the Church of Scotland prevailing at the time
of the Disruption, that departure from those tenets in
any matter of substance would be a violation of that
profession or testimony which may be called the unwritten
charter of her foundation, and so necessarily involve a
breach of trust in the administration of funds contrib-
uted for no other purpose but the support of the Free
Church — the Church of the Disruption? Was the Free
Church by the very condition of her existence forced to
cling to her Subordinate Standards with so desperate a
grip that she has lost hold and touch of the Supreme
Standard of her faith? Was she from birth incapable
of all growth and development? Was she (in a word)
a dead branch and not a living Church?"[76] We must,

[75] On all this Dr. J. N. Figgis, *Churches in the Modern State*,
is of very high value.

[76] Orr, report of Free Church of Scotland case, p. 573. S. C. 4 f.
1083 (1902).

surely, accept the point of view of Lord Haldane when
he argued that "the test of the personal identity of this
Church lies not in doctrine but in its life." To insist
on the strictest adherence to the letter of a trust means
that the dead hand shall regulate the living even when
they have outgrown that hand's control, sixty or six
hundred years after its decease. Is there any answer to
the protest of Mill when he urged that no person ought
thus to be exercising the rights of property six hundred
years after his death? [77] It is more plausible to take
one's stand on the spirit of the trust. It would not in
substance have been far removed from the doctrine of
cy près for the House of Lords to have granted the
right of self-development to the beneficiaries of a trust.
It is clear, for instance, that religious interpretation
has vastly changed since the advent of Darwinism.
Would the courts have deprived a church which had so
modernized its creed as to take account of the new
knowledge from enjoying gifts left to it in a pre-Dar-
winian age? It is not, at any rate, insignificant that the
justice of the courts had speedily to be remedied by Act
of Parliament.

It is no light stumbling-block that this cover of trusteeship has proved. It may be that the trustees of a club
will incur liabilities on that club's behalf, though the
rules have failed to provide for their indemnity. In that
event the members will be able to avoid payment on the
ground that they have contracted for no more than their
subscriptions, even though the club (and they as its
members) enjoy the benefit of the trustees' action. [78]
Yet it would appear to the man in the street more equi-

[77] 1 *Dissertations and Discussions*, p. 36.
[78] Wise *v.* Perpetual Trustee Co. [1903], A. C. 139.

table to make the club pay for that of which it enjoys the
benefit. It, for example, the committee of a football
club employs an incompetent person to repair a stand
which collapses, sanity would appear to require that just
as the club would have enjoyed the profits, so, on the
collapse of the stand, it is right that it should
suffer the penalties. Yet the courts, taking their stand
on the principles of the law of contract, held that the
members of the committee were responsible and must pay
as individuals.[79] This is surely the violation of the ordinary principle of English law that he who holds property
must bear its burdens no less than enjoy its advantages;
nor should an agency or trusteeship obscure the real
relation. A case can be conceived, can easily arise,
where, without any knowledge on the part of the trustees,
and by sheer misadventure on the part of one of their
servants, they become liable for damages and the members go scot free. This is surely the *reductio ad ab-
surdum* of legal formalism. Had the Privy Council in
Wise v. *Perpetual Trustee Co.* applied the perfectly
straightforward doctrine of *Hardoon* v. *Belilios*[80] no
injustice would have thus occurred.

And the contractual theory of voluntary associations
can result in fictions compared to which the supposed
fiction of corporate personality has less than the ingenuity of childish invention. If you buy a liqueur in a
club that does not, in the eyes of the law, constitute a
sale. What was before a joint interest of all the members has been magically released to you just at the
moment when you expressed your desire to the club

79 Brown *v.* Lewis, 12 T. L. R. 455 (1896).
80 [1901] A. C. 118.

waiter, with the result that you can drink in safety.[81] Is
it worth while thus to strain reality for the sake of
inadequate theory?

Certain property rights serve to bring out the failure
of the contractual attitude with striking clearness. The
luckless fate of Serjeants' Inn, of Clements' Inn, and
Barnard's Inn shows how disastrous can be the attempt
to conceal corporateness to the public interest.[82] No
one believes that the distribution of their property among
the surviving members fulfilled the pious purpose of their
founders. The property of the unincorporate association can now be taxed [83] (and for income tax at that) ;
but the courts did not tell us whether this was a new
method of double taxation or an attempt to recognize
the fact of corporateness. The fact that the fishermen
of the Wye had for a period certainly not less than three
centuries had a perfectly unquestioned user, had therein
acted exactly as, in like circumstances, a prescriptive
corporation would have acted,[84] did not persuade the
Lords to regard them as having rights against the technical owners of the land.[85] It were surely an easier as
well as a wiser thing to give to this obvious unit the title
of unity.

Yet another curiosity deserves some notice. The
courts do not regard a volunteer corps as a legal entity,
so that it cannot be bound by contract. It can become
bound only by particular members pledging their liability

81 Graff *v.* Evans, 8 Q. B. D. 373 (1882).

82 See a deeply interesting letter in the *Times* for April 10, 1902.

83 48 & 49 Vict., c. 51, and Curtis *v.* Old Monkland Conservative
Ass'n [1906] A. C. 86.

84 *In re* Free Fishermen of Faversham, L R. 36 Ch. D. 329 (1887).

85 Harris *v.* Chesterfield [1911], A. C. 623. Lord Loreburn read
a valuable dissenting judgment.

on its behalf, not for it as agents but for themselves as principals. So a commanding officer of a volunteer corps will be held responsible for uniforms supplied to the corps;[86] though, anomalous as it may seem, he is not responsible to the bankers of the battalion for its overdraft.[87] If a corps cannot have a liability for uniforms, why can a liability for its overdraft exist? And, further, if "it" is no legal entity at all, why do we use collective nouns with possessive pronouns and singular verbs?

Now in all conscience these are absurdities enough; yet note what has followed from the denial of a right to sue and be sued. It was the mere accident of his membership of the Middle Temple which made Lord Eldon grant to a body of Free Masons the right to a representative action. It might have been, as he said,[88] "singular that this court should sit upon the concerns of an association, which in law has no existence," but it was just because it had an existence in life that the law had to take some account of it. "The society must," as Eldon saw, "some way or other be permitted to sue." Why? Because without that permission the gravest injustice would occur and to refuse it is to negative the whole purpose for which the courts exist. It was, again, a great advance when a private Act of Parliament enabled a voluntary society to sue in the name of its chairman.[89] But it does not go far enough. The entities the law must recognize are those which act as such, for to act in unified fashion is — formality apart — to act as a corporation. When the Scottish courts upheld a verdict

[86] Samuel Brothers, Ltd. v. Whetherly, L. R. [1908] 1 K. B. 184.
[87] National Bank of Scotland v. Shaw [1913], S. C. 133.
[88] Lloyd v. Loaring, 6 Ves. 773, 778 (1802).
[89] Williams v. Beaumont, 10 Bing. 260 (1833).

against the libellers of "the Roman Catholic authorities of Queenstown," they knew that no corporation had been libelled, but a body of men to be regarded as a unit for practical purposes. That body had suffered in reputation from the libel; it was right and fitting that it should receive compensation.[90] And when a voluntary society in the pursuit of its functions libels a company without justice, it seems rational, even if it is legally an innovation, to make the society pay.[91]

Nothing has brought into more striking prominence the significance for practical life of this controversy than the questions raised in the last decade and a half by trade-union activity. Of the rights and wrongs of their policy great authorities have written;[92] and it is not now needful to discuss at length the decisions of the courts. But this much may at least be said: that just as surely as the decision of the House of Lords marked, in the great Taff Vale case,[93] a vital advance, so, no less surely, did its decision in the Osborne case[94] mark a reactionary step. The Taff Vale case decided, as it appears to us, quite simply and reasonably, that a trade union must be responsible for the wrongs it commits — a point of view which so impressed the Royal Commission that they did not recommend the reversal of the judgment.[95] The Osborne case decided that a method of action

[90] Brown v. Thomson & Co. [1912] S. C. 359.

[91] Greenlands, Ltd. v. Wilmshurst, L. R. [1913] 3. K. B. 507.

[92] See particularly the Report of the Royal Commission on Trade Disputes, 1906; the preface to the 1911 edition of Webb, *History of Trade Unionism;* and above all, the brilliant articles of Professor Geldart in 25 *Harv. L. Rev.* 579 and *Pol. Quart.* for May, 1914.

[93] [1901] A. C. 426.

[94] [1910] A. C. 87.

[95] Report, p. 8.

which a trade union thinks necessary for its welfare and protection may be illegal because it is political and not industrial in its scope — political objects being *eo nomine* beyond the province of a trade society. But that is surely a too narrow interpretation of the facts. Where does a political object end and an industrial object begin? It is obvious to anyone who has eyes to see that at every point modern politics is concerned with the facts of everyday life in its industrial aspect. Therein they clearly touch the worker, and the trade union is an association formed for his protection. On this view the political activity of trade unions means no more than giving emphasis to one particular branch of their industrial policy. It is, then, one would urge, open to the courts to declare the transaction void on grounds of public policy;[96] but it is probable that they would pay dearly for so doing in the loss of the respect in which they are held. It is wiser when dealing with the group person not to interfere with its individual life. The experience of the Privy Council as an ecclesiastical tribunal might herein have given a lesson to the House of Lords. There was it sternly demonstrated that the corporation of the English Church — a corporation in fact if not in law — will not tolerate the definition of its doctrine by an alien body.[97] The sovereignty of theory is reduced by the event to an abstraction that is simply ludicrous. It may well be urged that any similar interference with the life of trade unions will result in a not dissimilar history.

[96] As Lord Shaw did in the House of Lords, and, in part, Farwell and Fletcher Moulton, L. J. J., in the Court of Appeal below.

[97] See on this the Report of the Royal Commission on Ecclesiastical Discipline of 1906 *passim.*

VIII

We have traveled far, but at least there has been direction in our traveling. We have asked a question: is corporate personality a real thing? Is the collective will that is the inevitable accompaniment of that personality but a figment of the imagination? The thesis that has been here maintained is a simple one. It is that when the man in the street calls (let us say) Lloyds and the Stock Exchange corporations he is profoundly right in his perception. He has brushed aside the technicalities of form and penetrated to the reality, which is but a cloud serving not to reveal but to obscure. This, it may be pointed out, Erle, J., perceived nearly sixty years ago.[98] "According to the plaintiff," he said, "it is supposed to be a corporation created for the purpose of the navigation, and having the legal incidents of its existence limited for that purpose. But it appears to me that, by common law, the creation of a corporation conferred on it all the rights and liabilities in respect of property, contracts and litigation which existence confers upon a natural subject, modified only by the formalities required for expressing the will of a numerous body." Here, at any rate, is the basis of much-needed innovation. A corporation is simply an organized body of men acting as a unit, and with a will that has become unified through the singleness of their purpose. We assume its reality. We act upon that assumption. Are we not justified in the event?

After all, our legal theories will and must be judged

[98] Bostock v. North Staffordshire Railway Co., 4 E. & B. 798, 819 (1855).

by their applicability to the facts they endeavor to resume. It is clear enough that unless we treat the personality of our group persons as real and apply the fact of that reality throughout the whole realm of law, what we call justice will, in truth, be no more than a chaotic and illogical muddle.

English lawyers, it is said, have a dislike of abstractions. Such excursions as this into the world of legal metaphysics have for them the suspect air of dangerous adventure. But life, after all, is a series of precipices, and we have to act upon the assumptions we make. Here we urge a radical thesis; we say that the distinction between incorporate and voluntary association must be abolished. We say that the trust must be made to reveal the life that glows beneath, that we must have the means of penetrating beyond its fictitious protectiveness. No one doubts that the change will be vast. No one doubts that the application will need courage and high resolve. But it is in its very difficulty that we shall find its supreme worth.

IX

A last word remains to be said. If what we have here been urging is true, it reacts most forcibly upon our theory of the state. Thus far, for the most part, we have sought its unification. We have made it intolerant of associations within itself — associations that to Hobbes will appear comparable only to "worms within the entrails of a natural man." As a result we have made our state absorptive in a mystic, Hegelian fashion. It is all-sovereign and unchallengeable. It has, if it be the papal state, and the Pope its personification, the *plenitude potestatis;* be it imperial, its emperor is *legibus solutus;* be it Britannic, its parliament has, as De Lolme somewhat whimsically pointed out, no limit in power save the laws of nature. We seem, when we front the state, to cry with Dante that the *maxime unum* must be the *maxime bonum,*[99] and with Boniface VIII that there is heresy in political dualism.[100] Admirable enough this may be in theory; of a certainty it does not fit the facts. We do not proceed from the state to the parts of the state, from the One to the Many, on the ground that the state is more unified than its parts. On the contrary, we are forced to the admission that the parts are as real, as primary, and as self-sufficing as the whole. "The pluralistic world," said James,[101] "is . . . more like a federal republic than an empire or a kingdom. However much may be collected, however much may report itself as present at any effective center of consciousness or action, something else is self-governed and absent and unreduced to unity." But sovereign your state no longer is if the groups within itself are thus self-governing. Nor can we doubt this polyarchism. Everywhere we find groups within the state which challenge its supremacy. They are, it may be, in relations with the state, a part of it; but one with it they are not. They refuse the reduction to unity. We find the state, in James' phrase, to be distributive and not collective. Men belong to it; but, also, they belong to other groups, and a competition for allegiance is continuously possible. Here, as a matter of history, we find the root of Mr. Gladstone's attack on the Vatican decrees of 1870. An

99 De Mon., Ch. 15.

100 See the Bull Unam Sanctam, Ch. 1, Ex. Com. 1, 8.

101 *A Pluralistic Universe,* p. 321. The whole book has vital significance for political theory; see especially the fifth lecture.

allegiance that is unreduced to unity appeared to him without meaning. Yet it is obvious that every great crisis must show its essential plurality. Whether we will or no, we are bundles of hyphens. When the centers of linkage conflict a choice must be made.

Such, it is submitted, is the natural consequence of an admission that the personality of associations is real and not conceded thereto by the state. We then give to this latter group no peculiar merit. We refuse it the title of creator of all else. We make it justify itself by its consequences. We stimulate its activities by making it compete with the work of other groups coextensive with or complementary to itself. As it may not extinguish, so it may not claim preëminence. Like any other group, what it is and what it will be, it can be only by virtue of its achievement. So only can it hope to hand down undimmed the torch of its conscious life.

THE EARLY HISTORY OF THE
CORPORATION IN ENGLAND *

OURS is a time of deep question about the state.[1] Theories of corporate personality have challenged in decisive fashion its proud claim to preëminence.[2]   Its character of uniqueness seems hardly to have survived the acid test of skeptical inquiry.   The groups it has claimed to control seem, often enough, to lead a life no less full and splendid than its own.   The loyalty they can command, the fear they may inspire, are near enough to its own to seek comparison with it.   Yet dogmas that are none the less fundamental because they are hardly old still haunt our speculations.   It is barely a century and a half since Blackstone asserted in his emphatic fashion the right of the state to condition and control all corporate existence.[3]   Less than three centuries have elapsed since a civil war shocked the timid Hobbes [4] into a repetition of Richard of Devizes' anger at the danger

---

* Reprinted from the *Harvard Law Review,* Vol. XXX, No. 6.

[1] Cf. Barker, *English Political Thought from Herbert Spencer to To-day,* 175 ff., and Burns, *The Morality of Nations, passim.*

[2] Cf. E. Barker in the *Political Quarterly* for February, 1915; Figgis, *Churches in the Modern State,* and Saleilles, *De la Personnalité Juridique,* 41, 856, 364, 463–64, 533, 619.

[3] 1 *Comm.* 472.

[4] *Leviathan,* Bk. II, Ch. 29. For his timidity, cf. Croom Robertson's *Life,* 52.

of group-persons.[5] We perhaps too little realize that
a long history lies behind Blackstone's incisive sentences;
nor is the contemptuous phrasing of Hobbes an accurate
index to the English attitude. For, as Maitland has
pointed out,[6] few countries have enjoyed a richer variety
of group-life. Yet we have hardly come to ask the
fundamental questions that richness suggests. A history
of English state theory has still to be written.[7] We have
still to work out in detail the lines of their thought as to
its juridical nature and of its relation to those groups
of which they were so dramatically prodigal. Englishmen are a practical race, and they had discovered the
benefits of fellowship long before they speculated upon
their nature. Orcy of Dorsetshire had built for his
brethren a gild-house long before the stern hand of the
Norman conquerer had begun to effect the centralization
of law;[8] and the benefits of meat and drink in goodly
fellowship were not unknown in Anglo-Saxon Cambridge.[9]

But where men meet to eat and drink and, mayhap,
to pray, the subtleties involved in corporate existence
hardly seem to emerge. *Communitas*, it is true enough,
is the key to early English history; but it is a dangerous
and ambiguous word. "It swallows up," as Maitland
has happily remarked,[10] "both the corporation and the

---

[5] *Richard of Devizes' Chronicle*, 416. Cf. 1 Stubbs, *Constit. Hist.*,
6 ed., 455.

[6] Cf. Maitland's Introduction to Gierke, *Political Theories of the
Middle Age*, XXXVI.

[7] Though Maitland has indicated the lines on which such a history should be written. 3 *Coll. Papers*, 210-70.

[8] *Codex Dip.* (ed. Kemble), No. 1942.

[9] 1 Kemble, *Saxons in Eng.*, 513. On the Anglo-Saxon gilds generally, see 1 Gross, *Gild Merchant*, 174-91. Gneist has warned us
against overestimating their importance. 1 Verwalt. 139.

[10] *Township and Borough*, 12.

group of coöwners." That, indeed, is intelligible enough; for in the nineteenth century a great Lord Chancellor could still be puzzled about the nature of corporate ownership.[11] The abstractions of early jurisprudence are post-conquestual in origin; and we may even doubt whether the early communalism which has so much affected the economic speculation of our time is not in fact more truly individualist than we care to admit.[12] We dare not base our speculations upon the evidence anterior to the time when the iron hand of Norman William fashioned a conquered kingdom to his own desire. Of corporateness we shall speak with some skepticism, though we shall recognize that its roots are there. For the court rolls from which our main knowledge of internal organization is drawn date only from the end of the thirteenth century; the records of the King's Court are continuous only after the twelfth. Our earlier knowledge is rather of fields and farming methods, of taxation and military service, than of judicial or political unification. And where there is so dangerous an economy of words, our footsteps must needs go slowly.

II

Yet some sort of guesswork we may adventure. If corporateness be held in the balance the basis of it may at any rate be discovered. The theory of possession — the later turning point in corporate history — here helps us but little. It is to men that the land belongs. Our

---

11 Cf. Eldon, L. C., in Lloyd v. Loaring, 6 Ves. 773, 776–77 (1802).

12 Cf. Maitland, *Domesday Book and Beyond*, 342 ff. On the other hand Professor Vinogradoff stands by the older conception. *Growth of the Manor*, 18 ff., 150.

Anglo-Saxon village is full of freeholders.[13]   The men who drew up Domesday Book were not very certain whether St. Peter owns his church, or the priest who cares for it.[14]   The church will indeed hold land; and we may perhaps see therein a significant effort after a natural personification.   Yet we shall put our trust in the mysticism of a superstitious time rather than the advanced ideas of an inquiring jurisprudence.[15]   The land of England, of a certainty, is the king's, for William knew too well the dangers of continental feudalism to submit himself to its conflicts of allegiance.[16]   It is evidence enough that a corporate kingdom is not yet attained, for William at least is stout flesh and blood, and what he calls his own he uses for his purposes.[17]

Yet a certain attempt at noteworthy unification we deem not wanting.   England is divided into townships; and we shall exaggerate the automatism of medieval life if we believe that its affairs went of themselves.   A township court it seems clear that we must have.[18]   That court will pass by-laws,[19] and, if need be, enforce them.[20]

---

[13] This is of course the whole point of the second essay in Maitland, *Domesday Book and Beyond.* Cf. especially pp. 318 ff. It is interesting to note the kindred ideas of continental historians. Cf. especially 2 Flach, *Les Origines de l'Ancienne France*, 45, and Dargun, *Ursprung des Eigenthums 5 Zeitschrift für Vergleichende Rechtswissenschaft*, 55.

[14] 1 Pollock & Maitland, 2 ed., 498–500.

[15] Cf. 3 Gierke, *Deutsche Genossenschaftsrecht*, 195.

[16] 1 Stubbs, *Constit. Hist.*, 6 ed., 290.

[17] Cf. 3 Maitland, *Coll. Papers*, 246. "All lands were his lands, and we must be careful not to read a trusteeship for the nation into our medieval documents."

[18] Cf. Vinogradoff, *Growth of the Manor.* 194.

[19] Cf. *Northumberland Assize Roll* (Surtees Soc., vol. 88), 45.

[20] Cf. Massingberd, *Court Rolls of Ingoldmells*, 44; 1 P. & M., 2 ed., 613.

There was joint liability in taxation,[21] for the separate collection of geld from each individual was a task no administration could then have undertaken.[22] The village will grow and divide into parts;[23] surely the fact of division connotes the recognition of significant difference. The village is a police unit, and it will sometimes struggle against a forcible extinction.[24] It is of real importance that our great geld-book should write of local duties and local privileges in township terms.[25] The vill that farms its own dues has a healthy sense of its own individuality;[26] and the men who could hold and sell their land "*communiter*" we may not easily pass by.[27] Nor dare we minimize a waste land which, however vaguely, is yet the possession of the community.[28]

Admittedly this is no proof of formal corporateness; it is doubtful if your Anglo-Saxon peasant, even if he be lettered monk, would have grasped the transition from *communa* to *universitas*. But no one who looks at this evidence of an action which, whatever it is, is yet not individual, can fail to discern a soil which seems to promise fairly for the growth of abstract ideas. Land

[21] Cf. *Rot. Hund.*, I, 6; II, 8, etc.

[22] Hence Maitland's brilliant but untenable theory of the manor. *Domesday Book and Beyond*, 107-28.

[23] *Domesday Book and Beyond*, 14 ff. For a different view, cf. 2 Maitland, *Coll. Papers*, 84-86.

[24] Maitland, *Pleas of Gloucester*, Pl. 157. Vinogradoff, *English Society in the Eleventh Century*, 216.

[25] Cf. 1 *Domesday Book* 181 d (Frome), 275 b (Wyaston).

[26] Cf. 1 *Select Pleas in Manorial Courts* (Selden Soc.), 172 (Brightwaltham).

[27] 1 *Domesday Book* 213 d (Goldington). On the self-governing character of the medieval township the tenth appendix of Professor Vinogradoff's *English Society in the Eleventh Century* is an interesting balance to Maitland's skepticism.

[28] 2 Gross, *op. cit.*, 122.

that is somebody's land may soon, and easily, become
the land of some body. Men who act in union will come
rapidly to regard themselves as an unit. Local delimitation will make for the growth of separatism. The
men of Trumpington will somehow partake of its character. What that character is they may not as yet
speculate; but the basis of speculation lies ready to their
hand.

Whatever skepticism we may cherish as to townships,
some vague sort of corporate character we may not take
from hundreds and from counties. "The 'county,'"
wrote Maitland,[29] "is not a mere stretch of land . . .
it is an organized body of men; it is a *communitas*." In
truth that organized character is little short of an amazing thing. Devonshire boasted a common seal at the
time of the first Edward;[30] and comital grants seem to
fall no less trippingly from the pen of needy John Lack-
land than when boroughs were the subject of his corrupt
donations.[31] The county can be fined; and it seems like
enough that it kept a common purse against such mis-
fortune.[32] It will defend itself and hire a champion to
the purpose.[33] It has a court which is thoroughly representative in character. It seems to make by-laws;[34] and
it is a natural unit of parliamentary representation.
And if the hundred has failed to advance so far, the fine
for *murdrum* denotes an early unification; and a clause
in the Statute of Winchester shows us that the recogni-

---

29 1 P. & M., 2 ed., 534.

30 *Ibid.*, 535.

31 *Rot. Chart.* 122, 132. Maitland has noted that as late as 17
Edw. II an attempt was made to indict the county. 1 *loc. cit.*, 535.

32 Madox, *Hist. of Exchequer* (ed. of 1711), 386.

33 1 P. & M., 2 ed., 537.

34 *Ibid.*, 555, n. 2.

tion of its value remains at least to the close of the early middle ages.[35] The hundred has its court; nor does it evade the financial censure so beloved of the Angevin kings.[36] There is even some prospect that a property in land may not have been lacking to it.[37] So near, in truth, to corporateness are these units of administration that within a century and a half its absence gave deep cause for reflection to a chief justice of England.[38]

Most striking of all we find those vills which have gone beyond the stage of villadom and attained burghality. Wherein lay the secret of that transition we may not now speculate; nor dare we venture a guess as to the time of its beginning.[39] For us the important point is rather what was in the minds of those who administered the king's law when they spoke of boroughs. It is unquestionable that to the scribes of Domesday Book the borough is a piece of land like shire and manor and hundred;[40] yet in one curious passage the writer seems to draw a vivid distinction between the power of personality the county may have and that of the town. He will allow the shire to speak for itself; but the men in Huntingdon he seems to conceive of as in no sense or-

---

[35] Stubbs, *Select Charters* (ed. Davis), 467.

[36] 1 Stubbs, *Constit. Hist.*, 6 ed., 430.

[37] Maitland, *Domesday Book and Beyond*, 355, n. 2.

[38] See the opinion of Kenyon, C. J., in Russell *v.* Men of Devon, 2 T. R. 667, 672 (1788).

[39] All discussion of this problem must now start with Maitland's famous chapter in *Domesday Book and Beyond*, 172–219, as checked by Professor Tait in 12 *Eng. Hist. Rev.*, 776. Mr. Ballard has fortified Maitland's theory, perhaps a little too emphatically, in his *Domesday Boroughs*.

[40] Cf. 1 *Domesday Book* 132 a. (Hertford), 3 a (Sandwich).

ganically one.[41]   The borough is a piece of land and to
it corporateness, before the Conquest at least, seems
lacking.   There are men there, it is true enough; and
Henry I will grant to the men of English Cambridge
that the barges shall be nowhere loaded save at their
port.[42]   It is in a similar sense that his grandson
speaks.[43]   They talk of living men, and the borough
seems not yet to have attained the abstract character
implied in corporateness.   Yet soon a different language
will be spoken.   When the good burgesses of Okehamp-
ton sell their land they will pay to lord and reeve, but
to the borough as well;[44] and the drinking that the
friendly men of Whitby demanded implies the possession
of a common purse.[45]   We can see clearly enough how
men's thoughts move toward the idea of the borough as
an entity.   Bristol in 1188 had already an interest distinct from that of its citizens;[46] but such nice metaphysical differences puzzled the good draftsman of Dublin
when he copied the Bristol charter, and he hesitated to
make the bridge from an intelligible plurality of citizens
to the difficulty of a singular city.[47]   Bit by bit what
it was at first natural to attribute to the men of the
borough the borough itself will come to possess; so that
by the reign of King John it has become natural for that
reckless prodigal to cast about his free boroughs and
their rights.[48]   Magna Carta itself personifies a city

[41] 1 *Domesday Book* 208 a.
[42] Maitland, *Cambridge Borough Charters*, 2.
[43] 1 *Records of Nottingham* (Stevenson), 2.
[44] 1 Fraser, *Contested Elections*, 82.
[45] 1 Whitby, *Cart.* (Surtees Soc., vol. 69), 211.
[46] See Bickley, *Little Red Book*, where the charter is reproduced.
[47] *Hist. & Mun. Doc. Ireland* (Rolls Ser.), 2.
[48] See his charter to Lynn in *Rot. Chart.* 118; to Dunwich in
ibid., 159; to Stafford in 1 *Cal. Charter Rolls* 71.

of London to which rights have been annexed.[49] Lost-
withiel may allow a stranger to keep its tavern.[50]
Northampton will elect its reeve and coroner; [51] Shrews-
bury,[52] Ipswich,[53] and Gloucester [54] will follow that
fascinating example. A town from which its citizens
may take "common counsel" has a suggestive group-
quality about it. The city of Worcester paid forty
marks to the aid Henry II collected in 1177; [55] and when
Lion-hearted William grants to his "burgh and burgesses"
of Ayr five pennyworth of land, the reality of the distinction seems incapable of disproof.[56] What was that
communa of the city of Oxford which in 1214 had a
common purse wherewith it could pay penance for the
murder of poor scholars? [57]

We must not overstress this communalism, for in
truth it is ambiguous enough. What we shall recognize is the undoubted fact that the draftsmen of the
twelfth century see here, however vaguely, the terms of
corporate liability and are striving forward to express
it. It is an effort made unconsciously and it is an effort
rarely sustained. The transition from "borough" to
"burgesses" is too easy for the clerk not to make it with
great ease. But the materials of change are there. A
mercantile center the borough is to become with its
gilds and fraternities. It will send twelve men to the

49 *Magna Carta*, Ch. 9.
50 *Rep. Hist. Mss. Com.*, 1901, pt. i, 328.
51 1 *Records*, 25, 31.
52 *Rot. Chart.* 46.
53 *Rot. Chart.* 153.
54 *Rot. Chart.* 56.
55 *Pipe Roll* 23 Hen. II, 67.
56 See *Charters of Ayr*, 1.
57 Wood, *Hist. and Antiq. of the Univ. of Oxford*, s. a. 1214.

assize and two men to the parliament.[58]   It has a power
of self-direction which is earlier and more real than that
of all other communities in England.   But in these early
days it is an administrative area rather than a corporate
personality.[59]   It retains much of its old rural character.
Its heterogeneous tenure reminds it that a sense of corporate ownership is not yet at hand.   It has still to
fight its way to independence, and it will find that the
road thereto lies through the coffers of the king.   The
time when it will become a new type of community dates
rather from the age when kings will sell somewhat easily
their liberties that they may establish their sovereignty
with the profits so gained.   The *liber burgus* in a full
and corporate sense is perhaps the offspring of parliamentary representation.[60]   What is at this time significant is the fact that the desire for unity and the privileges that give it form come from below.   There is no
imposition from above.   The purchase price stands for
a common aim.   The men of London who took the county
of Middlesex to farm [61] had a fine sense of collective
effort.   The oath they would take within sixty years may
derive from foreign models; [62] but it stands for the
growth of a spirit which will not find it difficult to take
corporate form.   That of which the early history of
the English boroughs will leave a firm impression is the
fact that not even the pressure of medieval centralization can hinder their growth.   They will remain the
centers of commerce.   Their fairs, their markets, the

[58] Cf. 1 P. & M., 2 ed., 634.

[59] *Ibid.*, 636.

[60] Cf. *Ibid.*, 640–41.

[61] Stubbs, *Select Charters* (ed. Davis), 129.

[62] Stubbs, *Select Charters* (ed. Davis), 245; 1 Stubbs, *Constit.
Hist.*, 6 ed., 704–07; Round, *Commune of London*, 235.

protection they can offer to merchants, the immunities they have purchased — all these foster in them that precious spirit of localism which gives to each borough its own unique history. They broke the hard cake of feudal custom. They were to cast off the control of their lord. There was in them the potentiality of spontaneous development which is the fundamental basis of corporate life. That which they are no royal grant nor lordly privilege has made. But what they are to become depends on the powers of other men. The problem of their future is bound up with those powers.

III

Yet what is striking is the failure — the borough and the church apart — of these groups of men to pass from collectivism to a corporate character. The one step which seems to lie most readily before them is the one step they do not take. Manors and vills, counties and hundreds, these lose bit by bit the fine sense of unified separatism which had distinguished them. Soon after the Angevin dynasty has established itself we cease to expect such development. Individuals become the controlling factors in their history. As early as the twelfth century suit of service at the county court has become a resented burden.[63] Its direction passes to the sheriff; immunities deprive it of its representative character;[64] the possessory assizes made its jurisdiction comparatively unimportant. If it remains as an administrative area its control is exercised, at least from the time of Richard I,[65] by the conservators of the peace; and when under

[63] Maitland in 3 *Eng. Hist. Rev.* 418.

[64] 1 P. & M., 2 ed., 548.

[65] Stubbs, *Select Charters* (ed. Davis), 237. Cf. 1 Stubbs, *Constit. Hist.*, 6 ed., 570.

Edward III that office was established in something like its modern form,[66] it proves so successful as gradually to supersede the shire court as the unit of local adminis-tration. It remained, indeed, an electoral center; but its communal character is entirely lost. Even more tragic is hundredal history. They had begun quite early to pass into private hands. Offa of Mercia, so at least the Bishop of Salisbury claimed,[67] had granted to his pre-decessor the hundred of Ramsbury in Wiltshire. Three of the hundreds of Worcestershire belonged in the eleventh century to the church of the cathedral city.[68] In 1255 more than half the hundreds of Wiltshire were in private hands; nor is the tale of Devon, some seventy years later, less complete.[69] Communal control becomes in-dividual control. The units of local government cease to be bodies that may hope for corporateness and be-come living men. The hundred becomes an object of property, and as such its internal development ceases to burden or to influence the history of corporations.

Of manor and vill the history is a similar one. Seign-orial jurisdiction sweeps them into its sway. The kings are fairly generous in their grants; and even if the im-munity may conveniently be limited by the skill of royalist lawyers, still the great inquiry of Edward I shows that immunization has gone far.[70] But perhaps more serious still is the jurisdictional element implicit in the character of feudalism. The lord has tenants; he holds a court

[66] Cf. 1 Edw. III, St. II, § 16; 18 Edw. III, St. II, § 2; 34 Edw. III, Ch. 1.

[67] *Rot. Hund.* II, 231.

[68] 1 *Domesday Book* 172 b.

[69] 1 P. & M., 2 ed., 558.

[70] 1 P. & M., 2 ed., 572–73.

for those tenants.[71] That right will be exercised so far as royal claims will allow. Feudal justice was a potent weapon in the subjection of the free men.[72] Even if all feudal power be in its origin — as post-conquestual theory makes it — a royal power, still the significant fact remains that the primary nature of this legal machinery is its personal character. The courts are men's courts. The justice in them will be lord's justice; and however firmly the little community may cling to its pathetic antiquarianism it is many centuries before royal justice will begin once more to protect the force of custom. It is a steady tale of oppression that we read. The communities of these villages are feeble enough; and they become the easy prey of the king and his lords. That process of conquest and subjection seems steadily to have deprived these groups of what pretensions they had before possessed to corporateness. The land is recognized on a personal basis. If the freeholder retains vague rights of common, a period of inclosures will teach us for just how little that vagueness really stands;[73] and even Bracton seems to think of them in terms which suggest a personal origin.[74] The Statute of Merton is a weapon in the lord's hand of which he will not fail to make good use. That "sufficient pasture" which he is to leave for the use of freeholders seems on the whole a serious invasion of the manorial community.[75] What

[71] Cf. *Domesday Book and Beyond*, 80 ff.

[72] *Ibid.*, 318 ff.

[73] Mr. Tawney's *Agrarian Problem in the Sixteenth Century* has recently told most brilliantly that pitiful story.

[74] Bracton, f. 230, 230 b.

[75] See the weighty remarks of Professor Vinogradoff, *Villeinage in England*, 272–74. He thinks that the Statute of Merton actually changed the common law.

is the criterion of sufficiency save custom? And who shall give custom the binding force of law?

These communities, in fact, become but little more than quasi-geographical expressions. The power they had once possessed of a suggestive self-government passes to the hands of natural persons. There is little enough need in such a result to speculate deeply about the nature of their personality. The rules of law will fit lord and king and freeholder easily enough. The need for their expansion, in this context at least, loses its force. "The figure of the ideal person vanishes," say Maitland,[76] "or rather at times it seems to become a mere mass of natural persons." Certainly this is true of all medieval groups save those of the borough and the church. Their collectiveness crumbles into dust at the approach of men.

Nor does it appear that the lawyers of this age had very different notions. The word *communitas* is a large and ambiguous one. Neither the writers of textbooks nor chronicles use it with any precision. The *communitas bacheleriae Angliae*[77] can have been in no legal sense a corporation. What Bracton will say of the *universitas* will, indeed, show some continental influence; but at best he is troubled and confused by what he has thereof to say.[78] Exactly those things of which we should in this context expect some speech — the things which on the continent at least were troubling vastly the Italian lawyers — are absent from his survey.[79] The relation of the corporate body to the crown — the funda-

[76] 1 P. & M., 2 ed., 492.

[77] Stubbs, *Select Charters* (ed. Davis), 331. Cf. 2 Stubbs, *Constit. Hist.*, 6 ed., 87.

[78] Cf. Maitland, Bracton and Azo (Selden Soc.), 87, 90.

[79] Maitland has pointed out that Bracton has nowhere realized that the ecclesiastical body is an *universitas*. 1 P. & M., 2 ed., 496.

mental problem in the theory that was to be evolved —
he will not even discuss. Surely the cause of such con-
spicuous absence can but be apparent on the surface.
If there is lacking a theory of corporations it is because
that which men later deem a corporation is not to be
found.

The borough, admittedly, is different; but the borough
will not, at any rate before the fourteenth century, assist
us to evolve a corporate theory. It will not aid us
because the theory which governs its relations to the
state is one which denies the necessity of speculation as
to its character. Every borough is some person's borough. Every borough derives its privileges and immunities from a grant to be produced at will. Spontaneous
it may be their growth is; and that spontaneity will
preserve their communalism for a day more receptive to
the approach of theory. But act they must not without royal warranty. That which they will obtain is a
matter of gold and silver. The king drives a hard and
fisty bargain. The most famous definition of a corporation which the new world has given to the old seems
best to fit the matter. It is with franchises, financial,
juristic, economic, that we are concerned. We seem to
have a scale of values from the vast freedom of London
to the emulant anxiety of a tiny township. But no im-
munity can be obtained by any process of self-institution.
The rights are the rights of the lord or the king, and
it is very clear that they are for sale. And if they are
for sale they are revocable, for the will of kings is arbitrary, and each burst of temper will beget repurchase.

Sufficiently late, indeed, this concession theory remains.
The stout-hearted Tudors recked little of group-cor-
porateness in their effort after unity; and the making

and unmaking of boroughs was a weapon they brought
not seldom into use.[80]   Those cities which forfeited their
charters under the *quo warranto* of Charles II illustrated
no different theory.[81]   The "spoils of towns" with which,
as North tells us,[82] Jeffreys returned from his Bloody
Assize is a significant response to Monmouth's appeal
against the "Court Parasites and Instruments of
Tyranny" who had urged the right of forfeiture.[83]   But
it is in the beginnings of our history that we must search
for the origin of these ideas.   All goes back to the king.
When Archbishop Thurstan wished his men of Beverley
to have the privileges of the citizens of York he must
have the royal permission to that end.[84]   Henry II's
clerks had quickly some questions to ask (also some fines
to levy) when the butchers and pilgrims of London sought
to set up their gilds.[85]   Aylwin of Gloucester, who was
perhaps somewhat Frenchified by travel, was soon brought
to see the advantage of an English model when the exchequer fined him one hundred pounds for his Gloucester
experiment;[86] and, six years later, if Thomas from
beyond the Ouse escaped more lightly, the fine of twenty
marks is proof of royal control.[87]   As late as 1305 the
townsmen of Salisbury could only escape the burden of
an episcopal tallage which had grown ruthless by placing
themselves on the royal hands.[88]   Even London is not

---

[80] 1 Hallam, *Constit. Hist.* (Everyman's ed.), 47.

[81] 2 *Ibid.,* 411.

[82] North's *Examen,* 626.

[83] See the interesting citation in Carr, *Corporations,* 170–71.   The
Commons ordered it to be burned by the common hangman.

[84] Stubbs, *Select Charters* (ed. Davis), 131.

[85] Madox, *Hist. of Exchequer* (ed. of 1711), 390.

[86] *Ibid.,* 391.

[87] Madox, *Firma Burgi,* 35.

[88] 1 *Rot. Parl.,* 175–76.

sufficiently powerful to withstand the royal anger. The part it played in the historic crisis of Henry III's reign was sufficient to entail the temporary abolition of its mayoralty.[89]   Edward I (who treated York in similar fashion) [90] kept the liberties of the city in his hands for twelve years when the mayor sought to restrain the justices in eyre from entering it.[91]   When London chafed at the exactions of Richard II, he seized the occasion of a chance riot to revoke its rights [92] and to remove the Common Pleas to York; [93] and only the compassion of the queen secured their restitution.[94]   Edward I held London liable for the trespass of its officers; [95] and Dunwich suffered in a similar fashion.[96]   Nor did the fact of incorporation matter.   When the citizens of Wainflete took toll unjustly the fact that they had no charter served in no way to protect them,[97] for such towns can sue or be sued as the men of the king.[98]   Even an amorphous body like the "Knights of the bishopric of Durham" can lie in the royal mercy.[99]   The mere enumeration of the towns vested in the king is evidence of his substantial power; [100] and when he grants out his powers for money — as the venality of Richard I did with unceas-

---

[89] 1 Stubbs, *Constit. Hist.*, 6 ed., 588.

[90] 1 *Rot. Parl.* 202.

[91] 1 Stubbs, *Constit. Hist.*, 6 ed., 590.

[92] Higden, *Polychronicon*, IX, 268.

[93] 7 Rymer, *Foedera*, 213.

[94] Higden, *Polychronicon*, IX, 274.

[95] Madox, *Hist. of Exchequer*, 698.

[96] Madox, *Firma Burgi*, 154. For a similar instance of Dover, see Ryley, *Plac. Parl.*, 287.

[97] Madox, *Firma Burgi*, 64, and other instances there cited.

[98] Madox, *Firma Burgi*, 65.

[99] *Ibid.*, 85.

[100] See the striking statistics in Madox, *Firma Burgi*, 4 ff.

ing hand [101] — he draws a firm distinction between possession and ownership.[102]

Corporateness — we do not say the fact of incorporation — is clearly here preserved; and it is preserved because it is profitable to the crown.   Where men act in group-unity you can fine them, if the single assumption be made of an action which derives from royal kindliness. The king concedes powers: he is real enough.   And so long as the relation of a borough is for the most part with him, a speculation as to the nature of burghality is here as elsewhere unneeded.   But with the borough a new day will presently dawn.   The England of the fourteenth century will begin to untie the jealous knot of separatism.   It will begin a hundred-years' struggle with France and find a sense of unity in that suffering, while the horrors of the Black Death will spell consolidation.[103] There were new needs to satisfy; and new ideas are required for their satisfaction.

IV

Let us go back to our churches.   Of ecclesiastical communities medieval England has in truth a plethora, for our ancestors were pious men, willing enough, as the charters bear witness, to buy their salvation at the expense of their property.   And these communities are voluntary in character with a definite purpose behind them; it is not difficult to feel that their wills are to serve those purposes.[104]   Who owns their possessions?

[101] Stubbs, *Select Charters* (ed. Davis), 258.

[102] Cf. Madox's phrase, "He had a compleat seisin of [the town] with all its parts and adjuncts," *loc. cit.,* 14.

[103] Cf. 1 Cunningham, *Growth of English Industry*, 378 ff.

[104] Cf. 1 P. & M. 2 ed., 510.

That is a more troublesome question. Lands from the earliest times are church lands; and the opening words of English law ascribe a special sanctity to the property of God and of the church.[105] But what is the church that owns them and what is the nature of their possession? The early rules of law are rather fitted to deal with the problems of natural or of immortal men than of a group which raises a metaphysical inquiry.[106] It is simple enough when the property of the diocese is at the disposal of the bishop;[107] but for a cellular and separatist England it is too simple by far. If the church is owned, it will also own; and Bracton has noted the difference between the ownership and the right of presentation to its control.[108] If the church owns land, some speculation there must be about the nature of that church; and there are lawyers enough (canonist at that) anxious to weave theories that will give the ecclesiastical community the full benefit of its powers. Mysticism, of course, we shall have early, for St. Paul had given to Christians the picture of an ecclesiastical organism,[109] and men like John of Salisbury and the great Cardinal of Cusa will push the comparison to the point of nauseation.[110] Crude as is this anthropomorphic conception, it is not without its influence on law. If the body ecclesiastic is to be given substantiality, a head must control its action; and the abbatial church will be so much the possession of its

[105] Laws of Ethelbert, Ch. I, Stubbs, *Select Charters* (ed. Davis), 66.

[106] Cf. 3 Holdsworth, *Hist. Eng. Law*, 363.

[107] 1 P. & M., 2 ed., 497.

[108] Bracton, f. 53.

[109] Epist. Rom., XII, 4, 5; Epist. Cor., XII, 12, 14; Epist. Col., I, 18, 24.

[110] Cf. Gierke, *Political Theories of the Middle Age*, 132.

abbot that Domesday Book can indifferently equate him with church and convent.[111]   That is perhaps the more natural when it is remembered that the monks are legally dead and thus no longer the subjects of rights.   Certainly as late as Edward IV that need of a head for corporate activity will give much trouble.[112]   But restrictions must be laid on that power since, after all, the rights and purposes of founders must be protected. Maitland has printed a Register of Writs from the reign of Henry III which contains the royal writ protecting the convent against the forcible alienation of a former abbot — a protection of canonical law;[113] and the Statute of Marlborough in obviating the limitation of personal actions by the death of the wronged abbot in some sort emphasizes conventual rights.[114]   As the years go by these convents will bring their actions in a name which betokens incorporate aggregation;[115] the "dean and chapter of St. Paul's" is neither dean nor chapter.   It has a connecting link about it — shall we say a seal?[116] — which perhaps we may best term its corporate personality.   And when Bracton talks of a body that endures forever, even though death may thin its ranks, though the language is vague and hesitant it is clearly reflective of new ideas.[117]

And what is perhaps of fundamental import is the thought to which Innocent IV gave decisive expression.[118]

[111] 1 P. & M., 2 ed., 504.

[112] Y. B. 18 Hen. VI, f. 16.   Y. B. I Edw. IV, f. 15, 31, etc.

[113] 2 *Coll. Papers,* 144, No. 43.   Cf. *Corpus Juris,* 3, X, 3, 10.

[114] *Stat. of Marlborough,* Ch. 28 (52 Hen. III).

[115] Cf. Bracton, *Note-Book,* Pl. 482, 654, etc.

[116] Cf. Y. B. 20 Edw. III, 96, 98 (Rolls Series).

[117] Bracton, f. 374 b.   The comparison is to a flock of sheep which remains the same though the individual sheep die.

[118] 3 Gierke, *Genossenschaftsrecht,* 279 ff.

Whether he in fact perceived the vast significance which lay behind his attribution of fictitious personality to communities may perhaps be doubted.[119]   But the phrase, whatever its author meant it to imply, gave exactly the impulse to the current of men's thoughts for which they had long been waiting. For immediately we have the acts of a person, the nature of that person may be matter of debate. Inevitably the phrase of a Pope begets discussion.[120]   What is more important is the means it gives us of passing from anthropomorphic terms (though retaining the memory of them) to representative action. If the group-person is to act, it will prove no small convenience to designate those through whom its action may be effective. It is difficult to persuade all men that you are right. Yet it seems clear enough that in the early church, as at Elvira,[121] for instance, and at Nicæa,[122] unanimity was essential; nor is there any suggestion of ought save unanimity at the fifth and sixth œcumenical councils.[123]   It seems plausible, indeed, to urge that not until the Council of Ferrara did the majority principle obtain its full sway in the corporate church.[124]   But long before this time the concept of representative action had been clearly understood. The

[119] Cf. on this Mr. H. A. Smith's pertinent criticism, *Law of Associations*, 152–57. He seems to me to have shown good ground for doubting Dr. Gierke's picture of Innocent as a great speculative lawyer.

[120] 3 Gierke, *Genossenschaftsrecht*, 227–85.

[121] 1 Hefele, *Hist. des Concils*, 131.

[122] *Ibid.*, 320.

[123] 4 *Ibid.*, 164.

[124] 2 *Ibid.*, 399, 402. Even then it is a two-thirds majority; and the attitude to the dissent of a single archbishop to the resolutions on the *Filioque* clause is very striking. 2 Hefele, *Hist. des Conciles*, 461.

Glossators had begun, if with hesitation, to call the delict of a majority of a church the delict of the church itself.[125] Roffredus in the middle of the thirteenth century was discussing corporate personality with the comfort which comes from understanding;[126] and Johannes Andreæ found little difficulty in emulating that significant example.[127] It becomes evident to men that what is important is not so much unanimous opinion as corporate opinion; and they begin to realize that corporate opinion is largely a matter of form to which the verdict of a majority will give substance.[128] And by the time of the post-Glossators — and very notably in the great Bartolus [129] — the idea of the group as a corporation is fully and strikingly developed.[130]

Nor was it difficult to apply these new doctrines to the great orders which were springing up at the behest of Francis and of Dominic. Dominic especially is one of the greatest of federalist statesmen. Almost from the outset the order was cognizant of representation as the basis of corporate action.[131] It does not seem unnatural to suppose that the idea passed from the Black Friars to the convocation of the English church.[132] But one of the primary objects of convocation is fiscal; and the kings must have soon discovered that representation is an admirable method of countering such absential re-

---

125 *E. g.,* the gloss to L. 160, § 1, D. 50, 17, 10 C. 1, 2, *Verbo Corrigimus.*

126 Cf. his *Quaestiones Sabbathinae,* 23, 27.

127 Joh. Andr. Nov. s.c. 16, in VI. 3, 4, n. 4.

128 Gloss. to c. 56, C. 12, q. 2, *Verbo Accusandi.* Cf. 3 Gierke, *Genossenschaftsrecht,* 345, for a striking example.

129 Cf. C. N. Sidney Woolf, *Bartolus,* 123–24, 160–61.

130 3 Gierke, *Genossenschaftsrecht,* 354.

131 Barker, *The Dominican Order and Convocation,* 4 ff., 18.

132 *Ibid.,* 49, 51.

calcitrance as that of Geoffrey of York.[133]   Certainly little by little the idea seems to follow a secular path. But majority action did not come lightly into parliamentary affairs.   As late as 1290 the barons could bind their absent peers only *quantum in ipsis est* — and we do not know the extent of that power.[134]   Contumacy, of course, merited and met with punishment; but the medieval idea that each group in the realm may bargain separately about its ratability struggled long and hardily before it died.   What slew it was the creation, in 1295, of a fully representative parliament.[135]   The "Common assent of the realm" of which the *Confirmatio Cartarum* makes such impressive mention,[136] means finally that, for fiscal purposes at least, the kingdom has become incorporate.   "It was no longer," says Stubbs,[137] "in the power of the individual, the community, or the estate, to withhold its obedience with impunity."   Somewhere or other the men of the kingdom, great and humble alike, are present in Parliament.   That *commune consilium regni* which henceforward figures so largely in the preamble of statutes is the sign of a change drawn from ecclesiastical example.   The administrators of the thirteenth century are learning the lessons of the canon law.   Surely in this aspect we are to read the statute of Mortmain as the result of a growing acquaintance of the common lawyers with the nature of groups which the canonists have already long envisaged as immortal.[138]

The ecclesiastical community, moreover, comes with

[133] 1 Stubbs, *Constit. Hist.*, 6 ed., 562.
[134] 2 *Ibid.*, 253.
[135] Stubbs, *Constit. Hist.*, 6 ed., 256.
[136] Stubbs, *Select Charters* (ed. Davis), 490.
[137] 2 Stubbs, *Constit. Hist.*, 6 ed., 257.
[138] 3 Holdsworth, *Hist. Eng. Law*, 367.

increasing frequency to court. It thus compels men to speculate upon its nature. They will learn why the new abbot will set aside an irregular conveyance of his predecessor.[139] They will theorize as to why monastic tort is at bottom conventual tort.[140] Even the conception of the church as a perpetual minor will at any rate make them see that the church lands are not the possession of its incumbent.[141] The canons of Hereford may be sued where its particular canon has done wrong.[142] Even if, as Maitland has pointed out,[143] our lawyers will learn less than might be hoped from examples that derive from quasi-despotism, the mere fact of meeting is important. It is important because it prevents the knowledge of new ideas as to corporateness from perishing at birth. The clergy are a litigious race; and the rules of their legal governance must have compelled a frequent resort to the *Corpus Juris* from which their inspiration was derived. There our English lawyers will learn how majority action is corporate action and how the corporation is a person. And if they are slow to see the significance of so much abstractness, there will yet come a time when the movement from church affairs to the problems of the lay world may be made.

V

That Bracton could call the town an *universitas* is perhaps accident rather than design.[144] Yet it is the borough which compels our lawyers to recognize the sig-

139 1 P. & M., 2 ed., 504.

140 Y. B. 49 Edw. III, Mich. Pl. 5.

141 1 P. & M., 2 ed., 503. Bracton, f. 226 b is the fundamental passage.

142 *Placit. Abbrev.* 53.

143 1 P. & M., 2 ed., 508.

144 Bracton, f. 228 b.

nificance of theory. At what day the *liber burgus* becomes in a full sense corporate we may not with any
precision speculate; but, of a certainty, the older authorities were wrong who ascribed that change to the
middle fifteenth century.[145] The *communitas* of the
borough is gaining abstractness as the years of the first
Edward draw near their end.[146] In the reign of his
successor the courts are talking freely of the bodiliness
of towns.[147] The good citizens of Great Yarmouth betray a healthy anger when the townsmen of their smaller
brother "who are not of any community and have no
common seal" pretend to burghal rights.[148] The *Liber
Assisarum* has not a little to say of the physical substantiality of a city which is not its citizens.[149] Richard
II takes compassion upon the good men of Basingstoke
who have suffered the scourge of fire, and incorporation
is the form his pity takes — with a common seal thereto
annexed.[150] Nor, assuredly, may we belittle in this context the meaning of his extension to cities and to boroughs
of the provisions of Mortmain.[151] It is made thereby very
clear that the nature of corporateness is becoming known
to men. The citizens of Plymouth were not less clear
about its nature when they petitioned Parliament that
for the purchase of free tenements for life they might
become *un corps corporat.*[152] The union of the two

---

[145] As Merewether and Stephens did. Cf. 1 Gross, *Gild Merchant*, 93 ff.

[146] 2 Gross, *op. cit.*, 18.

[147] 1 *Ibid.*, 94.

[148] 4 *Close Rolls*, 19 Edw. II, 457–61.

[149] Liber Ass. 62, 100, 321.

[150] 5 *Charter Rolls* 336.

[151] 2 Stubbs, *Constit. Hist.*, 6 ed., 509.

[152] 3 *Rot. Parl.* 663.

Droghedas into a single county — a corporate county the record will make it [153] — suggests that we have passed to the language of a new jurisprudence. We have synthesized men into the abstraction of a new being. What has happened is less the acquisition of new rights than the formulation of a means whereby collective action may be taken by that which is not the body of citizens even while it is still the citizen body.[154] The later use of the corporate term to mean that oligarchic body which will with such difficulty be reformed in the nineteenth century, is evidence of how easily the towns absorbed the possibilities laid open by representative action. [155]

The point to which such evidence must drive us is surely the admission that by the time of Edward III the concept of burghality has undergone a change. Not, indeed, that the meaning of that change has been grasped in any sense that is full and complete. If the courts cannot separate John de Denton from the Mayor of Newcastle, the ghost of anthropomorphism can still trouble the joys of corporate life.[156] Yet within less than a century the meaning of such confusion is clearly understood.[157] But the attribution of property to a corporation as distinct from its members is already made at the earlier time;[158] and the great Fortescue will be willing to protect the corporator's property against seizure

---

[153] 1 Gross, *op. cit.*, 94, n.

[154] Cf. Merewether & Stephens, *Hist. of Boroughs*, 242.

[155] 2 May, *Constit. Hist.*, 494 ff.; Maitland, *Township and Borough*, 12.

[156] Y. B. 17, 18 Edw. III, 70 (ed. Pike).

[157] Y. B. 8 Hen. VI, Mich. Pl. 2, 34, and cf. 1 P. & M., 2 ed., 493.

[158] 17 Ass. Pl. 29. Cf. also Y. B. 8 Hen. VI, Mich. Pl. 2.

for the debts of the corporation.[159] The lawyers, moreover, begin to wander from the realm of fact to that in which the delights of fancy may be given full rein. The judges can sit back in their chairs and speculate about its torts and treasons,[160] while Mr. Justice Choke — surely with some memory of the common law in his mind — will inform us that it lies beyond the scope of excommunication.[161] And since a corporate person must needs have a voice, the seal will be given to it whereby it may in due form have speech.[162] Trespass against its property the courts will not hesitate to admit[163] if they still shrink somewhat from admitting its sufferance of certain grave forms of wrong.[164] Surely the "gladsome light" of this jurisprudence is a new and a refreshing thing.

A new commerce, moreover, is beginning, and it casts its shadows across the pathway of our history. The Black Death and the Hundred Years' War brought with them distress in their trail. The social movements which are their consequence are too vast for a local authority to control, and from separatism we pass to the national consolidation which reached its zenith under the Tudors.[165] What is perhaps above all important is its resultant emphasis on the class structure of industrial society.[166] The emergence of the capitalist seems to synchronize with the

---

[159] Y. B. 20 Hen. VI., Pl. 18.

[160] Y. B. 21 Edw. IV, Pl. 13, 14.

[161] *Ibid.*, Pl. 14.

[162] Y. B. 21 Edw. IV, Hil. Pl. 9. I need not say how much this analysis owes to Maitland.. See especially 1 P. & M., 2 ed., 488–93 and 678 ff.

[163] Y. B. 21 Edw. IV, Pl. 13.

[164] *Ibid.;* and cf. 22 Ass. Pl. 67.

[165] Cf. 1 Cunningham, *Growth of English Industry*, 375 ff.

[166] Cf. Mr. Unwin's pregnant remarks. *Industrial Organization in the XVIth and XVIIth Centuries*, 16–19, 85–93.

emergence of new forms of business organization. As early
as 1391 Richard II, whose reign seems generally to have
marked the onset of a new time, was granting a charter
to what is at least the *communitas* of the English merchants in Prussia;[167] and Henry IV was not slow to emulate the novelties of his predecessor.[168] The organization
of foreign merchants in England will be encouraged, since
a unit permits with satisfactory ease of the assessment the
kings hold dear.[169] The very phrases which suggest the
corporate idea begin everywhere to make their appearance. Henry VII made the Englishmen of Pisa a corporation in 1490.[170] The great trading companies which
are in some sort the parents of empire begin to buy their
charters. Henry VII provided the Merchant Adventurers
with what protection the written privilege of an English king might afford;[171] and it has been significantly
pointed out by Dr. Cunningham that the object of the
grant was rather the encouragement of commercial speculation than the governmental regulation of commerce.
These companies seem to arise with all the spontaneity
that marks the communalism of our earliest history.
Their appearance is very striking, since the simpler forms
of such business organization as the partnership were already well known.[172] But the partnership seems too narrow in its scope for the larger ideas of fellowship these
fifteenth century Englishmen have inherited from their
ancestors. Why they should have chosen the corporate
form of life is perhaps not wholly clear. But the step is

---

167 7 Rymer, *Fœdera*, 693.
168 *Ibid.*, 360, 464.
169 1 Cunningham, *op. cit.*, 420–22.
170 12 Rymer, *Fœdera*, 389–93.
171 1 Cunningham, 416.
172 Ashley, *Economic History*, pt. ii, 414.

taken, and from the time of Elizabeth it is in them rather
than in the municipal corporation that the historian
of corporate theory must be interested.   Moreover,
after 1515 they could not escape from the king's hands
even if they remained a voluntary society; the ministers
of Henry VIII recked but little of formal matters.[173]
The companies, for the most part, deal with a foreign
trade in their earlier history.   They want privileges because they are journeying into far, strange lands; and it
is surely one of the happiest thoughts of Philip and Mary
(whose grandparents had tasted the rich fruits of mari-
time adventure) which led them to incorporate a company of which the great Sebastian Cabot was the governor.[174]

We may not surely deny that this corporateness is inherited from burghal organization.   These merchants
have learned the value of their fellowships from the gilds
of the towns; and not seldom they strive, in all the bitterness of a novel rivalry, with the older crafts and mysteries
of the towns.[175]   It is perhaps from the analogy of the
medieval towns that we shall find the connection.[176]   Its
whole point lies in the organization of a group of men
into something like an unity; and once the charters are
forthcoming, the incidents of corporateness are not wanting.   The sense of exclusiveness must have been fostered
by the stress of the keen foreign competition they had
from the outset to face.   Englishmen have had pride in
their isolation, and they did not find it difficult to com-

[173] See 6 Hen. VIII, c. 26.   This succession of acts seems to have
ended in Edward Sixth's reign.

[174] 2 Hakluyt, *Voyages* (Maclehose ed.), 304.

[175] Lambert, *Two Thousand Years of Gild Life*, 158, for Hull;
Latimer, *Hist. of the Merchant Venturers of Bristol*, 26.

[176] Ashley, *op. cit.*, pt. ii, 217.

bine against alien rivals.[177] We can imagine that a
medieval government which understood the difficulties of
evolving a foreign policy would welcome the spontaneous
development of groups of men who for the royal protection we term incorporation would call a new world into
being.[178]

These companies are, at the outset, at least, devoted
for the most part to external trade; so John Cabot and
his sons, in return for no more than an exclusive right to
traffic (whereof the fifth part of the capital gain will
fill the coffers of the avaricious Tudor), will engage to
plant the English flags in lands "which have hitherto been
unknown to Christians." [179]   That Master Hore of London whose "goodly stature and great courage" perhaps
inclined him to the "study of cosmography" planned his
establishment of the Newfoundland fisheries in return for
a similar monopoly.[180]   But gradually the expedient becomes of obvious advantage in internal commerce. When
burghal monopoly of trade begins to break down, it became clear that the crafts were no longer able to cope
with the scale of national development. It was obvious
that the essential need was either a fully developed
national control or no control at all. And it is perhaps
singularly fortunate that this industrial expansion should
have synchronized with the accession of so able and vigorous a sovereign as Elizabeth.[181]

The patents of monopoly which she granted with so
royal a hand were a definite and systematic attempt after
industrial unity. They continued in a new fashion the

177 I Cunningham, *op. cit.*, 417–20.
178 2 Cunningham, *op. cit.*, 214.
179 12 Rymer, *Fœdera*, 595.
180 1 Cunningham, *op. cit.*, 505.
181 2 *Ibid.*, 25.

regulation which had made the crown the center of the economic system. Granted at first rather to individuals than to groups of men, the opportunities of profit they opened up soon and naturally attracted the courtiers into the race for wealth. So that if. Elizabeth was somewhat hard in her dealings with inventors,[182] she was apparently woman enough to make the road that led to her favorites' hearts a gilded one. Little by little the recipient of her bounty becomes a group rather than an individual, until, under the Stuarts, the collective monopoly is the more typical form.[183] In the mining monopoly of Master Thurland of the Savoy, Pembroke and Cecil and Leicester are all most willing to share.[184] Corporations, indeed, we shall hesitate to call groups that are often no more than amorphous partnerships. But that form of organization is far from wanting, and its meaning is very clearly conceived. When Sir Thomas Smith, who toyed with chemistry in the intervals, doubtless, of his political and legal studies, claimed to have found at length the philosopher's stone, a corporation was founded to do him honor for so signal a triumph.[185] Drake seems fully to have realized the meaning of such organization;[186] and we may be sure that the great Sir Humphrey Gilbert when he incorporated "The Colleagues of the Fellowship for the Discovery of the Northwest Passage"[187] was by no means sacrificing the practical to his sense of stateliness. The list of monopolists which

[182] Price, *English Patents of Monopoly*, 16.

[183] *Ibid.*, 35.

[184] *Ibid.*, 50.

[185] *The Society of the New Art.* See the amusing account of its adventures in Strype, *Life of Sir T. Smith*, 100 ff.

[186] S. P. Dom. Eliz., XCV, 63.

[187] S. P. Dom. Eliz., CLV, 86.

Sir Robert Cecil communicated to the House of Commons in 1601 contained not a few groups of men.[188]   That "Fellowship of English Merchants for the Discovery of New Trades" wherein, mayhap, the Muscovy Company concealed its commercial cousinship with barbarians in dignified phrasing,[189] shows us in what direction men's minds are tending.   The relation, in fact, between monopolies and joint-stock enterprise is the dominant note of the time.[190]   The resuscitation of local companies is giving new vigor to the collective efforts of men.[191]   It is suggestive of the recognition of value in such effort that a definite encouragement of their creation should meet with the approval of the crown.[192]

All this we take to mean that the significance of corporateness has been firmly grasped.   And when men tell us of the causes of their desire for it, they speak with a definite perception of its character far different from the misty conceptions of medieval time.   The East India Company becomes "a body corporate and politic" because only in such fashion can it cope with problems so vast as that of an eastern civilization.[193]   The immortality of a corporation was what tickled the palates of the Miners Royal.[194]   Unity of assent and need of better government led Henry VIII to give the merchants of Andalusia the rights a moment of friendship with the em-

[188] Price, *op. cit.*, 148 ff.

[189] 3 Hakluyt, *op. cit.*, 83.

[190] Unwin, *op. cit.*, 164.

[191] Lambert, *op. cit.*, 236, 273, 316; Hibbert, *Gilds*, 77.   The Statute of Artificers had, of course, much the same purpose.

[192] Winchester, in Lambert, *op. cit.*, 382; and cf. 2 Cunningham, *op. cit.*, 36.

[193] The charter of 1600 in Prothero, *Statutes and Constitutional Documents*, 448 ff.

[194] Stow, *Survey* (ed. Strype), 246.

peror led the latter to confirm.[195]   Thomas Thurland,
whom much mining had made somewhat impoverished,
turned his holdings into a company in admirable anticipation of modern methods.[196]   When in 1605 the "free
traders" of the time sought means of hindering this corporate growth, the merchants who favored it were very
ready with their answer.   They insisted that only with
such an organization could they have the adequate protection of the law.   The trade needed regulation, and its
corporate character provided the simplest means to that
end.   Competition, moreover, would prevent the maintenance of quality and would be subversive of all good order.
The Privy Council accepted their statement and the
charter was renewed.[197]   The arguments seem to come
with a familiar note to a generation not less puzzled by a
similar question.   But even more striking, perhaps, were
the words of one who mirrored in himself the resplendent
qualities of that spacious time.   When the House of
Commons, on the 20th of November, 1601, debated the
merits of monopolies as an economic system, there were
not a few who strove to distinguish between grants made
to persons and grants made to the corporate groups of
men.   Francis Bacon, at any rate, saw clearly the illogic
of such distinction.   "If her Majesty," he said,[198] "make
patent or a monopoly into any of her servants, that we
must go and cry out against; but if she grant it to a
number of burgesses, or a corporation, that must stand,
and that, forsooth, is no monopoly."   The history of half
a thousand years is in that significant equation.

195 *Letters and Papers of Hen. VIII*, No. 6640.
196 Price, *op. cit.*, 50.
197 S. P. Dom. Jac., I, XII, 59, 64.
198 Prothero, *op. cit.*, 112.   Cf. also p. 115.

VI

If it was thus a new world that had developed, traces
of the old still linger about its confines. If the corporation becomes a fully developed legal person, it is still
dependent upon royal caprice. The king concedes it
privileges; it is from his bounty that it takes its origin.
In the last years of Edward III two judges did not shrink
from holding that only the crown could erect a corporation.[199] When the citizens of Norwich pleaded their
crimes to Sir John Fortescue, their liberties *de alto et
basso* were seized into the royal hands.[200] Madox has
pointed out[201] that in the Tudor age gildation and incorporation are used transferably by the statutes; but
from the Conquest the lawfulness of gilds depended upon
royal permission. We cannot avoid the conclusion that
the power to incorporate is no more than part of the general prerogative by which vast powers of regulation in-
hered in the king. The chartered companies demanded
their charters because without them life would have been
less than tolerable. While their members may have had a
common law right to pass freely without the realm for
any cause,[202] yet the king could prohibit any emigration
on grounds of public safety;[203] and the wisdom of Richard
II chose to ordain, as the wisdom of James I chose
to repeal, that none should pass out of the kingdom without royal license,[204] while it was understood —
men soothe themselves a little easily with phrases — that

[199] Y. B. 49 Edw. III, f. 4, per Candish and Knivet, JJ.
[200] Madox, *Firma Burgi,* 291.
[201] *Ibid.,* 29.
[202] Fitzherbert, *New Natura Brevium,* f. 85.
[203] Dyer, 165.
[204] 5 R. II, repealed by 4 Jac. I, Ch. 1, § 22

his power was not to be abused in the depression of commerce.[205] Who is there who can call the crown to answer? Your medieval merchant has sufficient experience of the ills he might not remedy. He will prefer to purchase his charter — the equivalent of a continuous passport — and avoid the costliness of legal controversy. The East India Company, in a later reign, was to have some hard experience of what that purchase meant.[206]

Nor was this theory of concession in any way diminished by such powers as those possessed by pope and palatine. If the popes did set up their religious corporations,[207] the marital difficulties of Henry VIII soon drew a clear distinction between right and courtesy. The power of the Bishop of Durham[208] was clearly derived from the *jura regalia* bestowed on him by the Conqueror in return for an inconvenient proximity to Scotch marauders. Even more striking was the Elizabethan delegation of this power to any person or persons who should erect a hospital,[209] whereof Coke significantly remarked that "these words do extend to anybody politic or corporate" [210] — an interpretation to which an earlier Tudor had already given utterance.[211] The corporation by prescription — which seems to originate in this time, and thereby to prove the general acceptance of this concession-theory[212] — takes for granted the written fact of

205 Hargrave, *Law Tracts*, 91–92 (Hale, *De Portibus Maris*, pt. 2, VIII).

206 3 Macaulay, *History of England* (Everyman's ed.), 241.

207 Y. B. 14 Hen. VIII, 2.   209 39 Eliz. Ch. 5.

208 Grant, *Corporations*, 11.   210 2 Co. Inst. 722.

211 32 Hen. VIII, c. 7. Cf. Dyer, 83 b. The reaction from this view does not seem to come until 9 Geo. II, c. 36. Cf. 2 M. & W. 890.

212 Y. B. 2 Hen. VII, 13. Cf. Anon. dofft. 556, and Jenkins *v.* Harvey, 2 C. M. & R. 339; 10 Coke Rep. 27.

royal approval. That which exists by implication surely
does no more than define with firmness what hitherto has
been vaguely deemed the royal will.[213] And since the
Courts hold firmly that, if they exist without royal authority, attack on these corporate privileges is a valuable
procedural plea,[214] it is surely plain that the early prerogative of the crown suffers no derogation.[215] The legal
construction of charters seems to make evident the same
tendency of thought. The charter, as Coke tells us,[216]
is no less effective than an act of Parliament. It may not
be interpreted in a manner other than that most favorable
to the crown.[217] It limits by its very circumstances.
These, surely, are the thoughts of men who deal with the
rights of property. They are the thoughts of men who
do not dream of questioning a royal prerogative which
lies at the basis of the state.

But it is perhaps the extent of regulation and of con-
fiscation which marks most clearly the character of this
attitude. Everyone knows of that famous Ipswich procedure when the right to form a merchant-gild was
granted to its burgesses.[218] When the merchant-gild
passes from our view and the crafts take their place, we
find that the crown has supplanted the earlier autonomy
by the conference of municipal regulation.[219] The his-

213 Y. B. 12 Hen. VII, 29.

214 Anon. Dyer, 100. Cf. Pl. Q. W. 618.

215 Y. B. 20 Edw. IV, 2; *Ibid.* 22 Edw. IV, 34; 12 Hen. VII, 27.
Cf. Broke, *Abr. Corp.,* No. 33.

216 8 Coke Rep. 8. Cf. Hale, *Jurisdiction of Lords House* (ed.
Hargrave), 20 ff.; Plowden 214.

217 Priddle *v.* Napper, 11 Coke Rep. 8 (1612); Knight's Case, 5
Coke Rep. 56 (1688); Willion *v.* Berkley, Plowden 243 (1662).

218 2 Gross, *op. cit.,* 114 ff.

219 15 Hen. VI, Ch. 6.

tory of their relations may well suggest the thought that town and craft struggled mightily together in an age when civil war prevented too close an attention to their rivalries. But with the advent of the Tudor, there came significant innovation. The king has heard with displeasure that the "companies corporate" have used their rule and governance to make "among themselves many unlawful and unreasonable ordinances . . . for their own singular profit and to the common hurt and damage of the people." It is therefore rendered unlawful for any fellowship to make its by-laws without the approval of certain great judicial functionaries.[220] The act was no mere threat. Discontented members could drag their officers before the court;[221] and many of the companies thought it valorous to be discreet and seek the ratification of what rules they had already.[222] Nor is it unimportant in this connection to note that the great Statute of Artificers took from the crafts their control over their servants.[223] No man, surely, can have mistaken the implications of this policy. Were he so blind the dissolution of monasteries and chantries would have stricken him with sight.[224]

It is the strident voice of Coke which raps out an elegy on this early history.[225] "A corporation aggregate of many," he said, "is invisible, immortal, and rests only in intendment and consideration of the law." From treason and outlaw and excommunication he deemed its nature to exclude it. Loyalty was a virtue of the mind to which

220 19 Hen. VII, Ch. 7.
221 Williams, *History of the Founders' Company*, 13, 16.
222 Milbourne, *Hist. of Vintners' Company*, 39.
223 5 Eliz. Ch. 4, §§ 4, 11, 14, 28.
224 2 Ashley, *op. cit.*, 135.
225 The Case of Sutton's Hospital, 10 Coke Rep. 1 (1612).

it could make no pretension. It exists but *in abstracto,* so that it lies ready to the king's hands. They are precise words. "The King giveth and the King taketh away" is no inapt summary of their purport, though we who know the history of their future may well shrink from the addition of the wonted blessing. Two centuries were to elapse before the charge of high treason gave Stuart Kyd the leisure which he turned to service of corporate realism.[226]   Seventy years later England discovered a road more fitted to corporate travel.[227]   Within forty years, the greatest of English historians wrote large the epitaph of corporate fictions. The new theory of the state his words are making may yet prove his truest memorial.[228]

226 The second volume of Kyd's work (1794) is actually dated from the Tower.

227 Companies' Act, 25 & 26 Vict. Ch. 89.

228 Maitland's translation of, and introduction to, Gierke was published in 1900. Cf. Saleilles' impressive remarks in 23 *L. Quart. Rev.* 189. I ought to say that I have not discussed the relation of fictions to the concession theory because I am convinced that in order to do so at all adequately it is necessary to consider the history of the corporation to the end of the seventeenth century. I hope to deal with this subject in a later paper. Sir F. Pollock's essay in the *Gierke Festschrift* is, of course, our main authority on this head.

THE THEORY OF POPULAR
SOVEREIGNTY

I

ALEXIS DE TOCQUEVILLE has wisely insisted upon the natural tendency of men to confound institutions that are necessary with institutions to which they have grown accustomed.[1] It is a truth more general in its application than he perhaps imagined. Certainly the student of political and legal ideas will in each age be compelled to examine theories which are called essential even when their original substance has, under pressure of new circumstance, passed into some allotropic form. Anyone, for instance, who analyses the modern theory of consideration will be convinced that, while judges do homage to an ancient content, they do not hesitate to invest it with new meaning. The social contract is no longer in high place; but those who bow the knee to the fashionable hypothesis of social solidarity half-consciously offers it its old-time worship.[2]

Of the general theory of sovereignty a similar truth may be asserted. It has fallen from its high estate. Distinguished lawyers have emphasized the unsatisfactory character of that bare statement we associate, perhaps wrongly, with the great name of Austin.[3] When we ex-

* Reprinted from the *Michigan Law Review*, Vol. XVII, No. 3.
1 *Souvenirs d'Alexis de Tocqueville*, pp. 111-2.
2 I owe this conception to my friend Dean Pound.
3 Cf. Prof. Dewey in the *Political Science Quarterly* for 1893.

amine the historic perspective of sovereignty, it becomes
sufficiently obvious that its association with the modern
state is no more than the expression of a particular environment which is already passing away.[4] Sovereignty,
after all, is no more than the name we give to a certain
special will that can count upon unwonted strength for
its purposes. There is nothing sacred or mysterious
about it; and, if its sense is to be at all meaning, it can
secure obedience only within limits. We cannot, indeed,
with any certainty predict or define them, though we can
indicate political unwisdom deep enough to traverse their
boundaries. In the modern democratic community, it has
become customary to associate that sovereignty with the
people as a whole. The theorist insists that only the
state — the people, so he will say,[5] viewed as a political
unit — can exercise supreme power. The conception is
not new; nor is it, so far as rigid accuracy is concerned,
more useful than when it was first suggested. For supreme power in any full sense, or as more than a merely
transient thing, it is clear enough no state possesses. Irresponsibility is politically non-existent, for the simple
reason that our acts entail consequences. Policy is embarked upon at our peril; and if the courts use noble
words about an infallible crown or a state that refuses
responsibility, there are other means of reversing their
judgments. It was to a sovereign parliament that the
Declaration of Independence was issued; and the Dred
Scott decision did not survive the Civil War it in part
entailed.

Nor is this all. A state must, as a general rule, act
by agents and ministers to whom the exercise of power

4 Cf. Laski, *Authority in the Modern State,* Chapter I.
5 Esmein, *Elements de Droit Constitutional* (6 ed.), p. 1.

is entrusted. The power so confided may, as in America, be limited, or plenary, as in Great Britain. But in neither case is it in actual fact more than a permission to perform such acts as are likely to secure public approval. Nor does the issue of legality at all nearly concern us. The judiciary looks not to the inherent nature of acts so much as to their source; and it may well approve what is condemned by the common opinion of men. That is important only in so far as it sets in motion sanctions which well may overawe the majority into silence. It is not evidence of moral judgment, though the character in which it is clothed may well arrest the impulse to resistance. But it is not without importance that the experience of mankind has, at every period of public excitement, denied the equation of law with morals.

This theory of popular sovereignty has had amazing influence; nor should the novelty of the democratic state blind us to its antiquity. "It is a distinctive trait of medieval doctrines," says Gierke,[6] "that within every human group it decisively recognizes an aboriginal and active right of the group taken as a whole." There is a sense, indeed, in which the theory may be said to be coeval with the very birth of political doctrine; though it was not until the middle ages that its full significance began in any adequate fashion to be perceived. Certainly no reader of Aquinas[7] or Marsiglio[8] can complain of the thoroughness with which the implications of popular control were, at least in theory, demonstrated; but it was not until the Reformation provided some signal instances of successful rebellion that it became a working-part of

6 *Political Theories of the Middle Ages* (ed. Maitland), p. 37.
7 *Summa Theolog.*, II. 1. q. 90. a. 3. q. 105. a. 1.
8 Marsiglio, *Defensor Pacis*, I, Ch. 9–15.

the theory of the state. Even then it was but partially operative; for it was an inevitable result of the Counter-Reformation that bureaucratic absolutism should, in general, extend its triumphs to the secular sphere. Nor is England a complete exception to the rule. John Lilburne's eager gestures did not make effective headway against the stern disapproval of Cromwell and Ireton;[9] and the parliamentary system which the Revolution of 1688 made permanent was but partially, at best, an application of national sovereign power. Neither the House of Commons nor the electorate could claim in any real sense to be representative of the people at large. Catholic and Dissenter alike still groaned, like Lambard's justice, under stacks of burdensome statutes. The real impetus to a more direct expression of popular will comes from French speculation in the eighteenth century, on the one hand, and from the American Revolution on the other.

It is hardly worth while to examine in curious detail whether the appeal to more liberal doctrine meant exactly what it said. The sceptical might urge that the early Federalists were prone to emphasize rather the dangers of democracy than its merits; and the greatest of them, Hamilton, seems, in the just perspective of a century, to take his stand by Burke as an apostle of generous conservatism. Montesquieu and Voltaire were subtle dissolvers of a despotic system; but neither embraced with any ardour the prospect of a popular government.[10] The active source of innovation is Rousseau; and the theory he consecrated for his disciples in the

9 Cf. Pease, *The Leveller Movement* (1916).
10 Cf. the useful essay of M. Ameline. *L'Idee de la Souverainete* d'après les ecrivains francais du XVIIIme siècle. Paris, 1904.

Revolution certainly requires a somewhat more critical examination than it has received. In its classical conception, whether in France or in America, it is open to a variety of interpretations; nor is it obvious that, for the practical purposes of government, it possesses the merits of clearness and utility. That is not to allege its lack of influence. On the contrary, it is matter of record that it has, again and again, been the basis of popular action; and it is still, for most, the theoretic basis of popular government. Certainly it is undeniable that when Rousseau declared sovereignty to be in the people as a whole, he gave birth to a plethora of constitutions of which some, at least, were intended to give partial substance to his ideas. Nor did the Revolutions of 1848 have a very dissimilar objective.

But, in the technical sense of full administrative application, it is seriously questionable whether the theory of Rousseau is in fact a working hypothesis. What he emphasized was the distinction between state and government, and it was to the former alone that he gave unlimited power.[11] It is, however, obvious that no system of politics is workable which involves so frequent an elicitation of the sovereign's will. The business of the modern state is too complex to be conducted by perpetual referenda; and, in actual practice, governments which can obtain the necessary support are able to act as they on occasion deem warranted. Rousseau's doctrine, in any case, will mean no more than majority rule. We shall not easily surrender the convenience that has been administratively secured by the transition from the impossible medieval system of unanimous judgments. But the hypothesis of majority rule herein implied is itself too

[11] *The Social Contract.* Bk. III, Ch. 1.

simple to cover the facts. What, in fact, Rousseau's
system, like any other, does is to leave power in the hands
of that minority which is able most effectively to manipu-
late the will of the inert mass of the population.

It is clear, in brief, that popular sovereignty, if it
means that the whole people is, in all but executive detail,
to govern itself, is an impossible fiction. There are, indeed, occasions when it may have been operative; at least
it was theoretically possible for the citizen-body of Athens
to make its sovereign decisions as a unity. But once
we turn to the modern state, with its absence of the nu-
merical limits within which the Greek cities were confined, it is obvious that, for the general purposes of daily
life, popular sovereignty is non-existent. We cannot
avoid, that is to say, the device of representation. The
scale of our social life involves specialization of function.
Political business has to be confined to a small group of
men whose decisions, generally speaking, are accepted by
the vast majority. We still make, indeed, Rousseau's
distinction between state and government. We still, that
is to say, vaguely realize that there is no necessary co-
incidence between the wills of each; and, if they conflict,
it is the former alone which possesses the ultimate power
to get its will obeyed.[12] Government, if it is to be secure,
must so act as to obtain at least the passive consent of
the major portion of the community. But so long as
that border remains uncrossed, so long, that is to say, as
the policy of government is normally sagacious, it is possible to assert that whatever is necessary for complete
political effectiveness is no longer the exclusive and jeal-
ously-guarded possession of the state.

There is herein implied a second and vaguer sense in

[12] *The Social Contract,* Bk. III, Ch. 18.

which the notion of popular sovereignty has become accepted. Historically, it perhaps goes back to the teleo-
ology of Aristotle's *Politics*, at least in the sense in which
it is given ethical justification. For its practical bearing,
the sense insisted upon by Hume when he urged[13]
the paramountcy of public opinion is a sufficient expression of its meaning. No one will deny that any government can, often enough, secure obedience from an unwilling people; but no one will deny either that the ultimate power in any state belongs to the majority and
that the latter, if it be roused, will get itself obeyed. But
this is too abstract a sense for any practical value to be
attached to it. For there is, as Sidgwick pointed out,[14]
a "fundamental distinction between power that is unconsciously possessed — and therefore cannot be exercised
at all — and power consciously possessed." Certainly
deliberate organization is necessary if opinion is to flow
into channels where it can be effective. The majority of
men, moreover, is so habituated to obedience that, normally speaking, the sanction of penalties is hardly necessary to obtain it. In a democratic state, at least, it
is rarely necessary for government to act upon the supposition that disobedience is contingent. Its possibility,
doubtless, is a factor in restraining the selfish exercise of
governmental power. But it is essentially a reserve
weapon the use of which belongs rather to the realm of
prophecy than of analysis.

Here, indeed, we verge upon the teleological factor by
which Aristotle justified the existence of the state. Its
object, he said, is to secure the good life; and popular
sovereignty is therefore in turn justified by the argument

13 *Essays* (World's Classics ed.) p. 24.
14 *The Elements of Politics*, p. 630.

that government should not proceed against the will of the governed. The cause of such hesitation is variously explained. Most usually it is the assumption of a certain popular instinct for right of which Aristotle himself seems to have accepted the reality.[15] At the moment, it is sufficient to remark that the argument raises more difficulties than it solves. It in reality asks what degree of opposition ought to deter a government from proceeding with its policy; or, more positively, it asks what concessions should be made to a strong popular desire. We cannot answer these questions. To them, indeed, Royer-Collard made the response that the only sovereign is right conduct and that the action of government will move as it compels.[16] But, for most, the definition of right conduct would appear less easy than he seemed to make it. We enter here into the realm of the impalpable. It is sufficient to indicate the immense difficulty that is involved in seeking not merely the justification, but even the very sources, of political power.

A corollary that has been deduced from this attitude is worthy of some notice. The authors of the *Federalist* were compelled, of course, to accept the dogma wholeheartedly, though it is interesting, in view of Hamilton's attitude to democracy, to note that they nowhere attempted any analysis of its meaning. What, with them, it seemed to imply was the necessity of a careful limitation of the power to be entrusted to the various branches of government; and they were urgent, with historic precedent immediately behind them, in insisting upon the reserve power of revolution. "If the representatives of the

---

[15] Pol. Bk. III, Ch. 11, 1281 b.
[16] Cf. Laski, *Authority in the Modern State,* Ch. 4.

people," said Hamilton,[17] "betray their constituents, there is then no resource left but in the exertion of that original right of self-defence which is paramount to all positive forms of government"; and he even conceived of the constituent states as an organized security against national usurpation. The American constitution, indeed, once the power of judicial review began to be exercised, was perhaps the first attempt at the protection of this vaguely ultimate popular opinion by something like definite safeguards. The power of rebellion, as the Civil War was to show, of course remained; but it was postponed by an intermediate defence. Yet it will be remarked that the only distinction between this view and that which merely emphasizes the ultimate control of public opinion, is the more serious attempt of the American constitution to make public opinion effective. It gives it instruments of which to make use; but it does not organize it to use them.

A more subtle interpretation of Rousseau's formula has been attempted by Dr. Bosanquet. He sees that ultimate power must reside in the community as a whole; but he insists that the conception is meaningless unless the power finds some determinate expression. He places sovereignty, therefore, in the state, and he defines the state as "the entire hierarchy of institutions by which life is determined." [18] Sovereignty, in his view, really belongs to the general will, to the acts, that is to say, of the state's best self. But this, surely, does no more than move the inquiry back to a further stage. The state must find organs for the expression of its selfhood; and Dr. Bosanquet gives us no criterion by which to recognize

17 *The Federalist,* No. 28.
18 *The Philosophical Theory of the State* (2nd edition), p. 150.

the expression. The sovereignty of the general will, indeed, is very like the assertion that right and truth must prevail; but it does not tell us how certainly to discover the presence of right and truth. It is, moreover, questionable whether the identification of the community as a whole with the state is adequate. It is, perhaps, less untrue for the ancient world, by the views of which Dr. Bosanquet has been profoundly influenced, than for our own day; but a state which comprises, to take a single example, the Roman Catholic church and the Secularist Societies seems almost wilfully to have taken steps to obscure any knowledge of its purposes.

This, indeed, Dr. Bosanquet would deny. "If, for example," he writes,[19] "we speak of the 'sovereignty of the people' in a sense opposed to the sovereignty of the state — as if there were any such thing as 'the people' over and above the organized means of expressing and adjusting the will of the community — we are saying what is, strictly speaking, meaningless." It is difficult to see why that should be the case. Even if we admitted the justice of regarding the state as identical with society we still should have no means of knowing when an act was sovereign. For social obligations conflict; and unless, for practical purposes, we take as paramount the duty of obedience to government, we have no rule of conduct herein. Nor is it useful to accept such a criterion; for churches, to take only a single example, refuse to accept as final a governmental decision which, as they conceive, violates their own ethos.[20] The fact is that Dr. Bosanquet is so concerned with the discovery of a unity inherent in

19 Ibid., p. 282.
20 Cf. my Problem of Sovereignty, Chs. II–V. for a full analysis of this question.

the social fabric that he slurs over the presence of disharmonies. Unity of purpose, in a broad sense, society well may possess; but the methods by which its constituent parts propose to achieve that purpose are not only various, but, often enough, mutually destructive. So long as the size of the modern state renders it necessary to entrust power to a small group of selected persons, it is difficult to see how controversy can be avoided where the acts of those persons arouse differences of opinion that are fundamental. Dr. Bosanquet, like Rousseau, makes government simply an instrument for effecting the will•of the sovereign state; but he gives us no means of knowing when that will has received expression.

At this point an interpretation emerges which has all the merit of simplicity and clearness. The people, it is admitted, cannot directly govern itself; but it can directly delegate, through the device of universal suffrage, the business of government. The national assembly, whether Congress or Parliament, then in fact becomes the people, and it derives the right therefrom to exercise completely sovereign powers. Popular sovereignty, that is to say, implies representative government. Some institution, or set of institutions, has to be erected in which the will of the people as a whole may find expression. The most eminent of Rousseau's disciples did not hesitate to accept this view. "The nation," said the Constitution of 1791,[21] "from which alone all powers derive, can exercise them only by delegation. The French constitution is representative; its representatives are the legislative body and the King." The Belgian constitution expresses a similar idea. "All powers," it asserts, "emanate from the nation; they are exercised in the manner established

[21] *Constit. of 1791.* Tit. II, Art. 2.

by the Constitution." [22]   The sovereignty of the King in
Parliament has a basis in nowise different; and it has been
given classically emphatic expression in Burke's insistence
that the private member ideally represents the nation as
a whole.[23] Statesmen of distinction, indeed, have not hesitated to affirm that resistance to the representative
assembly is resistance to the state itself. M. Briand, for
example, based his opposition to the demands of the
French civil service on the ground that they could not
secure the support of the Chamber. "The civil servants,"
he said,[24] "are confronted by the national representatives,
that is to say by the nation itself." "Against whom,"
asked M. Barthou,[25] "are the postal workers on strike?
. . . it is against you, gentlemen, against the whole
nation. . . . The question is whether we are to abandon
general interests, we who represent the national sovereignty." "The system of representation," said Brougham in his famous speech upon the Reform Bill of 1832,[26]
"consists altogether in the perfect delegation by the
people of their rights and the care of their interests to
those who are to deliberate and to act for them."

But it is, as a distinguished authority has admitted,[27]
at least an open question whether the theory of popular
sovereignty is compatible with representative government. The element of representation, he says, "means
that, within the limit of the powers conferred upon them,
the members are called upon freely and finally, to repre-

[22] *Belgian Constitution*, Art. 25.

[23] *Speech at Bristol Works* (World's Classics ed.), II, 165.

[24] *Journal Officiel*, May 14, 1907.

[25] *Ibid.*

[26] House of Lords, Oct. 7, 1831. Speeches (Philadelphia, 1841),
II, 49.

[27] Esmein, *Elements de Droit Constitutionnel* (6 ed.), p. 391.

sent in the name of the people, what is considered to be the will and voice of the latter." There is herein implied exactly that theory of a restricted mandate which Burke[28] and Mill[29] so emphatically rejected. Rousseau himself, indeed, insisted that sovereignty cannot be represented because that is to admit, what is illogical, the possibility of its alienation. To part with paramount power was, in his view already to betray it.[30]

Certainly it must be admitted that the theory of representation contains much that is the merest fiction. It is often difficult to know upon what issues a member has been returned. There are innumerable problems upon which, in any real sense, a public opinion cannot be said to exist. James Mill expended much thought upon the methods by which the interests of the representative assembly could be kept in harmony with those of the electorate,[31] and his greater son emphasized the ease with which the power supposedly delegated by the people may be perverted to sinister ends.[32] Even when the assembly has been elected with enthusiasm, it may cease rapidly to possess popular favor before the expiration of its term of power. "A prime minister," says Sir Sidney Low,[33] "may continue to govern for a period that may even extend over years in defiance of public opinion"; and a remark of M. Clémenceau, who is at least experienced, is to the same effect.[34]

Clearly there is herein the serious problem of being

28 Speech at Bristol, cited above.
29 *Representative Government* (Everyman's ed.), p. 323.
30 *Contrat Social*, Bk. III, Ch. 15.
31 *Essays upon Government*, p. 27.
32 *Representative Government*, p. 248, f.
33 *The Government of England* (1914), p. 113.
34 Duguit, *Le Droit Social*, p. 132 n.

certain that a representative assembly does in fact mirror the opinion it is supposed to reflect. It is useless to call the sovereignty of the people effective if the organs through which it works fail to do justice to popular desire. But what, at bottom, is justice to such desire? What popular desire must be accepted by the statesman? No one would urge that he should deliberately translate each whim as it occurs into the solid form of statute. It then seems true, as de Tocqueville insisted,[35] that our utmost democratic enthusiasm ought not to deny the necessity of safeguards against the tyranny of the majority. Are there, in fact, popular desires to which attention ought not to be paid, because they are wrong? We most of us condemn the continuance of the war with America after 1776; but it seems unquestionable that it was popular.[36] The unjustifiable execution of Admiral Byng was a sacrifice to the rage of the majority. It is, indeed, difficult to avoid the conclusion that, from the very situation by which he is confronted, the legislator will tend to emphasis less the sovereignty of the people than the sovereignty of what his reason and conscience tell him to be right conduct. He will find himself, that is to say, not very distant from the denial of all institutional sovereignty, as with Royer-Collard,[37] or from the belief in the supremacy of reason, as with Benjamin Constant.[38] The danger, in such a position, is, of course, the danger of paternalism. The legislator deals less with the popular will than with the popular need. We must not, indeed,

[35] *Democracy in America.* Part I, Ch. 15; and cf. Mill's comment, *Dissertations and Discussions*, Vol. II, p. 114.

[36] Lecky, *History of England in the XVIIIth Century* (Popular ed.), Vol. IV, pp. 165, 435.

[37] Cf my *Authority in the Modern State*, Ch. 4.

[38] *Cours de Politique Constitutionelle*, Vol. I, p. 177 f.

draw too careful a line of demarcation between them; for they become insensibly transfused in the hands of a skilful statesman.

But the kind of difficulty that is involved any observer can see for himself who watches a party in search of an issue. Lord John Russell in 1851 deliberately exploited the dormant anti-Catholic prejudices of Great Britain to secure a popularity that was waning.[39] Mr. Lloyd-George has admitted that the Insurance Act of 1911 was passed in the teeth of popular disapproval;[40] and the Opposition that had blessed it upon its appearance, did not fail to use and stimulate the antagonism that made itself felt. Issues are sometimes deliberately recommended to a party as worthy of exploitation.[41] "For nearly twenty years," says Sir Sidney Low,[42] "the National Union of Conservative Associations had been passing occasional resolutions in favor of "Fair Trade" and Retaliation, without attracting the slightest attention. But a single leading statesman uttered a few sentences . . . and instantly the whole country was in a ferment." The French system of politics makes the problem even more intricate by the way in which the Chamber of Deputies is constructed. It is impossible for the electorate directly to choose a ministry; and the most popular cabinet may be overturned through the accidental ill-chance of a private intrigue that has resulted in an unlooked-for interpellation.

It is here worthy of notice that the books abound in lamentations upon the breakdown of the representative

---

39 Cf. my *Problem of Sovereignty*, p. 142 f.
40 Cf. the *London Times*, Nov. 24, 1913.
41 *New York Nation*, Vol. 107, p. 282.
42 *Governance of England* (1914), p. 130,

system. There may be a clear advantage in the simplicity
of majority-rule; certainly the psychological strength of
a government which can claim effectively to have a majority behind it is enormous.[43] There are yet vast difficulties in its operation. We seem, on the whole, determined that there shall be no restrictions upon the
franchise; but not even the enthusiasm of Mill has convinced us that opinions ought to have their place in the
assembly proportionately to their strength. In the result,
there are many opinions that do not get represented at
all; and the majority actually exerted by the party in
power may be out of all relation to its strength in the
country. Yet the evil of proportional representation is
the not less grave danger that it may, on the one hand,
hinder the effective management of government while, on
the other, by leading, as it seems to lead, to the group-
system, it may deprive the electors of their choice of
leaders.

But even if we could suppose that the representative
assembly is an accurate reflex of public opinion, difficulties of an urgent kind remain. In every country in
the world the pressure of public business has made the
legislative body little more than the creature of the executive; and it is only a rare frankness which, like that of
Lord Hugh Cecil,[44] will admit its desirability on the
ground that it promotes the efficient conduct of public
business. "The theoretical and practical deductions from
this doctrine," remarks an acute observer,[45] "are that

---

[43] One of the gravest weaknesses of the Bolshevik government in
the eyes of the western democracies is the doubt whether it has the
support of the majority of the population.

[44] Hansard, 4th series, Vol. 90, p. 915. March 7th, 1901.

[45] Holland, *Imperium et Libertas*, p. 257.

the House of Commons is to become a mere body for registering the decrees of a secret committee." In our own day, this prophecy has become so largely fulfilled that deep search has been made by members of Parliament to make the House of Commons once more an adequate vehicle of effective control.[46] Even in America, where the theory of the separation of powers has given an immense safeguard to the legislature, the growth of presidential influence has been immense; and in France, while the group-system makes the French prime minister more humble than his English colleague, his influence has increased by leaps and bounds in the last decade.

It is, of course, greatly uncertain whether the sovereign people can in fact fulfil the functions that theory expects from it. Montesquieu, indeed, specifically excluded it from either a control over executive details or a share in legislation. He thought such direct participation the chief vice of ancient states; and he limited its competence to the selection of its rulers.[47] That attitude, in some measure at least, has been in recent times strengthened by our experience of direct legislation. The statistics suggest that an electorate is, roughly, twice as interested in the selection of men as in the determination of measures; and if there is important argument upon the side of direct government, it is the argument of theory rather than experience.[48] We need not argue, with de Lolme, that nature has given to but few men the capac-

---

[46] Cf. Hansard, 5th series, Vol. 95, p. 1494. (Sir Godfrey Collins); *Ibid*, Vol. 96, p. 1552 (Mr. Herbert Samuel); *Ibid.*, Vol. 100, p. 1282 (Mr. Herbert Samuel).

[47] *Esprit des Lois*, Bk. II, Ch. 2; and cf. Bk. XI, Ch. 6.

[48] Lowell, *Public Opinion and Popular Government*, pp. 152-240, esp. pp. 225-7.

ity to deal with legislation,[49] to admit that neither economic pressure nor education, neither the absence of leisure nor the possession of knowledge, permits the average elector to pass an opinion upon political questions that could be accepted as intellectually final. Nor is this all; for it is obvious enough that the average elector is not greatly interested in the political process. He demands results; but he does not greatly care about the methods by which those results are attained. It is sometimes difficult to doubt that we approach the epoch so greatly feared by de Tocqueville when he predicted that men might one day be willing to exchange power for material comfort.[50] In that event the sovereignty of the people would be no more than an antiquarian memory.

In sober fact, it is difficult to avoid the conclusion that the dogma attempts to give a specious exactitude of form to that principle of consent for which, in some fashion, room must be found in the modern state. But, as a dogma, it is of no juristic worth. It is, by its very nature, incapable of translation into terms of some specific authority to whose enactments the courts may look for final reference. The organs from which power is in England today derived are not in appearance different from those in active existence at the Revolution, even though their substance has so vastly changed. Legally, also, the alignment of constitutional power in the United States stands where it did in 1787; practically the absorption of much influence by the executive on the one hand, and voluntary groupings like the trade-unions, on the other,

---

[49] *Constitution de l'Angleterre*, Bk. II, Ch. 5, where there is a very interesting analysis.

[50] Cf. my *Problem of Administrative Areas*. (Smith College Studies, Vol. IV, No. 1). (Reprinted *supra*.)

are the facts which most prominently confront the observer. It is, indeed, obvious that the way in which our political institutions function renders it impossible at any moment to ascribe to their true author the roots of any political act. One of the greatest events in English history is the foundation of the Bank of England; but it is impossible to measure the comparative credit which attaches to Paterson and Montague and the original subscribers. It was their influence which made the experiment successful, though the enacting authority was a hesitant House of Commons and a frankly suspicious Upper Chamber.

The truth surely is that we should regard the idea of popular sovereignty as expressive of what is the most real problem in modern politics. In some sort it goes back to Plato; for the institutions of which we make use are an attempt to answer his uncompromising rejection of the democratic system. Plato, in substance, denied the value of any general public opinion; and it is at least clear that the philosophic justification of democratic government must begin by showing that his argument is unsound. Even when that is done, there is a second difficulty, of which he was unaware, to be confronted. For, since direct government is, in the modern state, for the most part impossible, it is necessary to show that the organs of the modern state are capable of clothing that opinion with reality. Sovereignty of the people, in fact, means that the interest which is to prevail must be the interest of the mass of men rather than of any special portion of the community; and it is, further, an implicit insistence that this general interest is the criterion of political good. In that regard, it is obviously but little different from the Benthamite criterion, and it may perhaps be usefully observed that the "greatest happiness principle" is as little exact where practical utility is concerned as its predecessor. For here, as in every political question, the real problem lies not so much in the announcement that the interest of the people as a whole must be the ultimate governing factor, as in the means taken to secure the supremacy of that interest. Practice, in this regard, limps painfully behind the theory it is to sustain.

Nor is the reason difficult of access. It is our fashion to make of political theory the search for that ultimate unity of interest which the ideal purpose of the state suggests may one day be found. It is at least permissible to doubt whether the unity so postulated is more, at least thus far in history, than a fantastic dream. The idealist philosophy may tell us[51] that the "pure" instance only is important. The difficulty yet is that the variations with which practice must reckon make the "pure" instance at best of doubtful application. It is unnecessary to regard history, with Lord Acton, as the record of the crimes and follies of mankind to see that there has, thus far, been no state in which an actual identity of interest between rulers and subjects can be admitted. For the fact surely is that those who possess the engines of power will, for the most part, tend to regard their private good as identical with the general good. That is, in fact, contrary to much of the evidence we possess. At the best, it equates the intention to do good with the achievement of good itself. It is yet not enough, as Plato again and again insisted, to will what is right; it is also necessary to know what it is right to will. Whatever

[51] Barker, *Political Thought from Herbert Spencer*, p. 80. There is, in this whole chapter, a very powerful criticism of the view I am here concerned in urging.

theory may say, an analysis of the modern state reveals it as a complex of interests between which there is no necessary or even predominant harmony. The right of employers, for instance, to engage or discharge their workmen as they please is inconsistent with the latter's interest in security of tenure; and yet, in the immediate conditions of the modern industrial state, it is a right which law will protect. The definition of right and wrong by the courts, in brief, will inevitably reflect, though not in detail, the dominant ideas of the time; and it is not in the least clear that those dominant ideas will necessarily represent an attempt to secure the equal happiness of the members of the state. The social interests which are translated into legal rights are almost always the rights of a limited group of men.

This, indeed, does no more than indicate the general nature of the problem. Perhaps, also, it suggests a method of approach to social questions which, if less metaphysically exact than such analyses as those of Green and Bosanquet, would, if rightly used, lead to results of more practical character. In the analysis of political problems the starting-point of inquiry is the relation between the government of a state and its subjects. For the lawyer, all that is immediately necessary is a knowledge of the authorities that are legally competent to deal with the problems that arise. For him, then, the idea of sovereignty has a particular and definite meaning. It does not matter that an act is socially harmful or unpopular or morally wrong; if it issues from the authority competent to act, and is issued in due form, he has, from the legal stand-point, no further problems.

For political philosophy, on the other hand, legal competence is no more than a contingent index to the facts it needs. The political philosopher is concerned with the discovery of motives, the measure of wills, the balance of interests. It is important for him that an act, in theory the will of Parliament, is in fact the will of a subordinate official in the Colonial office.[52] He cannot neglect the implications of the perversion of a legislature to selfish ends by a criminal adventurer like Tweed. The sovereignty of Parliament will interest him as a legal instrument, but its workings he will have to view in the light of the numerous defeats it has suffered.

He will, in fact, be driven to the perception that, politically, there is no such thing as sovereignty at all. He will find himself, rather, in the presence of different wills, some of which, from their strength, have more importance than others. He will ascribe to none a moral pre-eminence by the mere reason that it claims political priority. He will be satisfied simply with the ascription to these wills of a power which is never constant and rarely capable of prophetic announcement. It is possible that he will discover in the will of government something to which, from the nature of social organization, a special obedience is due. It is possible, also, that he will be driven to insist that the history of politics must make us careful in the erection of safeguards about the exercise of power. He will see that, ultimately, the basis of all power is in the consent offered to action by each individual mind; and he may therefrom induce the conclusion that liberty is the capacity to resist. Certainly the atmosphere of his endeavor will correspond, within its range, to the task of history as Ranke defined it.

Not, of course, that his effort will end there. A politi-

[52] Cf. Charles Buller's famous description in Wakefield, *Act of Colonisation* (ed. of 1914), p. 279 f.

cal metaphysic must be had, but to be useful it must be grounded in historic experience. Only in this fashion can we avoid the danger noted by de Tocqueville and cease to confound institutions that are ancient with the eternal needs of social organization. Nothing is easier than to pass from legal right to moral right, but nothing, at the same time, is more fatal. Certainly the history of popular sovereignty will teach its students that the announcement of its desirability in nowise coincides with the attainment of its substance.

THE PLURALISTIC STATE *

EVERY student of politics must begin his researches with
humble obeisance to the work of Aristotle; and therein, I take it, he makes confession of the inspiration and
assistance he has had from the effort of philosophers.
Indeed, if one took only the last century of intellectual
history, names like Hegel, Green, and Bosanquet must
induce in him a certain sense of humility. For the direction of his analysis has been given its perspective by their
thought. The end his effort must achieve has been by no
other thinkers so clearly or so wisely defined.

Yet the philosophic interpretation of politics has suffered from one serious weakness. It is rather with
staatslehre than with *politik* that it has concerned itself.
Ideals and forms have provided the main substance of its
debates. So that even if, as with Hegel and Green, it
has had the battles of the market-place most clearly in
mind, it has somehow, at least ultimately, withdrawn
itself from the arena of hard facts to those remoter
heights where what a good Platonist has called[1] the "pure
instance" of the state may be dissected. Nor has it seen
political philosophy sufficiently outside the arena of its
own problems. Aristotle apart, its weakness has lain

---

* Reprinted from the *Philosophical Review*, Nov. 1919.

[1] Barker, *Political Thought in England from Herbert Spencer to
Today*, p. 68 f.

exactly in those minutiæ of psychology which, collectively, are all-important to the student of administration. Philosophy seems, in politics at least, to take too little thought for the categories of space and time.

The legal attitude has been impaired by a somewhat similar limitation. The lawyer, perhaps of necessity, has concerned himself not with right but with rights, and his consequent preoccupation with the problem of origins, the place of ultimate reference, has made him, at least to the interested outsider, unduly eager to confound the legally ancient with the politically justifiable. One might even make out a case for the assertion that the lawyer is the head and centre of our modern trouble; for the monistic theory of the state goes back, in its scientific statement, to Jean Bodin. The latter became the spiritual parent of Hobbes, and thence, through Bentham, the ancestor of Austin. On Austin I will make no comment here; though a reference to an ingenious equation of Maitland's may perhaps be pardoned.[2]

It is with the lawyers that the problem of the modern state originates as an actual theory; for the lawyer's formulæ have been rather amplified than denied by the philosophers. Upon the historic events which surround their effort I would say one word, since it is germane to the argument I have presently to make. We must ceaselessly remember that the monistic theory of the state was born in an age of crisis and that each period of its revivification has synchronized with some momentous event which has signalized a change in the distribution of political power. Bodin, as is well known, was of that party which, in an age of religious warfare, asserted, lest it

2 Cf. *The Life of F. W. Maitland,* by H. A. L. Fisher, p. 117.

perish in an alien battle, the supremacy of the state.[3]
Hobbes sought the means of order in a period when King
and Parliament battled for the balance of power. Bentham published his *Fragment* on the eve of the Declaration of Independence; and Adam Smith, in the same year,
was outlining the programme of another and profounder
revolution. Hegel's philosophy was the outcome of a
vision of German multiplicity destroyed by the unity of
France. Austin's book was conceived when the middle
classes of France and England had, in their various ways,
achieved the conquest of a state hitherto but partly open
to their ambition.

It seems of peculiar significance that each assertion of
the monistic theory should have this background. I cannot stay here to disentangle the motives through which
men so different in character should have embraced a
theory as similar in substance. The result, with all of
them, is to assert the supremacy of the state over all
other institutions. Its primary organs have the first
claim upon the allegiance of men; and Hobbes's insistence[4] that corporations other than the state are but the
manifestations of disease is perhaps the best example of
its ruthless logic. Hobbes and Hegel apart, the men I
have noted were lawyers; and they were seeking a means
whereby the source of power may have some adequate
justification. Bentham, of course, at no point beatified
the state; though zeal for it is not wanting in the earlier
thinkers or in Hegel. What, I would urge, the lawyers
did was to provide a foundation for the moral superstructure of the philosophers. It was by the latter that the

---

[3] The background of his book has recently been exhaustively out-
lined by Roger Chauviré in his *Jean Bodin* (Paris, 1916), esp. pp.
312 f.   [4] *Leviathan*, Ch. 44.

monistic state was elevated from the plane of logic to the plane of ethics. Its rights then became matter of right. Its sovereignty became spiritualized into moral pre-eminence.

The transition is simple enough. The state is today the one compulsory form of association;[5] and for more than two thousand years we have been taught that its purpose is the perfect life. It thus seems to acquire a flavor of generality which is absent from all other institutions. It becomes instinct with an universal interest to which, as it appears, no other association may without inaccuracy lay claim. Its sovereignty thus seems to represent the protection of the universal aspect of men — what Rousseau called the common good — against the intrusion of more private aspects at the hands of which it might otherwise suffer humiliation. The state is an absorptive animal; and there are few more amazing tracts of history than that which records its triumph over the challenge of competing groups. There seems, at least today, no certain method of escape from its demands. Its conscience is supreme over any private conception of good the individual may hold. It sets the terms upon which the lives of trade-unions may be lived. It dictates their doctrine to churches; and, in England at least, it was a state tribunal which, as Lord Westbury said, dismissed hell with costs.[6] The area of its enterprise has consistently grown until today there is no field of human activity over which, in some degree, its pervading influence may not be detected.

But it is at this point pertinent to inquire what exact

[5] I say today; for it is important to remember that, for the Western World, this was true of the Church until the Reformation.

[6] A. W. Benn, *History of English Rationalism in the Nineteenth Century*, Vol. II, p. 133.

meaning is to be attached to an institution so vital as this. With one definition only I shall trouble you. "A state," writes Mr. Zimmern,[7] "can be defined, in legal language, as a territory over which there is a government claiming unlimited authority." The definition, indeed, is not quite correct; for no government in the United States could claim, though it might usurp, unlimited power. But it is a foible of the lawyers to insist upon the absence of legal limit to the authority of the state; and it is, I think, ultimately clear that the monistic theory is bound up with some such assumption. But it is exactly here that our main difficulty begins to emerge. The state, as Mr. Zimmern here points out, must act through organs; and, in the analysis of its significance, it is upon government that we must concentrate our main attention.[8]

Legally, no one can deny that there exists in every state some organ whose authority is unlimited. But that legality is no more than a fiction of logic. No man has stated more clearly than Professor Dicey[9] the sovereign character of the King in Parliament; no man has been also so quick to point out the practical limits to this supremacy. And if logic is thus out of accord with the facts of life the obvious question to be asked is why unlimited authority may be claimed. The answer, I take it, is reducible to the belief that government expresses the largest aspect of man and is thus entitled to institutional expression of the area covered by its interests. A history, of course, lies back of that attitude, the main part of which would be concerned with the early struggle of the modern state to be born. Nor do I think the logical

---

7 *Nationality and Government*, p. 56.

8 Cf. my *Authority in the Modern State*, pp. 26 ff.

9 Cf. *The Law of the Constitution* (8th ed.), pp. 37 ff.

character of the doctrine has all the sanction claimed
for it. It is only with the decline of theories of natural
law that Parliament becomes the complete master of its
destinies.   And the internal limits which the jurist is
driven to admit prove, on examination, to be the main
problem for consideration.

There are many different angles from which this claim
to unlimited authority may be proved inadequate. That
government is the most important of institutions few,
except theocrats, could be found to deny; but that its
importance warrants the monistic assumption herein implied raises far wider questions. The test, I would urge,
is not an *a priori* statement of claim. Nothing has led
us farther on the wrong path than the simple teleological
terms in which Aristotle stated his conclusions. For
when we say that political institutions aim at the good
life, we need to know not only the meaning of good, but
also those who are to achieve it, and the methods by which
it is to be attained. What, in fact, we have to do is to
study the way in which this monistic theory has worked;
for our judgment upon it must depend upon consequences
to the mass of men and women. I would not trouble you
unduly with history. But it is worth while to bear in
mind that this worship of state-unity is almost entirely
the offspring of the Reformation and therein, most
largely, an adaptation of the practice of the medieval
church. The fear of variety was not, in its early days,
an altogether unnatural thing. Challenged from within
and from without, uniformity seemed the key to self-
preservation.[10] But when the internal history of the state

10 Cf. Professor McIlwain's introduction to his edition of the
Political Works of James I, and my comment thereon, *Pol. Sci. Quarterly*, Vol. 34, p. 290 (reprinted in this volume).

is examined, its supposed unity of purpose and of effort
sinks, with acquaintance, into nothingness. What in fact
confronts us is a complex of interests; and between not
few of them ultimate reconciliation is impossible. We
cannot, for example, harmonize the modern secular state
with a Roman Church based upon the principles of the
Encyclical of 1864; nor can we find the basis of enduring
collaboration between trade-unions aiming at the control
of industry through the destruction of capitalistic organization and the upholders of capitalism. Historically,
we always find that any system of government is dominated by those who at the time wield economic power;
and what they mean by "good" is, for the most part, the
preservation of their own interests. Perhaps I put it too
crudely; refined analysis would, maybe, suggest that they
are limited by the circle of the ideas to which their interests would at the first instance give rise. The history
of England in the period of the Industrial Revolution is
perhaps the most striking example of this truth. To
suggest, for instance, that the government of the younger
Pitt was, in its agricultural policy, actuated by some
conception of public welfare which was equal as between
squire and laborer, is, in the light of the evidence so
superbly discussed by Mr. and Mrs. Hammond, utterly
impossible.[11] There is nowhere and at no time assurance
of that consistent generality of motive in the practice
of government which theory would suppose it to possess.

We cannot, that is to say, at any point, take for
granted the motives of governmental policy, with the
natural implication that we must erect safeguards against
their abuse. These, I venture to think, the monistic
theory of the state at no point, in actual practice, sup-

[11] See their brilliant volume, *The Village Laborer* (1911).

plies. For its insistence on unlimited authority in the governmental organ makes over to it the immense power that comes from the possession of legality. What, in the stress of conflict, this comes to mean is the attribution of inherent rightness to acts of government. These are somehow taken, and that with but feeble regard to their actual substance, to be acts of the community. Something that, for want of a better term, we call the communal conscience, is supposed to want certain things. We rarely inquire either how it comes to want them or to need them. We simply know that the government enforces the demand so made and that the individual or group is expected to give way before them. Yet it may well happen, as we have sufficiently seen in our experience, that the individual or the group may be right. And it is difficult to see how a policy which thus penalizes all dissent, at least in active form, from government, can claim affinity with freedom. For freedom, as Mr. Graham Wallas has finely said,[12] implies the chance of continuous initiative. But the ultimate implication of the monistic state in a society so complex as our own is the transference of that freedom from ordinary men to their rulers.

I cannot here dwell upon the more technical results of this doctrine, more particularly on the absence of liability for the faults of government that it has involved.[13] But it is in some such background as this that the pluralistic theory of the state takes its origin. It agrees with Mr. Zimmern that a state is a territorial society divided into

12 Cf. his article in the *New Statesman*, Sept. 25, 1915. I owe my knowledge of this winning definition to Mr. A. E. Zimmern's *Nationality and Government*, p. 57.

13 Cf. my paper on the *Responsibility of the State in England.* 32 *Harv. L. Rev.*, p. 447 (reprinted in this volume).

government and subjects, but it differs, as you will observe, from his definition in that it makes no assumptions as to the authority a government should possess. And the reason for this fact is simply that it is consistently experimentalist in temper. It realizes that the state has a history and it is unwilling to assume that we have today given to it any permanence of form. There is an admirable remark of Tocqueville's on this point which we too little bear in mind.[14]   And if it be deemed necessary to dignify this outlook by antiquity we can, I think, produce great names as its sponsors. At least it could be shown that the germs of our protest are in men like Nicholas of Cusa, like Althusius, Locke, and Royer-Collard.

It thus seems that we have a twofold problem. The monistic state is an hierarchical structure in which power is, for ultimate purposes, collected at a single centre. The advocates of pluralism are convinced that this is both administratively incomplete and ethically inadequate. You will observe that I have made no reference here to the lawyer's problem. Nor do I deem it necessary; for when we are dealing, as the lawyer deals, with sources of ultimate reference, the questions are no more difficult, perhaps I should also add, no easier, than those arising under the conflict of jurisdictions in a federal state.

It is with other questions that we are concerned. Let us note, in the first place, the tendency in the modern state for men to become the mere subjects of administration. It is perhaps as yet too early to insist, reversing a famous generalization of Sir Henry Maine, that the movement of our society is from contract to status; but there is at least one sense in which that remark is significant. Amid much vague enthusiasm for the thing itself,

14 *Souvenirs*, p. 102.

every observer must note a decline in freedom. What we
most greatly need is to beware lest we lose that sense of
spontaneity which enabled Aristotle to define citizenship
as the capacity to rule not less than to be ruled in turn.[15]
We believe that this can best be achieved in a state of
which the structure is not hierarchical but coördinate, in
which, that is to say, sovereignty is partitioned upon some
basis of function. For the division of power makes men
more apt to responsibility than its accumulation. A man,
or even a legislature that is overburdened with a multiplicity of business, will not merely neglect that which he
ought to do; he will, in actual experience, surrender his
powers into the hands of forceful interests which know
the way to compel his attention. He will treat the unseen
as non-existent and the inarticulate as contented. The
result may, indeed, be revolution; but experience suggests
that it is more likely to be the parent of a despotism.

Nor is this all. Such a system must needs result in a
futile attempt to apply equal and uniform methods to
varied and unequal things. Every administrator has told
us of the effort to arrive at an intellectual routine; and
where the problems of government are as manifold as at
present that leads to an assumption of similarity which
is rarely borne out by the facts. The person who wishes
to govern America must know that he cannot assume
identity of conditions in North and South, East and
West. He must, that is to say, assume that his first duty
is not to assert a greatest common measure of equality but
to prove it. That will, I suggest, lead most critical observers to perceive that the unit with which we are trying
to deal is too large for effective administration. The
curiosities, say of the experiment in North Dakota, are

[15] *Politics,* Bk. III, Ch. 1, 1275a.

largely due to this attempt on the part of predominating interests to neglect vital differences of outlook. Such differences, moreover, require a sovereignty of their own to express the needs they imply. Nor must we neglect the important fact that in an area like the United States the individual will too often get lost in its very vastness. He gets a sense of impotence as a political factor of which the result is a failure properly to estimate the worth of citizenship. I cannot stay to analyze the result of that mistaken estimate. I can only say here that I am convinced that it is the nurse of social corruption.

Administratively, therefore, we need decentralization; or, if you like, we need to revivify the conception of federalism which is the great contribution of America to political science. But we must not think of federalism today merely in the old spatial terms. It applies not less to functions than to territories. It applies not less to the government of the cotton industry, or of the civil service, than it does to the government of Kansas and Rhode Island. Indeed, the greatest lesson the student of government has to learn is the need for him to understand the significance for politics of industrial structure and, above all, the structure of the trade-union movement.[16] The main factor in political organization that we have to recover is the factor of consent, and here trade-union federalism has much to teach us. It has found, whether the unit be a territorial one like the average local, or an industrial like that envisaged by the shop-steward movement in England, units sufficiently small to make the individual feel significant in them. What, moreover, this

[16] A book that would do for the English-speaking world what M. Paul-Boncour did twenty years ago for France in his *Fédéralisme Economique* would be of great service.

development of industrial organization has done is to
separate the processes of production and consumption in
such fashion as to destroy, for practical purposes, the
unique sovereignty of a territorial parliament. It is a
nice question for the upholders of the monistic theory to
debate as to where the effective sovereignty of America
lay in the controversy over the Adamson law; or to consider what is meant by the vision of that consultative industrial body which recent English experience seems likely,
in the not distant future, to bring into being.[17]

The facts, I suggest, are driving us towards an effort
at the partition of power. The evidence for that conclusion you can find on all sides. The civil services of England and France are pressing for such a reorganization.[18]
It is towards such a conclusion that what we call too
vaguely the labor movement has directed its main
energies.[19] We are in the midst of a new movement for
the conquest of self-government. It finds its main impulse in the attempt to disperse the sovereign power because it is realized that where administrative organization
is made responsive to the actual associations of men,
there is a greater chance not merely of efficiency but of
freedom also. That is why, in France, there has been
for some time a vigorous renewal of that earlier effort
of the sixties in which the great Odillon-Barrot did his
noblest work;[20] and it does not seem unlikely that some
reconstruction of the ancient provinces will at last compensate for the dangerous absorptiveness of Paris. The
British House of Commons has debated federalism as the

17 See the *Report of the Provisional Joint Committee of the Industrial Conference.* London, 1919.

18 See my *Authority in the Modern State*, Ch. 5.

19 Cf. Cole, *Self-Government in Industry, passim.*, esp. Ch. 3.

20 Odillon-Barrot, *De la centralization.*

remedy for its manifold ills;[21] and the unused potentialities of German decentralization may lead to the results so long expected now that the deadening pressure of Prussian domination has been withdrawn. We are learning, as John Stuart Mill pointed out in an admirable passage,[22] that "all the facilities which a government enjoys of access to information, all the means which it possesses of remunerating, and therefore of commanding, the best available talent in the market, are not an equivalent for the one great disadvantage of an inferior interest in the result." For we now know that the consequent of that inferior interest is the consistent degradation of freedom.[23]

I have spoken of the desire for genuine responsibility and the direction in which it may be found for administrative purposes. To this aspect the ethical side of political pluralism stands in the closest relation. Fundamentally, it is a denial that a law can be explained merely as a command of the sovereign for the simple reason that it denies, ultimately, the sovereignty of anything save right conduct. The philosophers since, particularly, the time of T. H. Green, have told us insistently that the state is based upon will; though they have too little examined the problem of what will is most likely to receive obedience. With history behind us, we are compelled to conclude that no such will can by definition be a good will; and the individual must therefore, whether by himself or in concert with others, pass judgment upon its validity by examining its substance. That, it is clear

---

21 *Parliamentary Debates,* June 4th and 5th, 1919.

22 *Principles of Political Economy* (2d ed.), Vol. II, p. 181.

23 On all this, cf. my *Problem of Administrative Areas* (Smith College Studies, Vol. IV, No. 1), *supra.*

enough, makes an end of the sovereignty of the state in its classical conception. It puts the state's acts — practically, as I have pointed out, the acts of its primary organ, government — on a moral parity with the acts of any other association. It gives to the judgments of the State exactly the power they inherently possess by virtue of their moral content, and no other. If the English state should wish, as in 1776, to refuse colonial freedom; if Prussia should choose to embark upon a Kulturkampf; if any state, to take the decisive instance, should choose to embark upon war; in each case there is no *a priori* rightness about its policy. You and I are part of the leverage by which that policy is ultimately enacted. It therefore becomes a moral duty on our part to examine the foundations of state-action. The last sin in politics is unthinking acquiescence in important decisions.

I have elsewhere dealt with the criticism that this view results in anarchy.[24] What it is more profitable here to examine is its results in our scheme of political organization. It is, in the first place, clear that there are no demands upon our allegiance except the demands of what we deem right conduct. Clearly, in such an aspect, we need the means of ensuring that we shall know right when we see it. Here, I would urge, the problem of rights becomes significant. For the duties of citizenship cannot be fulfilled, save under certain conditions; and it is necessary to ensure the attainment of those conditions against the encroachments of authority. I cannot here attempt any sort of detail; but it is obvious enough that freedom of speech,[25] a living wage, an adequate education,

---

[24] *Authority in the Modern State*, pp. 93–4.

[25] Cf. the brilliant artcle of my colleague, Professor Z. Chafee, Jr., in 32 *Harv. L. Rev.*, 932 f.

a proper amount of leisure, the power to combine for social effort, are all of them integral to citizenship. They are natural rights in the sense that without them the purpose of the state cannot be fulfilled. They are natural also in the sense that they do not depend upon the state for their validity. They are inherent in the eminent worth of human personality. Where they are denied, the state clearly destroys whatever claims it has upon the loyalty of men.

Rights such as these are necessary to freedom because without them man is lost in a world almost beyond the reach of his understanding. We have put them outside the power of the state to traverse; and this again must mean a limit upon its sovereignty. If you ask what guarantee exists against their destruction in a state where power is distributed, the answer, I think, is that only in such a state have the masses of men the opportunity to understand what is meant by their denial. It is surely, for example, significant that the movement for the revival of what we broadly term natural law should derive its main strength from organized trade-unionism. It is hardly less important that among those who have perceived the real significance of the attitude of labor in the Taff Vale and Osborne cases should have been a high churchman most deeply concerned with the restoration of the church.[26] That is what coördinate organization will above all imply, and its main value is the fact that what, otherwise, must strike us most in the modern state is the inert receptiveness of the multitude. Every student of politics knows well enough what this means. Most would, on analysis, admit that its dissipation is mainly

[26] J. Neville Figgis, *Charles in the Modern State*. The recent death of Dr. Figgis is an irreparable blow to English scholarship.

dependent upon an understanding of social mechanisms now largely hidden from the multitude. The only hopeful way of breaking down this inertia is by the multiplication of centres of authority. When a man is trained to service in a trade-union, he cannot avoid seeing how that activity is related to the world outside. When he gets on a school-committee, the general problems of education begin to unfold themselves before him. Paradoxically, indeed, we may say that a consistent decentralization is the only effective cure for an undue localism. That is because institutions with genuine power become ethical ideas and thus organs of genuine citizenship. But if the Local Government Board, or the Prefect, sit outside, the result is a balked disposition of which the results are psychologically well known. A man may obtain some compensation for his practical exclusion from the inwardness of politics by devotion to golf. But I doubt whether the compensation is what is technically termed sublimation, and it almost always results in social loss.

Here, indeed, is where the main superiority of the pluralistic state is manifest. For the more profoundly we analyze the psychological characteristics of its opposite, the less adequate does it seem relative to the basic impulses of men. And this, after all, is the primary need to satisfy. It was easy enough for Aristotle to make a fundamental division between masters and men and adapt his technique to the demands of the former; but it was a state less ample than a moderate-sized city that he had in mind. It was simple for Hobbes to assume the inherent badness of men and the consequent need of making government strong, lest their evil nature bring it to ruin; yet even he must have seen, what our own generation has emphasized, that the strength of governments consists only

in the ideas of which they dispose. It was even simple
for Bentham to insist on the ruling motive of self-interest;
but he wrote before it had become clear that altruism
was an instinct implied in the existence of the herd. We
know at least that the data are more complex. Our main
business has become the adaptation of our institutions
to a variety of impulses with the knowledge that we must
at all costs prevent their inversion. In the absence of
such transmutation what must mainly impress us is the
wastage upon which our present system is builded. The
executioner, as Maistre said, is the corner-stone of our
society. But it is because we refuse to release the creative
energies of men.

After all, our political systems must be judged not
merely by the ends they serve, but also by the way in
which they serve those ends. The modern state provides
a path whereby a younger Pitt may control the destinies
of a people; it even gives men of leisure a field of passionate interest to cultivate. But the humbler man is
less fortunate in the avenues we afford; and if we have
record of notable achievement after difficult struggle, we
are too impressed by the achievement to take due note
of the anguish upon which it is too often founded. This,
it may be remarked, is the touchstone by which the major
portion of our institutions will be tested in the future;
and I do not think we can be unduly certain that they will
stand the test. The modern state, at bottom, is too much
an historic category not to change its nature with the
advent of new needs.

Those new needs, it may be added, are upon us, and
the future of our civilization most largely depends upon
the temper in which we confront them. Those who take
refuge in the irrefutable logic of the sovereign state may

sometimes take thought that for many centuries of medieval history the very notion of sovereignty was unknown.
I would not seek unduly to magnify those far-off times;
but it is worth while to remember that no thoughts were
dearer to the heart of medieval thinkers than ideals of
right and justice. Shrunken and narrow, it may be, their
fulfillment often was; but that was not because they did
not know how to dream. Our finely articulated structure
is being tested by men who do not know what labor and
thought have gone into its building. It is a cruder test
they will apply. Yet it is only by seeking to understand
their desires that we shall be able worthily to meet it.

THE BASIS OF VICARIOUS
LIABILITY *

I

IF a master choose to give orders to his servant, no one
can fail to understand why he should be held liable for
the consequences of their commission.[1]   Nor is the case in
substance different when he ratifies his servant's act.   To
stamp what is done for him with the seal of his approval
is tacitly, but obviously, to accept the act as his own;[2]
and that is true no less where the ratification is implicit,
than where it is expressly made manifest.[3]   No one, moreover, deems it necessary to take objection to liability
which is consequent upon a general negligence.[4]   I may
knowingly employ a clearly incompetent person.[5]   I may
consciously fail to provide proper means for the perform-

* Reprinted from the *Yale Law Journal*, December, 1916.

[1] *Doctor and Student*, I. ix; Lucas *v.* Mason (1875) 10 Ex. 251;
Smith *v.* Keal (1882) 9 Q. B. D. 340.

[2] Bishop *v.* Montague (1600) Cro. Eliz. II, 824; Padget *v.* Priest
(1787) 2 T. R. 97; Ewbank *v.* Nutting (1849) 7 C. B. 797; Dempsey
v. Chambers (1891) 154 Mass. 330.

[3] Goff *v.* G. N. R. Co. (1861) 3 E. & E. 672; Walker *v.* S. E. Ry.
Co. (1870) 5 C. P. 640.

[4] Wanstall *v.* Pooley (1841) 6 Cl. & F. 910; Dansey *v.* Richardson
(1854) 3 El. & Bl. 144; Cox *v.* Central Vermont Ry. Co. (1898) 170
Mass. 129.

[5] Cutler *v.* Morrison (1910) 43 Pa. Sup. Ct. 55; Martin *v.*
Richards (1892) 155 Mass. 381.

ance of the allotted work.[6] I may fail to give my servant information which I know to be essential to the right completion of his task.[7] I may fail to take adequate precaution against the commission of a tort in my presence.[8] In cases such as these, where the master is directly involved, it is essential to any scheme of law that he should be held liable for such damage as his servant may cause.

The problem is far different where express authority does not exist. A state in which it is an accepted doctrine that the sins of the servant may, even when unauthorized, be visited upon the master, has won a tolerable respect for its law. Yet the thing is sufficiently novel to be worth some careful investigation. In no branch of legal thought are the principles in such sad confusion. Nowhere has it been so difficult to win assent to what some have deemed fundamental dogma.[9] Nor is this all. What principles — even if of a conflicting kind — have yet emerged are comparatively new in character. They do not go back to that venerable time when Richard I endowed the Anglo-Saxon race with legal memory. There is no trace of them in Bracton.[10] The Year-Books do not aid us.[11] Coke — it seems marvelous

6 Mitchell v. Boston & Maine R. R. Co. (1894) 68 N. H. 96.

7 Fletcher v. Baltimore & P. R. R. Co. (1897) 168 U. S. 135.

8 M'Laughlin v. Pryor (1842) 4 Man. & G. 58.

9 See Mr. Baty's fierce attack in his brilliant, if perverse, *Vicarious Liability* (1915). Dean Thayer in the posthumous paper published in 29 *Harv. L. Rev.* 801 has suggested some interesting possibilities of future development.

10 Cf. Bracton ff. 115b, 124b, 158, 171a, 172b, 204b.

11 Prof. Wigmore in 7 *Harv. L. Rev.* 315 has cited some evidence to the contrary, but it is hardly decisive. The cases which foreshadow the modern doctrine are conceived with special duties. Cf. Cowell, *Institutes*, p. 207; Southern v. Howe, Cro. Jac. 468; Noy, *Maxims*, Ch. 44. For the general rule, see Rolle, *Abridgment, tit.* Action on the Case, pl. 95; Waltham v. Mulgar (1606) Moore, 776.

enough — is silent upon them; or, at any rate, it is a
different tale he has to tell. Our theories come in with
the Revolution of 1688, and they bear the impress of
a single, vivid personality. So that if they have a history, it is short enough to raise deep questions. And,
indeed, it must be admitted that the problems inherent
in our principles are very formidable. There is no field
of law into which they do not seem to enter. Contract,
tort, negligence — in all of these they have their word
to say, and it is a word of growing import for our time.[12]
The age has passed when each man might bear untroubled
the burden of his own life; to-day, the complexities of
social organization seem, too often, to have cast us, like
some Old Man of the Sea, upon the shoulders of our fellows. Where, above all, the men of Mediaeval England
gloried in their own labor, we, or, at least many of
us, take pleasure in dividends that have been vicariously
earned. It is an age of abundant service. Vast numbers are working for other men and obeying their commands. Service implies action. A tells B to perform
some work. When B's work entails less to C, what is
the relation of A to the transaction? We have maxims
and to spare upon this question. *Respondeat superior*
is an argument which, like David, has slain its tens of
thousands. Its seeming simplicity conceals in fact a
veritable hornet's nest of stinging difficulties. It is the
merest dogma, and in no sense explanation. For while
everyone can see that the master ought to answer for
acts he has authorized, why should he be liable either
where no authorization can be shown, or where express
prohibition of an act exists? Latin may bring us com-

---

[12] Cf. Dr. Baty's remark that the modern law is injuring industry,
op. cit., p. 154.

fort but it will not solve our problems.   Nor is the case
improved if we substitute *qui facit alium facit per se* in
its place.   Like most of its kind that antique legend is
simply a stumbling-block in the pathway of juristic progress.   It is one of those dangerous generalizations which
shivers into untruth upon the approach of fact.   Where
another does no more than fulfil your command, you may
with accuracy be said to act.   That is as legally clear
as it is morally unimpeachable.   But what of cases where
your servant performs acts incidental to your business
without express authority for their performance?   What
of acts done in positive disobedience to command?   Can
we be said actually to have performed acts which at first
acquaintance we are anxious to repudiate?   Is Parker,
for instance, to suffer if a subordinate officer, who happens to be a genius, wilfully disobeys orders, and puts
his glass to an unseeing eye? [13]   What is to occur when
the servant's action is colored by personal motive?
Clarity, it is obvious, begins now to pale into that obscurity where what is most visible is the natural confusion of life.   Our vaunted simplicity perishes before
the realism of the event.   We have, it is clear, to go
further than the jingles of legal convenience if we are
to arrive at a working hypothesis; unless, indeed, we
accept the subtle Pyrrhonisms of a distinguished authority, and assume at the outset a fundamental disharmony
between reason and law.[14]

13 Though of course Parker hoped — and felt — that Nelson would
disregard his generous caution.

14 Mr. Justice Holmes in 5 *Harv. L. Rev.* 14.   Cp. Paley, *Moral
Philosophy,* Bk. III, Pt. I, Ch. 11: "These determinations stand, I
think, rather upon the authority of the law than upon any principle
of natural justice."

II

We shall be less pessimistic. Our skepticism is the consequence of a too great reliance upon the historic method. We have laid insistence rather upon the origins of law than upon the ends it is to serve.[15] When the history of the modern extension of vicarious liability is examined, no one can question the high degree of its mysteriousness.[16] We may barely guess what motives underlay the striking and decisive dicta of Chief Justice Holt in a series of cases, the more difficult, in that they were not adequately reported,[17] but largely gained their strength from remarks made *obiter*, and from that vivid imagination which enabled Lord Holt to suggest compelling analogies.[18] We see signs of a struggle with the mediaeval doctrine in the partial persistence of the old ideas.[19] Yet, by 1800, the novelties have forced their way to acceptance.[20] The rare genius of Willes and Blackburn makes of them, in some sort, not the least vital contribution of nineteenth-century jurisprudence to

[15] Cf. Mr. Justice Holmes' impressive words, 10 *Harv. L. Rev.* 457 ff.

[16] See Dean Wigmore in 3 *Select Essays in Anglo-American Law,* 474.

[17] Cf. Mr. Baty's remarks, *op. cit.* 23–4.

[18] Turberville *v.* Stampe (1697) Com. 459, 1 Salk. 13, Ld. Raym. 264; Middleton *v.* Fowler (1699) 1 Salk. 282; Jones *v.* Hart (1699) 2 Salk. 441, Ld. Raym. 736; Lane *v.* Cotton (1701) 12 Mod. 489; Hern *v.* Nichols (1709) Holt 462, 1 Salk. 289.

[19] Randle *v.* Deane (1701) 2 Lut. 1496; Naish *v.* East India Co. (1721) Com. 421.

[20] Cf. the change between Naish and Bush *v.* Steinman (1799) 1 B. & P. 404. Blackstone in 1 *Comm.* 429 is suggestive for the trend of opinion towards the middle of the century.

the growth of Anglo-American law.[21]   It becomes possible to assert that, special authority apart, the duties
assigned to a servant give him the power to bind his
master in such contracts as come within the scope of his
employment.[22]   But the law goes further, and makes the
master generally liable for his servant's torts so long
as they are fairly and reasonably to be traced to his
service;[23] though no burden is thrown upon the employer
where no such connection can be shown.[24]   When the act
committed is a crime, authorization, important statutory
exceptions apart, is still necessary; for the law still
places motive at the basis of criminal liability.[25]   Yet,
even when these limitations are considered, the scope —
as Jessel thought too vast[26] — of this extension is indeed
remarkable.   Almost within a century the doctrines of
hallowed antiquity are reversed.   No attention, as it
seems, is paid to historic antecedent.   The whole change

[21] The fundamental cases are Seymour v. Greenwood (1860) 6 H.
& N. 359; (1861) 7 ibid. 355; Goff v. G. N. R. Co. (1861) 3 E. & E.
672; Limpus v. Gen. Omnibus Co. (1867) 1 H. & C. 526; Barwick v.
Joint Stock Bank (1867) 2 Ex. 259; Poulton v. L. & S. W. R. Co.
(1867) 2 Q. B. D. 534.

[22] See Fitzherbert, *Natura Brevium*, 120b; *Doctor and Student*,
II, xlii; Noy, *Maxims*, p. 58; Nickson v. Brohan (1710) 10 Mod. 110;
Hibbs v. Ross (1866) 1 Q. B. D. 534; Watteau v. Fenwick Co. (1892)
67 L. T. N. S. 831; Langan v. G. W. Ry. Co. (1874) 30 L. T. N. S.
173, especially the remarks of Bramwell, B.

[23] Limpus v. Gen. Omnibus Co., *ut supra;* Stevens v. Woodward
(1881) 50 L. J. (Q. B.) 231; Dyer v. Munday [1895] 1 Q. B. 742.

[24] McManus v. Crickett (1800) 1 East, 106; Croft v. Alison (1821)
4 B. & Ald. 590; Stevens v. Woodward, *ut supra,* 318; Allen v.
L. & S. W. R. (1870) 6 Q. B. D. 65; Abrahams v. Deakin [1891]
1 Q. B. 516.

[25] R. v. Huggins (1730) 2 Str. 882; Bagge v. Whitehead [1892] 2
Q. B. 355.

[26] Smith v. Keal (1882) 9 Q. B. D. 351.

is, so one may urge, outstanding proof of oft-contro-
verted fact that judges can and do make law. Clearly,
good reason is essential for so striking a revolution of
opinion.

Here is the crux of the problem; for it must be admitted, that so far in legal theory if we have a multiplicity of theories, none has brought widespread satisfaction. Some, indeed, are frankly impossible. It is
not very helpful to be told by authority so distinguished
as Parke,[27] as Alderson,[28] as Cranworth,[29] that *qui facit
per alium* is the basis of the liability; for, as we have
seen, that, in strict fact, can be true only where the
master's assent is proved. The quasi-scientific mind of
Lord Brougham ascribed the doctrine to the fact that
"by employing him, I set the whole thing in motion, and
what he does, being done for my benefit, and under my
direction, I am responsible for the consequence of doing
it"[30] — a niggardly determinism which, from its concealed fictions, serves only to darken counsel; and it has
the additional demerit of being logically as extensible
to the work of an independent contractor, where vicarious
liability does not ordinarily apply, as to that of a servant,
or agent where it does. Mr. Justice Willes, of whose
opinion Mr. Baty seems to approve,[31] grounds our dogma
on the fact that "there ought to be a remedy against
some person capable of paying damages to those in-

27 Quarman *v.* Burnett (1840) 6 M. & W. 509.

28 Hutchinson *v.* York, Newcastle Ry. Co. (1850) 5 Ex. 343.

29 Bartonshill Coal Co. *v.* Reid (1858) 3 Macq. 266.

30 Duncan *v.* Finlater (1839) Cl. & F. 894, 910. I ought to add
that this theory seems to command the assent of Dean Wigmore,
3 *Select Essays in Anglo-American Law*, 536. See Parke's criticism
of it in Quarman *v.* Burnett, *ut supra.*

31 Baty, *op. cit.*, p. 154.

jured." [32] But it is clear that if this is the path the law ought, as a general rule, to follow, it is going to have small concern with justice. The great Pothier ascribed its force to the necessity of making men careful in the selection of their servants; [33] yet it is clear that in the vast majority of cases that have arisen, no such negligence has ever been alleged. Nor will anyone dream to-day of accepting the view of the unctuous Bacon, that the liability arises from our failure to do our own work — a failure permitted by an indulgent law on the condition that we bear an absolute responsibility for such delegation. [34] Sir Frederick Pollock — with far more reason — urges that as all business is a dangerous enterprise, boldness must pay its price. [35] The "implied command" theory has nothing rational about it; it is one of those dangerous and disagreeable fictions which persist as a method from a primitive stage of law. [36] And Maitland has slain the equally hopeless fiction of an imaginary identification of master and servant derived from the jurisprudence of Rome. [37] Nor is the opinion of Lord Holt — which derives a special importance from its historical setting — in any way more adequate. It

[32] Limpus *v.* Gen. Omnibus Co., *ut supra.* One has a troubled feeling that Maitland might have endorsed this dictum, 2 P. & M. 533.

[33] Pothier, *Obligations* (trans. Evans), p. 72.

[34] *Abridgment* (ed. 1832), *tit.* Master and Servant (K.), IV, 336.

[35] See his paper on Employer's Liability in his *Essays on Jurisprudence and Ethics.*

[36] Below, Sec. IV.

[37] P. & M. II, 530. I say this with deep respect, for Mr. Justice Holmes has given his weighty support to this theory, 4 *Harv. L. Rev.* 345-64, and 5 *Harv. L. Rev.* 1-23; but as Wigmore (*op. cit.* 533 n. 1) has pointed out, his illustrations are mainly derived from West, *Symboleography,* of which the relation to the civil law makes it at once suspect.

seemed to him simply a principle of natural justice that
where one or two innocent persons suffer through the
fraud of a third, the suffering must be borne by the
master who, in employing that third party, enabled the
fraud to be committed.[38] The view is little more than
that later adumbrated by Lord Brougham, though it is
more plausibly arrayed. All torts are not deceits, and it
would be difficult, for example, to apply such a test to
the situation in *Lunt* v. *North-Western Ry. Co.*, where
the defendant's gatekeeper invited the plaintiff in entire
good faith to pass over a railway crossing,[39] or where a
tramway conductor honestly, but mistakenly, suspects
a passenger of tendering a counterfeit half-sovereign, and
gives him in charge.[40] Lord Bramwell gave up the law
altogether. "I have never been able," he told the Parliamentary Committee of 1876,[41] "to see why the law should
be so — why a man should be liable for the negligence of
his servant, there being no relation constituted between
him and the party complaining." Nor did Mr. Justice
Wright attempt any explanation of the law beyond its
universality.[42]

III

That universality is notable. The law of a business
world is not made for amusement. Some solid reality
there must have been in the reasons for its acceptance;

[38] In Hern v. Nichols, *ut supra*.

[39] (1886) L. R. 1 Q. B. 277.

[40] Furlong v. South London Tramways Co. (1884) 4 J. P. 329;
cf. Charleston v. London Tramways Co. (1888) 4 T. L. R. 629.

[41] (1887) Cd. 285, p. 46.

[42] Baty, *op. cit.* p. 150. For a valuable general commentary on
the tendencies of the modern law, cf. Charmont, *Les Transformations
du droit civil*, chap. xvi.

and its very persistence in the face of bitter criticism is itself suggestive. We make men pay for faults they have not committed. It seems, on the surface, extraordinary enough; unless, indeed, we are to conclude with Lord Bramwell that the whole thing is nonsensical, or with Sir Frederick Pollock that it is the entrance-fee payable for admission to a dangerous trade. But the rules of law have usually some purpose behind them. Men like Holt and Blackburn are something more than whimsical innovators.[43] The basis of our principles is to be found in the economic conditions of the time. Business has ceased to be mere matter of private concern. A man who embarks upon commercial enterprise is something more — even in the eyes of the law [44] — than a gay adventurer in search of a fortune. The results of his speculation are bound to affect the public; and the state, as the guardian of its interests, is compelled to lay down conditions upon which he may pursue his profession. The emphasis does not lie, as Sir F. Pollock has suggested, in an *ipso facto* danger in business, but in the removal of certain zones of fact without the sphere of ordinary litigation. The basis of the rule, in fact, is public policy. One knows, of course, that "public policy" is a doctrine for which the judges have cherished no special affection. "I, for one," said Burrough, J.,[45]

[43] I hope to trace in a later paper the early history of *respondeat superior*.

[44] Cf. Mr. E. A. Adler's stimulating papers in 28 and 29 *Harv. L. Rev.*

[45] Richardson *v.* Mellish (1824) 2 Bing. 252; cf. Wallis *v.* Smith (1882) 21 Ch. D. *per Jessel* at p. 266; Rex *v.* Hampden (1637) 3 S. T. 1293; *Wilkes' Case* (1768) 19 S. T. 1112 *per* Mansfield, C. J.; and above all Egerton *v.* Brownlow (1853) 4 H. L. C. 1 *per* Pollock, C. B.

"protest . . . against arguing too strongly upon public policy; it is a very unruly horse, and when you get astride it, you never know where it will carry you. It may lead you from the sound law. It is never argued upon at all but when other points fail." But such an attitude is, in truth, but the prophetic anticipation of the Victorian distrust of governmental interference. It is becoming more and more clear that we may not be content with an individualistic commercial law.[46] Just as that individualism was the natural reaction from the too strict and local paternalism of mediaeval policy — perhaps aided by the inherent self-centredness of Puritan thought [47] — so we are compelled to turn away from every conception of the business relation which does not see the public as an effective, if silent, partner in every enterprise. That is the real meaning of Factory and Employers' Liability Acts as of compulsory education, and the establishment of a minimum wage. It is simply a legal attempt to see the individual in his social context. That, at which we industrially aim, is the maximum public good as we see it. In that respect, the employer is himself no more than a public servant, to whom, for special purposes, a certain additional freedom of action, and therefore a greater measure of responsibility has been vouchsafed.[48] If that employer is compelled to bear

[46] See the striking remarks of Mr. Justice Holmes in 10 *Harv. L. Rev.* 457, 467, and his speech to the Harvard Law Review Association on Feb. 15, 1913, in *Speeches* (1913) pp. 98–102; above all his remarks in Lochner *v.* N. Y. (1904) 198 U. S. 45, 75–6.

[47] See Levy, *Economic Liberalism, passim,* and the last chapter of Gooch, *Political Thought from Bacon to Halifax.* For the way in which state regulation has become essential, cf. Pic, *Legislation Industrielle* (1908) Chs. 2 and 7.

[48] Cf. Duguit, *Transformations du Droit Public,* especially Chs. 2 and 7.

the burden of his servant's torts even when he is himself personally without fault, it is because in a social distribution of profit and loss, the balance of least disturbance seems thereby best to be obtained.[49]

What, then, we have to ask ourselves is whether the positive benefits to be derived from the present rule do not in fact outweigh the hardships it may on occasion inflict. We cannot run a human world on the principles of formal logic. The test of our rule's worth must, in fact, be purely empirical in character. We have to study the social consequences of its application, and deduce therefrom its logic. We have to search for the mechanism of our law in life as it actually is, rather than fit the life we live to *a priori* rules of rigid legal system.[50] The way in which the modern conception has grown is, in fact, very comparable to the method by which special liabilities are attached to innkeepers,[51] to those who have wild animals,[52] to those who start a fire,[53] to those who engage as public carriers.[54] The meaning of the legal sword of Damocles forged for their penalization is rightly

[49] Cf. the remarks of M. Sainchelette in his *Responsibilité de la Garantie*, p. 124: La responsibilité du fait d'autrui n'est pas une fiction inventée par la loi positive. C'est une exigence de l'ordre social.

[50] What we have in fact to work out for vicarious liability are the principles indicated by Dean Pound in his various papers, especially in 5 *Col. L. Rev.* 339; 8 *ibid.* 605; 24 *Harv. L. Rev.* 591; 25 *ibid.* 489. A good instance of such application is Prof. Frankfurter's paper in 29 *Harv. L. Rev.* 353.

[51] This social conception is interestingly prominent in the judgment of Crompton, J., in Avards v. Dance (1866) 26 J. P. 437.

[52] Fletcher v. Rylands (1886) 1 Ex. 265, 3 H. L. 330; and see thereon the comment of Dean Thayer in the article cited above.

[53] Jones v. Festiniog Ry. Co. (1868) L. R. 3 Q. B. 733.

[54] Holmes, *Common Law*, chap. v. and Beale in 3 *Anglo-American Legal Essays*, 148.

to be found, not in the particular relation they bear to their charge, but in the general relation to society into which their occupation brings them. In such an aspect as this it may be urged that Holt found good reason for the incisive certitude of his dicta in an age which saw so enormous a growth of corporate enterprise. It was, says Dean Wigmore,[55] "a conscious effort to adjust the rule of law to the expediency of mercantile affairs." Something of this, it may be urged, was perceived by Bentham in a passage which has not perhaps received its due meed of attention. "The obligation imposed upon the master," he says,[56] "acts as a punishment, and diminishes the chances of similar misfortunes. He is interested in knowing the character, and watching over the conduct of them for whom he is answerable. The law makes him an inspector of police, a domestic magistrate, by rendering him liable for their imprudence." Even when we allow for the curiosities of the author's characteristic phraseology, it is yet clear that he has seized upon an important truth. If we allow the master to be careless of his servant's torts we lose hold upon the most valuable check in the conduct of social life.

The real problem in vicarious liability, in fact, is not so much the rectitude of its basal principles, as the degree in which they are to be applied.[57] Nor can we anticipate the manner in which that problem is to be solved. What must strike the observer in the study of

---

[55] *Op. cit.* III, 536. Anyone who reads Professor Scott's *History of Joint-Stock Companies to 1720* will realize the force of this dictum.

[56] *Collected Works*, I, 383. The passage occurs in his Principles of Penal Law.

[57] Cf. Prof. Frankfurter's remarks in regard to labor legislation, 29 *Harv. L. Rev.* 367.

the cases is that each is in itself a separate issue; the
employer of a railway conductor whose habit it is to
kiss the female passengers of pleasing appearance [58] must
be dealt with differently from a bank of which the cashier
fraudulently induces a customer to accept certain bills.[59]
"Each case," says Professor Frankfurter,[60] "must be determined by the facts relevant to it . . . we are dealing, in truth, not with a question of law but with the
application of an undisputed formula to a constantly
changing and growing variety of economic and social
facts.   Each case, therefore, calls for a new and distinct
consideration, not only of the general facts of industry,
but of the specific facts in regard to the employment in
question."   The issue in vicarious liability is not different from that in regard to labor legislation.   Just as our
conception of the constitutionality of statutes will depend
upon the contemporary interpretation of liberty,[61] so
the content of the liability enforced at any given moment
upon a master for his servant's torts, must be shifted to
fit the new facts it will continually encounter.   It is
not a very serious objection, in this age when incorporation has become but a formal informality, to urge that
the growth of the doctrine is a dangerous blow aimed
at the stability of property.[62]   The doctrine will grow

[58] Croaker v. Chicago & N. W. Ry. Co. 17 Am. Rep. 504.

[59] Mackay v. Com. Bank of N. B. (1874) L. R. 5 P. C. 394.

[60] Op. cit. p. 369.

[61] Cf. Pound, Liberty of Contract, 18 *Yale Law Journal*, 480, and
the argument of Prof. Frankfurter in Bunting v. Oregon (1916) reprinted by the National Consumers' League in *The Case for the
Shorter Workday*, pp. 9-15. See also the opinion in Holden v.
Hardy (1897) 169 U. S. 366, and the admirable remarks of M. Pic.
op. cit. pp. 548-9. They are concepts exactly similar to these which
I believe to lie at the base of vicarious liability.

[62] Baty, *op. cit.*, 165.

or contract according as the facts to which it is applied
seem to warrant growth or contraction. It will have in
view, not the history that is to be justified, but the end
that is to be attained. It will let the future take care of
itself by protecting it against the invasion of dogmas
which grow painfully antique. It will strive, in fact, to
make elastic that bed of Procustes in which the client of
law too often takes his rest. If, as Best, C. J., remarked,[63] our law is to be "bottomed on plain, broad
principles," it is well to see that they do not also, even
though unconsciously, include its superstructure. For
each age has to begin anew its legal thinking.

IV

The problem of scope of employment [64] has become
largely confused by the efforts of the courts to provide,
somehow or other, a test of negligence on the part of the
master. Thus, masters are to be held liable for their
servant's torts when the latter are acting "for the master's benefit" [65] when, as seems to be assumed, he is less
careful than we may demand — or in such wise that a
probable authority would from the nature of the case
have been given [66] — a fiction of implied command being,
so far as one can see, relied upon.[67] It seems far easier

[63] Strother v. Barr (1828) 5 Bing. 136, 153.

[64] Mr. Baty, in Chs. 5-7 of his *Vicarious Liability*, has provided a
perfect mine of admirable comment on the cases, to which I am
greatly indebted — though it is to be remembered that he enters
always from the standpoint of a complete disagreement with the
modern law.

[65] Barwick v. Eng. Joint Stock Bank, *ut supra;* Dyer v. Munday,
ut supra.

[66] Atty. Gen. v. Siddon & Binns (1830) 1 Tyr. 41.

[67] For a vigorous dissent from this attitude, see the remarks of
Bramwell, B., in Wier v. Bell (1877) 3 Ex. D. 238.

to attempt a humanist application of public policy to the problems presented by the cases.   The fiction of implied authority is so constantly breaking down, it so obviously results in patent anomalies as to be as dangerous as it is unsatisfactory.   When we have defined "scope of employment" as consisting in acts incidental or natural to the servant's occupation, we are only on the threshold of our difficulties.   For there has been the most widespread divergence of opinion as to what comes within the scope of such acts, and no statistical measurement is at all possible.   It is clear enough that if a driver employed by a jobmaster fails to keep watch over his customer's goods, that the master ought to pay; for he has held out the servant as capable in the performance of his duties — an obtainment of trust which carries with it a burden of responsibility.[68]   But when we explain the decision as based on negligence — after all, a fiction so far as the master is concerned — we have in reality advanced nowhere; for the negligence is that of the servant and the problem is the liability of the master.   It surely seems better to emphasize the fact that public policy obviously requires a means of forcing masters to keep continual watch over the conduct of their servants, and it is difficult to see how that end would otherwise be attained.   Nor is it difficult to understand why a bank should be held answerable for the faults of its manager.[69] From one point of view, and that the orthodox, it is, of course, possible to attribute the decision in *Barwick* to an "implied authority" on the part of the manager to act on behalf of his bank; but in a wider aspect it is clear, that where loss must occur, more good is likely to accrue

[68] Abraham *v.* Bullock (1901) 86 L. T. 796.
[69] Barwick *v.* Eng. Joint Stock Bank, *ut supra.*

from making a bank liable for a mistaken appointment, than from making a corn-dealer suffer for a not unnatural reliance on managerial dignity. The fiction is surely unsatisfactory; for it is hardly possible to suppose that the bank gave its servant to act dishonestly. It is surely better to explain the ground of the decision as an attempt to calculate the minimum social loss in a social situation where some loss is inevitable. So, too, if a teacher renders her employers liable for an unwise treatment of her charges,[70] it is not because it is part of her duty to act in such fashion as gives rise to penalization, but because the fact of her liability is more likely to prevent the recurrence of the act, than the argument that she was acting for her own benefit and therefore outside her authority; for no child is, on the whole, likely to be deterred from poking a fire at command by the consideration that a court might declare the order outside the implied authority of the teacher.

We do not therefore attempt the definition of the doctrine of implied authority for the simple reason that definition is impossible. We give up the doctrine. It is impossible, for instance, to say just when the occupation of a carter gives him implied authority to make a deviation, and at what point his journey becomes completely independent.[71] A "small détour" must obviously be relative to the day's journey, and it would be interesting to know exactly upon what principles the courts would be prepared to fix the proportion.[72] Nor is the task at

[70] Smith v. Martin [1911] 2 K. B. 775.

[71] Cf. Whatman v. Pearson (1838) L. R. 3 C. P. 422 with Joel v. Morrison (1834) 6 C. & P. 501; and Platten v. Rea (1857) 2 C. B. N. S. 606 with Cormack v. Digby (1876) 9 Ir. R. C. L. 567. See also the remarkable issue in Smith v. Spitz (1892) 156 Mass. 319.

[72] See Parke, B., in Whatman v. Pearson, ut supra.

all easier when the court refuses to consider the object the servant had in mind when he committed the tort. The manager of a saloon, for instance, is not usually sportively inclined to give his barman in charge (as it turns out erroneously);[73] and to declare that, because in fact the property he was suspected of stealing was safe, the manager could have no authority to act, is straining the bonds of common sense. An authority to have entire control is, in any rational aspect, an authority to act as best seems to fit the circumstances and if the measures taken to that end are mistaken, it is yet difficult to see exactly why the master should avoid the liability for the mistake.[74] Into what complications this system of delimitation may lead in any tangled issue that well-known case of *Owston* v. *Bank of New South Wales*[75] made very obvious.

It may also mistake the clear demands of humanity. A milkcart was involved in an accident, in the course of which a milk-boy was injured. A bystander offered her assistance to the driver in order to see the boy home safely. The cart started before she was properly settled in it, and she was injured by being thrown out.[76] It seems clear that the driver was acting on the socially admirable ground of ordinary human kindness; and it was not unreasonable, therefore, to expect his employers to be responsible. The court, however, took up an entirely different attitude. *Cox* v. *Midland Counties Ry. Co.*[77] decided that a station master cannot bind his com-

---

[73] Hanson v. Waller [1901] 1 K. B. 390.

[74] Bowler v. O'Connell (1894) 162 Mass. 319; Fogg v. Boston & L. R. R. Co. (1889) 148 Mass. 513; Brown v. Jarvis Engineering Co. (1896) 166 Mass. 75.   [75] (1879) 4 A. C. 270.

[76] Houghton v. Pilkington [1912] 3 K. B. 308.

[77] (1849) 3 Ex. 268.

pany for any surgeon's fees whom the former may summon; and it was, therefore, held by analogy that the acceptance of help by the driver was outside his implied authority. It is good law that a tramway-conductor who too forcibly ejects a passenger renders his company liable in damages;[78] if this occurs on a lonely road, cannot a surgeon's services be requisitioned save at the conductor's personal expense? Such reasoning is surely too pedantic to admit of acceptance. Nor can we place much faith in such a case as *Riddell* v. *Glasgow*[79] which apparently gives a rate-collector the choice between being disowned if he performs his duty efficiently, and being dismissed if he does not. The connotation of every such case ought surely to be the human circumstances in which it occurs. We are beyond that stage of strict law where men are bound by an empty formalism.

The case is more difficult when ethical defect in the servant's motive is the determining factor in his tort, or where he deliberately breaks his master's command. Here the modern doctrine is very new indeed, for as late as 1800 it was not admitted that wilful tort could be within the scope of employment.[80] Parke was very anxious to limit the liability of an employer to cases where negligence could be actually shown.[81] The origin of the new rule seems to have been the growth of corporate enterprise;[82] and with the classic judgment of Willes in *Limpus* v. *General Omnibus Co.* it became firmly

[78] Seymour *v.* Greenwood (1860) 6 H. & N. 359 (1862) 7 *ibid.* 355.

[79] [1910] S. C. 693; [1911] A. C. 209.

[80] McManus *v.* Crickett (1800) 1 East, 106.

[81] Sharrod *v.* L. N. W R. Co. (1849) 4 Ex. 585; and see the judgment of Bramwell, L. J., in Weir *v.* Bell, *ut supra.*

[82] Cf. Baty, *op. cit.*, p. 85.

established.[83] Its principle, in truth, is sufficiently clear.
The London General Omnibus Company had given
printed orders to its drivers not to interfere with the
vehicles of competing companies. The order was wilfully disobeyed, and yet judgment was given against the
company. The driver, as Willes pointed out, "was employed not only to drive the omnibus, but also to get as
much money as he could for his master, and to do it in
rivalry with other omnibuses on the road. The act of
driving as he did is not inconsistent with his employment,
when explained by his desire to get before the other
omnibus." He was in no way disturbed by the company's
instructions. He pointed out how easy it would be to
issue secret orders countermanding them, and for the
master thus both to benefit himself, and to keep on the
right side of the law.[84] That, surely, is a very necessary
and valuable limitation; for were the law otherwise, there
would be a positive incentive to employers to use their
humble servants as the screen for their wrongdoing.
The social object of prevention can only be obtained by
an effective and thoroughgoing penalization.

The case is similar when trespass becomes extended
to fraud.[85] The attempt to discredit the change on the
ground that fraud implies a state of mind on the part
of the defendant which does not in fact exist,[86] misses

[83] *Ut supra;* cf. also, Ward v. Gen. Omnibus Co. (1873) 42 L. J.
(C. P.) 265; Pittsburgh C. & St. L. R. R. Co. v. Kirk (1885) 102
Ind. 399.

[84] *Ibid.* at p. 539; cf. also McClung v. Dearborne (1890) 134
Pa. 396.

[85] As in *Barwick.*

[86] See the remarks of Bramwell, L. J., in Weir v. Bell, *ut supra:*
"I do not understand legal fraud; to my mind it has no more
meaning than legal heat or legal cold, legal light or legal shade."
But MacKay v. Com. Bank of N. B. (1874) 5 P. C. 394; Swift v.

the significant point, that in no case of vicarious liability is moral blame attached to the master. Liability for wrongful arrest is equally clear; for it is obvious that the action is entirely consistent with the scope of the servant's employment unless fiction is to be invoked,[87] and unless we are to be without means for protecting the public from needless suffering.[88] It is clearly simply a social interpretation of negligence. Because a servant does things in the stress of the moment which judicial reflection deems to have been actually unnecessary, there is no reason why the act should not bear its full consequences. One regrets the continual use of the fiction of "implied authority";[89] but that is no reason why the necessity of the rule should not lead to the discussion of what other reasons may be given for its usage. To narrow liability by considering authority actually expressed is to endanger very seriously our control of social life.[90] The employment of a servant to perform certain functions must, on the whole, mean his employment to perform them as he deems best fitted, in his interpretation of his instructions, to serve his master's interest.[91] It is not much consolation to an injured plaintiff to be told

Winterbotham (1873) L. R. 8 Q. B. 244; Brit. Mutual Bank v. Charmwood Forest Ry. Co. (1887) 18 Q. B. D. 714 have established it firmly. See also Pollock, *Torts* (6th ed.) p. 92 n. d.

[87] Moore v. Metropolitan Ry. Co. (1872) 8 Q. B. D. 36; Goff v. G. N. R. Co., *ut supra.*

[88] I have discussed below the unfortunate limitation of this doctrine through the misapplication of *ultra vires.*

[89] Mr. Baty in the fifth chapter of his book is able to exploit this weakness with great effect.

[90] In Lowe v. G. N. Ry. Co. (1893) 62 L. J. (Q. B.) 524. Matthew and Wright, J. J., really take this ground. It is the "must" of a railway porter's position that they consider.

[91] Cf. Furlong v. South London Tram. Co. (1884) 1 Cab. and E. 316.

that the defendant meant no harm; for, as Brian, C. J., said more than four hundred years ago, the courts do not try the thoughts of men.[92] We have here, as elsewhere, to follow the broad rule laid down by Shaw, C. J., in a famous case. "This rule," he said,[93] "is obviously founded on the great principle of social duty, that every man in the management of his own affairs, whether by himself, or by his agents, shall so conduct them as not to injure another; and if he does not, and another thereby sustains damage, he shall answer for it." Nor has the application of the rule shown it to be without justification.

And, after all, where the master most needs protection, he obtains it. He is not liable for the acts of his servant which are shown to be clearly unconnected with his service.[94] No master, for example, can possibly warrant the moral impeccability of his servants; and it is not difficult to see why Collins, M. R., should have held that when a servant has in view objects demonstrably and entirely his own, he should, in committing his tort, "have severed his connection with his master, and become a stranger."[95] The phrase is not perhaps of the happiest;

[92] Y. B. 17 E. IV. I.

[93] See Farwell v. Boston and Worcester R. R. Co. (1842) 4 Met. (Mass.) 49; and see the admirable remarks of Esher, M. R., in Dyer v. Munday, ut supra at p. 746, where he points out the real meaning of the term authority. Snee v. Trice (1802) 2 Bay (S. C.) 345 is an interesting example of how a special social situation will enable the master to escape responsibility.

[94] McManus v. Crickett, ut supra; Croft v. Alison (1821) 4 B. & Ald. 590; Hoar v. Maine Central R. R. Co. (1880) 70 Me. 65; Garvey v. Dung (1866) 30 How. Pr. (N. Y.) 315; Driscoll v. Scranton (1896) 165 Mass. 348; Pittsburgh F. W. & C. Ry. Co. v. Maurer (1871) 21 Oh. St. 421.

[95] Cheshire v. Bailey [1905] 1 K. B. 237 at p. 241.

it carries the crutch of fiction to sustain it. But everyone can see that it would not be right to hold a master
liable for the chance temptations to which an usually
reputed honest employee might succumb — the more so
as the temptation is rather the creation of the third party
than his own. It may even be suggested that, in this
respect, the master has been unduly protected; for when
a train conductor hits a boy for jumping on his car,
he is doing what he believes to be for his employer's good,
and ought duly to make him liable.[96]   To use a supposed
sudden cessation of authority at the moment when the
conductor's unlawful hand descends upon its victim's ear
is to strain rationality to the breaking-point.   Mr. Baty
complains [97] that a consideration of the servant's motive
ought alone to be sufficient to save his master from
liability.   But the truth here is that everything must
depend on the surrounding circumstances of the cases
with which the courts are called upon to deal.   The
reliance to be placed upon a coachman,[98] for instance,
is different in character from the reliance usually to be
placed upon a bank manager,[99] and it is reasonable that
a distinction should be made between them; and what is
true of a bank manager does not, as it seems, apply to a
clerk in a company.[100]   The rule must wait on the facts.

What is here suggested is the simple thesis that only a
social interpretation of the law will give us a satisfactory

[96] Radley v. L. C. C. (1913) 29 T. L. R. 680; cf. Central Ry. Co. v.
Peacock (1888) 69 Md. 257; New Orleans & N. E. R. Co. v. Jopes
(1891) 142 U. S. 18.

[97] Baty, op. cit. 109.   [98] As in Cheshire v. Banley, ut supra.
[99] Com. Bank of N. B., ut supra.

[100] Ruben v. Great Fingall Consolidated [1906] A. C. 439. See
also Houldsworth v. City of Glasgow Bank (1880) 5 A. C. 317 where
the cases are collected.

clue to the bewildering labyrinth that confronts us. If
the judges continue to apply general principles founded
on a dangerous and unsatisfying fiction, only confusion
of a lamentable kind can result. It is hardly possible,
as the case now stands, to avoid a perplexing variety
of opinion as to whether any given issue comes within
the scope of "implied authority" or not. But it is possible to have sufficient confidence in the good sense of
the courts to ask for a frankly communal application of
the law. The promotion of social solidarity is an end
it is peculiarly incumbent upon the law to promote, since
its own strength, and even life, depends upon the growth
of that sentiment. The fiction of implied authority is
no more than a barbarous relic of individualistic interpretation. It savors too dangerously of the time when the
courts held that they were to do no more than apply a
given remedy to a given set of facts concerning John Doe
and Richard Roe — with a lofty unconcern for the world
at large. We are passing beyond that stage. The meaning to be given to the scope of employment is bound
more and more to affect vitally the whole future of industry. It is according as lawyers realize this, that they
will be equipped to deal adequately with the facts of
life. It is, it is true, an interpretation they may not
find in the books. But law is perhaps in need of the
stimulus of a freer atmosphere.[101]

v

Such an attitude is the more important when the de-
personalization of industry is borne in mind. Machinery
and corporate enterprise have effected a revolution, the

101 Cf. Pound, "Law in Books and Law in Action," 44 *Am. L.
Rev.* 12.

very beginnings of which we are able only dimly to conceive.[102] The old, intimate relation between master and servant can hardly now return. The apprentice no longer marries his master's daughter, for the simple reason that his master no longer has a daughter, or, if he does, that daughter is a corporation who is not given in marriage. The modern business man is either a director or a manager and he sees nothing, often enough knows nothing, of his servants. That is, of course, the natural consequence of the scale of modern commercial enterprise, but it is a consequence of which the results need careful emphasis. And alongside this industrial impersonalism has gone the incredible development of machinery so that, as Mr. Birrell has grimly noted,[103] it is with arms and legs that the courts are largely concerned. Now these corporations are, in the eyes even of the law, juristic persons,[104] and since they act as an ordinary individual would act in a similar situation, that is to say by agents and servants, it is clearly reasonable, that they should, equally with individuals, be held vicariously liable for such acts as those agents and servants may perform. But it has not proved easy to establish this doctrine in anything like its necessary completeness. The law has accepted the concession theory of corporate personality, and the grim shadow of *ultra vires* has fallen

102 The reader will find in Mr. Sidney Webb's *Towards Social Democracy* (1916) a very brilliant and suggestive sketch of the modern change.

103 See his *Law of Employers' Liability*, pp. 3–5.

104 Cf. 29 *Harv. L. Rev.* 404 ff. The classic treatment of this problem is to be found in Maitland's famous introduction to his translation of Gierke's *Political Theories of the Middle Age*. Generally the fullest and most brilliant treatment is in Saleilles, *La Personnalite Juridique* (1910).

athwart the pathway of our needs. "The public," Lord Bramwell has told us,[105] "is entitled to keep a registered company to its registered business," and so a company may not go beyond the powers that have been conferred upon it in its origin. But the public had to be protected from the consequences of corporate enterprise, and the nineteenth century has gradually seen the extension to it of the principles of individual liability. It is so difficult, for instance, for a single individual to run a railway, that it would be intolerable if the mere problem of numbers prevented the attainment of justice. So trover,[106] trespass,[107] and nuisance [108] had all been successfully pled against the corporate person before the first half of the century had passed. Malicious prosecution,[109] libel,[110] fraud,[111] and false imprisonment [112] were little by little compelled to follow.

The hesitations that have been characteristic of our policy lie at the door of our conception of the corporation. So long as we think of it as a fiction created only for certain ends which are legal, the doctrine of implied authority logically prevents us from admitting that it can be guilty of authorizing illegal acts.[113] Having made it mindless, we are unwilling to admit it guilty of acts which seem to carry with them the stamp of conscious immorality. But immediately we surrender so inadequate

[105] A. G. v. G. E. Ry. Co. (1879) 11 Ch. D. 449, 503. Cf. 29 Harv. L. Rev. 405 f.

[106] Smith v. Birmingham Gas. Co. (1834) 1 A. & E. 526.

[107] Maund v. Monmouthshire Canal Co. (1840) 4 M. & W. 452.

[108] R. v. G. N. R. Co. (1846) 9 Q. B. 315.

[109] Citizens' Life Ass. Co. v. Brown [1904] A. C. 423, 436.

[110] Whitefield v. S. E. R. Co. (1858) 27 L. J. (Q. B.) 229.

[111] Barwick v. Eng. Joint Stock Bank, ut supra.

[112] Eastern Counties Ry. Co. v. Broom (1867) L. R. 2 Ex. 259.

[113] This seems to be Mr. Baty's view. Op cit. p. 69 ff.

a theory, the ground for the extension of vicarious
liability to the corporate person is very clear. It acts
and is acted for; it must then pay the penalty for its
habits. In a world where individual enterprise is so
largely replaced, the security of business relationships
would be enormously impaired unless we had the means
of preventing a company from repudiating its servants'
torts.[114] The reason is not that companies are well able
to pay; for it is not the business of law to see that a
debtor is solvent, but to provide a remedy for admitted
wrong.

The enforcement of such vicarious liability is more
urgent for another reason. The dissolution of individual business enterprise into the corporation system has
tended to harden the conditions of commercial life. The
impersonality of a company employing say five thousand
men is perhaps inevitable; but in its methods of operation,
it tends to be less careful of human life, more socially
wasteful than the individual has been.[115] But its consequences to society are equally momentous, and we dare
not judge it differently.[116] It is necessary, for instance,
to see to it that we have pure food and unadulterated
milk, and it can make no difference to us whether the
offender against our requirements be individual or corporate.[117] It is only by enforcing vicarious liability that

114 Cf. Gierke, *Die Genossenschafts Theories und die Deutsche
Rechtsprechung*, 801–3, and especially Loening, *Die Haftung das
Staates*, p. 89. See also Pollock, *op. cit.* at p. 127.

115 For an interesting suggestion that it should therefore be
judged differently, see M. D. Petre, *Life of G. Tyrrell*, II, 482.

116 Cf. C. D. Burns, *The Morality of Nations*, Chs. 1 and 2.

117 Pearks etc. *v.* Ward [1902] 2 K. B. 1, and Chuter *v.* Freeth
[1911] 2 K. B. 832; Stranahan Bros. Catering Co. *v.* Coit (1897) 55
Oh. St. 398 — a very striking case.

we can hope to make effective those labor laws intended
to promote the welfare of the workers;[118] for it is too
frequently the corporation that evades the statute or
attempts to discredit it.[119] It is useless to argue that
the responsibility rests upon the agent; for it is un-
fortunately too clear that men may act very differently
in their institutional relations than in their ordinary
mode of life.[120] The London Dock strike of 1911 suggested that a man who in his domestic capacity will display all the most amiable sentiments of an average retired grocer will, when acting for a great dock company,
show himself immovable and unrelenting. But if he
injure society in his activities it is surely clear that
means must be at hand to render his principal responsible. That, at any rate, was the basis of the great
judgment of Farwell, J., in the *Taff Vale* case.[121] No
one supposes that trade union officials will commit torts
unless there are trade unions for which to commit them.
There may be special reasons for taking the trade unions
outside the ordinary law,[122] but that is not to say that
the acts would not otherwise be corporately tortious in
character. No one can deny, for example, the reality

[118] Ruegg, *Law of Employer and Workman in England,* Lect. IV.

[119] Anyone who studies the *Reports of the Chief Inspector of
Factories in England,* or the *Bulletins of the Bureau of Labor,*
especially No. 142 of 1914, which deal with the enforcement of legislation, will be impressed by this state of affairs. For statistics as
to the part played by the great corporations in the extension of the
Fourteenth Amendment to labor legislation, see Collins, *The Fourteenth Amendment and the States.*

[120] See an interesting little essay by Father Tyrrell on the corporate mind in his *Through Scylla and Charybdis.*

[121] [1901] A. C. 426.

[122] See Mr. and Mrs. Webb's remarks in their introduction to the
1911 edition of their *History of Trade Unionism.*

of those entities we call England and Germany. Not
only do they act, but persons act on their behalf. It
seems then socially necessary to make them bear the
burden of a policy for which they are at bottom responsible.[123]

Nor is the case at all different when the association
we attempt to make corporately liable happens not to
have chosen the path of incorporation. There seems no
reason in the world why a technicality of registration
should be allowed to differentiate between societies not in
essence distinct. Yet as the law now stands active participation is essential to such liability.[124] Here contract has
betrayed us; for we regard the voluntary association as
no more than a chance collection of individuals who have
agreed to perform certain acts; and they could not, of
course, assent to the commission of illegalities.[125] "Because," says Mr. Baty.[126] "William Sikes is a bad man,
Lady Florence Belgrave is not to be taxed with abetting
burglary if she sends him soup." But it is not the soup
to which anyone — except Mr. Sikes and the philosophers
of the London Charity Organization Society — will object; the problem is as to the establishment by Mr. Sikes
of a fund which, though subscribed for legal purposes,
is yet used in an illegal manner.[127] No one really desires
to attack the private fortunes of associated individuals;
but it is eminently desirable that means should be had
of getting at the funds they collectively subscribe, when
legal — or illegal — results flow from their collective

[123] See 13 *Jour. of Phil. Psych. & Sc. Methods*, p. 85.
[124] Brown *v.* Lewis (1896) 12 T. L. R. 455.
[125] Cf. 29 *Harv. L. Rev.* 417 ff.
[126] Baty, *op. cit.* 52.
[127] As for instance, the money subscribed to arm the different
volunteer armies in Ireland recently.

action. If a religious order, which has not been incorporated, chooses to have the services of an architect, the mere fact that its members are scattered, and had never contemplated the use made of subscriptions by their representatives, ought not to hinder the architect from securing his rights by a representative action.[128] If an unincorporate aggregate acts as an individual body, it is surely good sense, it ought no less surely to be good law, to give it bodiliness.[129] That is why one can sympathize with decisions such as that in *Ellis* v. *National Free Labor Association*,[130] or, conversely, with that in *Brown* v. *Thompson and Co.*[131] The same is true of the liability of clubs acting through their committees. No one imagines that the committee of a football club would, as a group of respectable and individual householders, erect a grand stand; and if that stand collapses, a technicality of registration ought not to defeat the ends of justice.[132] An unincorporate individual is an unity for the fiscal purposes of the state;[133] it is difficult to see why its social needs should be refused a similar protection.

VI

The basis of modern legislation on employer's liability and workmen's compensation is very similar in character.

128 Walker *v.* Sur [1914] 2 K. B. 930.

129 See, for instance, the amazing remarks of Lord Halsbury in Daimler Co. *v.* Continental Tyre Co. [1916] 2 A. C. 307 at p. 316. Maitland might never have written so far as this view of the nature of a corporation is concerned.

130 [1905] 7 Fac. 629.   131 [1912] S. C. 358.

132 Brown *v.* Lewis, *ut supra,* and see also Wise *v.* Perpetual Trustee Co. [1903] A. C. 139.

133 48 & 49 Vict. c. 51; Curtis *v.* Old Monkland Conservative Association [1906] A. C. 86.

Both represent the typical modern reaction against mid-Victorian individualism. It is interesting to note the somewhat curious divergence in the attitude of lawyers and economists to these problems. To the economist, the necessity of such legislation is abundantly evident. It is simply that the needs of the modern state require that the burden of loss of life, or personal injury in industry, shall be charged to the expenses of production, shall be borne, that is to say, by the employer.[134] He knows well enough that eventually the cost will be paid by the community in the form of increased prices, but that is something it is not unwilling to pay. It is realized that if a workman is compelled to take upon himself all the risks of his employment, the results will be socially disastrous. For the real social unit at the present time is not the individual but the family. It is not merely the single worker who is employed; his wages in reality represent the maintenance of those who are dependent upon him. From the standpoint of public policy, therefore, for the employer to assert that risk must lie where it falls is simply impossible. We cannot allow the certificated managers of collieries to kill their miners with impunity.[135] If the carelessness of a porter breaks a scaffolding upon which a carpenter is standing, his

---

[134] For characteristic economic opinion, see Seager, *Principles of Economics*, p. 601; Taussig, 2 *Principles of Economics*, 334; 2 Chapman, *Work and Wages*, 401; Schaffle, *Theory of Labor Protection*, XIII; Carlton, *History of the Problems of Organized Labor*, p. 304; Seager, *Social Insurance, passim;* Eastman, *Work Accidents and the Law;* Barlow in 7 *Economic Jour.,* 345; and 11, *ibid.* 354; Willoughby, *Workingmen's Insurance*, p. 327; and above all, the classic eleventh chapter in Webb, *Industrial Democracy*, especially Vol. II, pp. 387–91.

[135] Howells *v.* Landore Siemens Steel Co. (1874) L. R. 10 Q. B. 62.

family ought not to starve through his injury.[136] The
need of the modern state is most emphatically that the
welfare of the workers should be the first charge upon
industry.[137]

But the law has approached the problem from so entirely different an angle as to place the workman in a
peculiarly unfortunate position until a fairly recent time.
It was considered essential that when a servant under-
took employment he should accept all the risks of service.
To do otherwise, said Abinger, C. J.,[138] "would be an
encouragement to the servant to omit that diligence and
caution which he is in duty bound to exercise on behalf
of his master."   There is a long history behind the enunciation of that pathetic self-reliance; though as a legal
fact Lord Esher has told us that it became good —
or bad — law "principally through the ingenuity of
Lord Abinger in suggesting analogies in *Priestley* v.
Fowler." [139] As a fact it was grounded upon a series
of most questionable hypotheses.   There could not be,
so the law held, where master and servant are concerned,
any mutual liability not based on a personal fault of the
former, since the servant knowingly and willingly under-
took the risks of service.   But this is not only the merest
fiction of a peculiarly vicious kind.   It created also one
law of negligence for strangers and another, far less
stringent, where masters were concerned.[140] The results
involved were patently unjust and discriminated unduly;
and it was natural that the first efforts of the trade-

---

[136] Morgan *v.* Vale of Neath Ry. Co. (1865) L. R. 1 Q. B. 149.

[137] This point is well worked out in Mr. Hobson's *Work and
Wealth.*

[138] Priestley *v.* Fowler (1837) 3 M. & W. 1 at p. 7.

[139] Birrell, *Law of Employers' Liability,* p. 25.

[140] Cf. Webb, *History of Trade Unionism,* p. 350.

unions after their legal recognition should have been devoted to the destruction of the fellow-servant doctrine.[141] This, after much effort, they were able to accomplish in England by the Employers' Liability Act of 1880.[142] Judicial interpretation has moreover explained that, in this context, the maxim *volenti non fit iniuria* ought to mean in reality just nothing at all.[143] The work thus admirably begun was supplemented and completed in the Workmen's Compensation Acts of 1897 and 1906. The effect of that legislation is perfectly clear. In certain specified cases it imposes upon the employer the liability of providing compensation to a workman or the dependents of a workman who is either killed or injured in the course of his employment. It it noteworthy that this method of social insurance is not confined to England alone but, in some form or other, is common to the continent of Europe.[144]

In this country, however, much of the old legal attitudes has survived, and the situation has become complicated by problems of constitutional interpretation.[145] Such statutes, says Judge Smith,[146] "are in direct conflict with the fundamental rule of modern common law

141 The sequence Reform Act 1867, Trade Union Acts 1871–6, Employers' Liability Act 1880 is surely very significant; see Webb, *loc. cit.*

142 43 & 44 Vict. Ch. 42.

143 Smith *v.* Baker [1891] A. C. 325.

144 Mr. A. P. Higgins in his *Law of Employer's Liability* has discussed the continental attitude.

145 Mechem in 44 *Am. L. Rev.* 221, and Smith in 27 *Harv. L. Rev.* 235, 344, are very typical of this. Cf. the weighty remarks of Freund in 19 *Green Bag* 80, and 2 *Am. Lab. Leg. Rev.* 43; and of Lewis in 38 *Ann. Am. Acad. Pol. Sc.* 119. See also the remarkable judgment in Ives *v.* So. Buffalo Ry. Co. (1911) 201 N. Y. 271.

146 27 *Harv. L. Rev.* 238.

as to the ordinary requisites of a tort"; and he points out, that the modern conception is really akin to the medievalism which apportioned blame irrespective of motive. But it may be questioned whether the statutes were ever intended to throw any light upon the theory of torts. That at which they aim is simply, for social reasons, to secure the worker against the dangers of his employment in the belief, that it is more advantageous for the burden to fall upon the employer.[147] It does not base that burden upon tort at all. On the contrary it withdraws it from the ordinary concepts of law by making it statutory. It places a statutory clause — the provision, in certain cases, for accident — as one of the conditions a master must observe if he wishes to engage in business.[148] The liability is made to arise not from any tort upon the part of the master, but upon the inherent nature of the modern economic situation.[149] It is not claimed that the master ought to pay because he gets the benefit of his servants' works,[150] any more than under the old doctrine of common employment the judges would have argued, that the workers ought to pay because they had the privilege of being employed.

The fact is that eighty years have passed since *Priestley* v. *Fowler*, and our social ideas have not stood still in that interval. The state has been brought to ask itself how the safety of the workers and their families may be best assured, and it has returned its answer. It is un-

---

147 For more drastically adverse criticism of the principle see Mignault in 44 *Am. L. Rev.* 719; Hirschfeld in 13 *Jour. Soc. Comp. Leg.* 119; and seemingly, Prof. Dicey in *Law and Public Opinion*, pp. 281–2; cf. Holmes, J., in U. S. 463, 541.

148 Cf Pound, 25 *Int. Jour. of Ethics*, p. 1.

149 Just as special liabilities are attached to carriers, etc.

150 As Prof. Mechem seems to think, *op. cit.* 227, 241–2.

necessary to attempt to bring the theory under any of the old maxims of vicarious liability.[151] The dogma underlying it may be new or it may be old; we need not be greatly concerned either at its novelty or its antiquity. The question to which we have to reply is a very different one. The test of our rule is whether it affords the protection that is intended. Much of the real problem is obscured by discussion of a supposititious case of an individual employer and a free and independent workman — without real existence in the industrial world we know — and then asking, if the former is to be responsible for accidents where no fault is anywhere to be discovered, and if the logic of the law of torts is thereby to be destroyed. We cannot sacrifice social necessity to the logic of the law of torts. The crux of this problem is the economic need of preventing the cheapening of human life,[152] and to that end our law must shape itself. We need not fear very greatly that the imposition of such liability on building contractors, for example, will force them out of business;[153] for the cost of labor has a convenient habit of expressing itself in terms of price. Nor can we rest content with the suggestion of a distinguished jurist[154] that it is expedient to let accidental loss lie where it falls. That may be an admirable maxim in the case of a stricken millionaire; but it is of too hard consequence where the sufferer has needy dependents.

It seems, on the whole, a better policy to set our faces

[151] As Judge Smith is anxious to compel us to do. 27 *Harv. L. Rev.* 254.

[152] Cf. Hutchins & Harrison, *History of Factory Legislation,* 254 ff.

[153] Quinn *v.* Crimmings (1898) 171 Mass. 255, 258.

[154] Holmes, *The Common Law,* 94 ff.

firmly forward, and shape the character of our law by the ends it has to serve. In such an aspect, if we admit that the state has the right, on grounds of public policy, to condition the industrial process, it becomes apparent that the basis of the vicarious liability is not tortious at all; nor, since it is withdrawn from the area of agreement, is it contractual. It is simply a statutory protection the state chooses to offer its workers. Whether, as such, it so discriminates against the employing class, as to come within the scope of measures contemplated by the Fourteenth Amendment, is another and a very different question. If we believe that it is not an infringement of liberty to read its meaning in its social context,[155] we shall perhaps be in no doubt as to the rightness of a negative response. We shall then argue that no other possibility in reality exists at the present time. We have to minimize the loss consequent upon the needs of life. The principles of law must be subordinate to that effort.

VII

There seems no valid *a priori* reason why the operation of our principles should cease at that border where tort becomes crime. *Actus non facit reum nisi mens rea* may be admirable in a state of nature; but it will not fit the facts of a complex social structure. So that we need fear no difficulties at the outset. The case is of course obvious where the crime is performed upon specific authority,[156] or is that natural and inevitable consequence of the servant's business.[157] The real problems, as in

[155] 3 Green, *Coll. Works*, 379.

[156] U. S. *v.* Nunnemacher (1876) 7 Biss. 111.

[157] As in the case of bookseller's assistant dealing with a libellous publication. Wilson *v.* Rankin (1865) 6 B. & S. 208, *per* Cockburn, *C. J.*

the case of civil liability, arise where the doctrine of implied authority begins to pale its ineffectual fire before the difficulties it has to confront.

Everything, it is clear, depends upon the nature of the crime. We shall not easily, for instance, charge a corporation with murder; but if a company's servants, acting for their master's benefit, send a gatling gun mounted upon an armored train through a village at night,[158] it is necessary to enforce adequate penalties against the source of such a crime. Again, we have statutes regulating the sale of liquor which are notoriously difficult to enforce. It is found essential, in these cases, to insist on the full responsibility of the license if the law is to be of any avail.[159] Lord Alverstone, indeed, has endeavored to formulate certain canons by which the breach of law may be tested;[160] but they can hardly be said to have much practical worth. The point at issue in this class of crime is simply and surely the enforcement of the law, and it may generally be suggested that the necessities of the case do not admit of our inquiring too closely into the delicate niceties of the situation.[161] Society has not usually suffered from a reasonable vigilance towards saloon keepers. And the same rule holds good when we pass the narrow line from drink to cards.[162]

We must have our food protected; and that, irrespective of the vendor's motive. It is here not merely a question

---

[158] Lippmann, *Drift and Mastery*, p. 80.

[159] State *v.* Fagan (1909) 74 Atl. (Del.) 693.

[160] Emory *v.* Nolloth [1903] 2 K. B. 264.

[161] Cf. however, Com. *v.* Riley (1907) 196 Mass. 60.

[162] Crabtree *v.* Hole (1879) 43 J. P. 779; Bond *v.* Evans (1888) 21 Q. B. D. 249. The remarks of Stephen, J., on the strange decision in Newman *v.* Jones (1886) 17 Q. B. D. 132 are particularly noteworthy.

of whether knowledge on the master's part may be assumed,[163] or whether the provision of food is so dangerous an occupation as to require special diligence,[164] but simply that the consequences of the alternative to a stern treatment are too serious to be admissible.   Arguments as to the reality of a corporate mind [165] pale into insignificance before the problem of public health.   We are, here, beyond the stage where it is sufficient to know that reasonable care was exercised.   It is essentially the consequences of action with which we have to deal,[166] for where public policy has such vital ends to serve it cannot rest content with the easy fatalism of good intention.[167] We dare not risk the nullification of our needs.   We authorize the master to sell in set fashion, and if the law is broken he must take the consequences.[168]   Cases such as these must clearly stand upon a special footing. "Where the statute," says the court in an Irish case,[169] "creates a direct and unqualified duty, the person to perform the duty cannot escape under the doctrine of *mens rea*."   Protection were otherwise an impossible task.

Parallel with such a situation is the law in regard to

[163] Nelson *v.* Parkhill (1892) 20 Sc. Sess. Cas. 4th Series, p. 24; Brown *v.* Foot (1892) 66 L. T. N. S. 649.

[164] R. *v.* Dixon (1814) 3 M. & S. 11.

[165] Pearks *v.* Ward [1902] 2 K. B. 1; Chuter *v.* Freeth [1911] 2 K. B. 832.

[166] Cf. however, Kearley *v.* Taylor (1891) 65 L. T. N. S. 261 for a case where distinct disobedience to express orders was held an admissible defence.

[167] See the judgment in Hosford *v.* Mackey [1897] 2 Ir. 292; Lehman *v.* Dist. of Columbia (1902) 19 App. D. C. 217.

[168] See the very able judgment in State *v.* Kettelle (1892) 110 N. C. 560, and that in Com. *v.* Savery (1887) 145 Mass. 212.

[169] Fitzgerald *v.* Hosford (1900) 2 Ir. Rep. 391. Cf. the judgment of Channell, J., in Anglo-American Oil Co. *v.* Manning [1908] 1 K. B. 536.

libel. It has been long and well settled that a master
— in the absence of statutes to the contrary — is responsible for the criminal libels committed by his servant without his knowledge or consent.[170] Those who
have the control of books and newspapers in their hands
have a weapon too powerful to bear no more responsibility than that of guilty intent. It is not merely, as
Tenterden, C. J., argued, that the proprietor of a book-
shop or of a newspaper ought to pay because he enjoys
the profits of the enterprise,[171] the fact is, that damage
by publication is very largely an irreparable damage,[172]
and that the law must protect the interest of personality
as best it may.[173]

Nor ought the corporation to avoid responsibility on
the ground that it is mindless.[174] Such a view has long
been regarded as untenable. No one would dream of
accusing a corporation of adultery, but there are offenses
clearly to be attributed to it where the act is directly
performed by its servants. "We think," said a strong
court,[175] "that a corporation may be criminally liable
for certain offences of which a specific intent may be a
necessary element. There is no more difficulty in im-
puting to a corporation a specific intent in criminal proceedings than in civil. A corporation cannot be arrested
and imprisoned in either civil or criminal proceedings;
but its property may be taken either in compensation

[170] R. *v.* Williams (1774) Lofft, 759; R. *v.* Topham (1791) 4
T. R. 126; R. *v.* Alexander (1829) Mood. & M. 437.

[171] As is well shown in the Mylius case.

[172] R. v. Gutch (1829) Mood. & M. 433.

[173] The limitation of 6 & 7 Vict. Ch. 96 should be noted.

[174] Holt, C. J., in 12 Mod. 559 (1702); State *v.* Great Works
Milling & Mfg. Co. (1841) 20 Me. 41.

[175] Telegram Newspaper Co. *v.* Commonwealth (1899) 172 Mass.
294.

for a private wrong, or as punishment for a public
wrong." Most people would agree that common sense
is on the side of such an attitude. It would be intolerable if corporate enterprise did not imply corporate responsibility. It is the determining factor in the action
of the servants who commit the crime on its behalf; so,
in a long series of cases, the rule has been extended from
the analogy of the individual.[176] We have not yet, indeed, been able to make criminal negligence extend to the
point of manslaughter;[177] though perhaps it may be
suggested that with the admission by an Australian court
of corporate *mens rea*,[178] there are real possibilities of
progress. It is not until we have admitted the necessity
of completely equating group-action with individual action in its social aspects that we can remain content.
It is, indeed, a happy augury, that this line of thought
should have been declared constitutional by the Supreme
Court of the United States.[179] It is difficult to take very
seriously the plea of Mr. Baty, that "even if the results
of summary process are not very serious, they involve
in the minds of ignorant persons a certain amount of
discredit." [180] Law is not made to suit the wrong notions
of ignorant persons. The real problem is simply whether
we dare afford to lose such hold as we possess over the
action of groups in the affairs of social life — the more
particularly in an age predominantly associational in

[176] Misfeasance in R. v. Brim. & G. Ry. Co. (1842) 3 Q. B. 223;
obstruction in R. v. G. N. Ry. Co. (1846) 9 Q. B. 315; under the
Lotteries Act in Hawke v. Hulton [1909] 2 K. B. 93 are typical
examples.

[177] R. v. G. W. Laundry Co. (1900) 12 Manitoba, 66; Union
Colliery Co. v. Queen (1900) 31 Can. Sup. Ct. 81.

[178] R. v. Panton, 14 Vict. L. Rep. 936.

[179] N. Y. C. & H. Ry. Co. v. U. S. (1908) 212 U. S. 481.

[180] Baty, *op. cit.* 219.

character.[181] It is, for the most part, a commercial
problem consequent upon the dissolution of individual
industrial action.[182] Its solution in the future must depend upon our manner of interpreting the business
functions.[183]

VIII

What has been here attempted is, in fact, a part of
the sociological analysis of law. We do not sufficiently
realize how greatly our legal ideas have been affected by
their peculiar relation to the history of landed property.
Primitive jurisprudence concerns itself, for the most
part, with the protection of individual rights. Certain
men are blameworthy; they have invaded the property
of other men. It is then necessary to obtain protection
against them. That ancient but tenacious individualism
is in truth the coronation of anarchy; and the time comes
when a spirit of community supersedes it. But either
because that notion is prematurely born, or else because
it is inadequately translated into terms of actual life,
it results in the cramping of single-handed effort. It
passes away; and the consequence is the beatification of
laissez-faire. But it becomes increasingly evident that
society be governed on the principles of commercial
nihilism. To assume that freedom and equality consist
in unlimited competition is simply to travesty the facts.

181 This is especially true of the United States. Cf. De Tocqueville's remarks in 2 *Democ. in America,* 97 ff. (trans. Reeve, 1889)
which are even more accurate at the present time.

182 Perhaps also of great ecclesiastical corporations, cf. Brown *v.*
Montreal (1874) 6 P. C. 157. Something of the same issue is involved
in First Church of Christ, Scientist, Applic. of (1897) 6 Pa. Dist.
Ct. 745, and the similar application in 205 Pa. 543.

183 Cf. Mr. Justice Brandeis in his *Business a Profession, passim.*

We come once more to an age of collective endeavor. We begin the re-interpretation of law in the terms of our collective needs.

Novelty for our principles, we may not in some sort deny; though, in truth, if it is by history that we are to be judged a plethora of antiquarianism might not be wanting.[184]   But it is on different ground that we take our stand.   It is our business to set law to the rhythm of modern life.   It is the harmonization of warring interests with which we are concerned.   How to evolve from a seeming conflict the social gain it is the endeavor of law to promote — this is the problem by which we are confronted.   We would base our legal decisions not on the facts of yesterday, but on the possibilities of to-morrow.   We would seek the welfare of society in the principles we enunciate.   We have been told on the highest authority that no other matter is entitled to be weighed.[185]

[184] Cf. the articles of Dean Wigmore cited above.
[185] Holmes, J., in 8 *Harv. L. Rev.* 9.

THE POLITICAL IDEAS OF JAMES I
*[1]

I

THE study of political ideas has been unduly neglected
in English-speaking countries. We have no such history as
Gierke's magistral survey of German associations, though
our group-life is even more prodigal of riches than that
which he recounted. No English monograph exists comparable with his study of Althusius, though the thought
of Locke, to take only a single example, provides the
materials for a not less magnificent analysis. Two brilliant volumes of Figgis, a classic preface of Maitland,
some penetrating criticism of Leslie Stephen, a solid essay
by Gooch —these represent almost the whole of what may
be rated as of first importance. The kind of work so
admirably done in France by Henri Michel and Dreyfus-
Brissac has so far found no imitators either in England
or America. It is a curious negligence, for the history
of political ideas is so closely related to that history of
political structure in which Anglo-Saxon writers excel
as to make explanation or excuse at least doubly difficult.
Nor should an America that is plethoric in political experiment be backward in tracing its affiliations; Harrington and Locke and Montesquieu thought to the purpose
of a later generation.

* Reprinted from the *Political Science Quarterly*, Vol. XXXIV,
No. 2.
1 *The Political Works of James I*. Edited by Charles Howard
McIlwain. Cambridge, Harvard University Press, 1918—cxi, 354 pp.

Professor McIlwain's volume is in the right tradition. It is, he tells us, the first of a series in which he and his colleagues propose to reprint those volumes that most of us have hoped to see one day in a bookseller's catalogue. Nothing is so greatly needed as to make accessible the classic texts of the Renaissance and Reformation. The existing copies of Althusius' book cannot exceed a score in number; only one copy, at least, has found its way into an American public library. The *De Concordantia Catholica* of the great Cardinal of Cusa, the *Vindiciae* of Duplessis Mornay, the *De Justa Potestate* of Rossaeus, — these and books like these we must have at our elbow if we are to understand the foundations of the modern state. After three centuries we ought, at least, to make vaunt that we have outstripped the massive complications of Melchior Goldast; yet Professor McIlwain tells us that later volumes must depend upon the success of his own. And if we are to be honest, we must admit that this postpones indefinitely the likelihood of their appearance, for we lack that *gelehrtes publicum* to whom such a volume is an event. Yet it is books like these we must have if historical science is to attain its ripest fruits.

Professor McIlwain merely reprints the works of James from the standard edition of 1616, but he adds thereto a preface of some hundred quarto pages. An Englishman may be allowed the remark that it is the most admirable contribution to its subject that has been made by an American scholar. It is at every point learned and exact, and it is rarely indeed that it is not convincing. Its main value lies not so much in the appraisal of James' ideas, to which little attention is given, as in the attempt to set them in their historic perspective. Something of this, indeed, Dr. Figgis had accomplished

in his *Divine Right of Kings;* but to him the theories of
James were a relatively unimportant incident, where to
Professor McIlwain they serve to demonstrate that England was plunged into the midstream of European political thought.   His narrative is, in fact, a full demonstration of the reason why, in the great counter-movement to
reform, England, together with Holland, was alone able
to avoid the primrose path of bureaucratic absolutism.
Little of what Professor McIlwain has to say is actually
new, and he rarely attempts its evaluation.   But his insistence upon More and Campanella as masters of the
controversial art is particularly arresting, and it forms
a welcome antithesis to the conventional picture of two
dreamy idealists weaving the vision of a fabulous empire.
Nor must we miss the illuminating appendix upon the
political literature of the Tudors.   No one acquainted
with that literature can doubt that Professor McIlwain
is right when he argues that political theory in England
begins with William Tyndale.   Fortescue is concerned
with *Politik;* it is Tyndale's *Obedience of a Christian
Man* which lays the foundation of an English *staatslehre.*
That is a valuable note to strike, for it rightly emphasizes
at once the roots from which the modern English state
has sprung and the main political problem which it is
the business of each age to answer.

II

That problem is the ground of obedience.   The
spectacle of the voluntary submission of vast numbers to
a small portion of themselves is an arresting one; for,
as Hume remarked, ultimate force is always on the side
of the governed.   The problem of securing unity in the
state is always typical of an age of crisis; and it was to

solve it that the thinkers of the Counter-Reformation above all struggled. Luther had broken into pieces the Christian Commonwealth of the medieval period; the religious wars had completed the disintegration of feudalism which the nationalist tendencies of the previous century had begun. "With the idea of the Commonwealth" — Professor McIlwain is speaking of the new state described by Bodin — "had come the need of re-stating the relations of its parts with one another, in particular, those of the King with his subjects." It was no easy task. The period of the Counter-Reformation shows everywhere a passionate worship of unity; even the *Politiques* embrace toleration on the low ground of expediency. "Diversity in an age of uniformity," says Professor McIlwain, "inevitably brings persecution, and the acceptance of uniformity as a principle means that each party demands the supremacy of its own doctrines." The questions thus raised are amongst the profoundest that have troubled mankind. How can a Catholic give Elizabeth her due allegiance when Pius V has urged her dethronement as a heretic? What, in an age when Augsburg had consecrated at least one heresy, is to be the nature of the papal power? What is the bond by which the new state is to maintain its hold upon its subjects? The problem did not confront the Romanists alone. Presbyterianism, at least in its Scottish development, insisted upon the separation of the "two kingdoms," and the allegiance of its adherents to a secular sovereign could never be entire. The Calvinists under Henry III found themselves preaching the sovereignty of the people and under Henry of Navarre the divine right of kings. Yet each group of thinkers is so convinced of its own rightness that, Robert Brown and William the Silent

apart, the ideal of liberty of conscience, as a human
right, is for them largely without meaning. The effort
is to rewin the unity which the facts have thrown into
jeopardy.

It is from that effort that the chief hypotheses of
modern politics are born. The divine right of kings,
the sovereignty of the people, the social contract, the conception of power as by its nature a trust, are all of
them answers to the questions of why and in what degree
men must obey their rulers. The Counter-Reformation
is thus the parent at once of liberal doctrine and absolutism. The persecuted, whether Jesuit or Puritan, become the inevitable creators of principles that make for
the redistribution of political power. They are driven
to revolutionary hypotheses as the necessary condition
of survival. Men like Hotman and Buchanan deny the
divinity of kings simply because they fear that kings will
uproot their faith. Power, so they urge, is dependent
upon conditions and the people must determine the nature
of those conditions. The retort is obvious when a
Protestant is on the throne; and Boucher and Rossaeus
do not fail to make it. For if power is ultimately in
the people and if the object of the state is virtue, clearly
enough the people will not tolerate a heretic upon the
throne, for his faith is incompatible with a virtue which
is defined by the decrees of Trent.

Only one answer was possible to such an outlook, and
that was the assertion of the self-sufficiency of the civil
power. Separation of church and state is only one side
of that hypothesis, for it was still possible and still
widely deemed desirable to put the state in place of the
medieval church and make its boundaries coextensive with
the limits of mind. That, at least, is the theory which

eventually lies at the bottom of practices like those of
Whitgift and Bancroft and Laud. But there were at
least two groups of thinkers for whom such acceptance
was impossible. No Catholic could admit that obedience
was due, at least in religious matters, to a heretic. No
Presbyterian could accept the implicit Byzantinism of
the Act of Supremacy; nor did what Maitland termed the
genial "etceteration" of Elizabeth make their problem
in any wise easier. Kings, for both, might rule by divine
right, but it was only so long as they confined themselves
to the secular domain.

It thus seemed that the problem of unity confronted
from the outset an impossible dilemma. The Anglican
state could, from at least half its members, exact an allegiance at no moment undivided or entire; and Elizabeth,
as Cecil argued, seemed, therefore, driven into persecution in order to maintain her political position. A member of the Anglican Church gave his Queen more than
Catholic or Puritan gave. For him there was no corner
of the field over which her *imperium* did not extend. But
each royal order demanded close scrutiny alike from
Puritan and Romanist. Their obedience had in it an
element of contingency which to the upholders of unity
made it both doubtful and dangerous.

The problem had clearly to be met; and the work of
showing the noncontentious character of the papal power
is mainly a construction of the Jesuits. Here, indeed,
as elsewhere, they were adapters rather than originators.
They owe much to Buchanan and Melville, more perhaps
than they would own. But in their hands political theory
was more finely wrought and more subtly fashioned than
by any thinker of the time except Althusius. Professor
McIlwain admirably explains the character of their effort.

He insists upon their connection with the schools of Presbyterian thought. "Brought into conflict," he writes, "with the power of secular governments that recognized no exemption from their oversight, the Jesuits, who had become the chief champions of the Catholic Church and the Papacy, were now forced as the Calvinists had already been to develop doctrines of a limitation of royal power in the interests of the people, on the one hand, and on the other of a separation of the fields of ecclesiastical and secular jurisdiction." They aimed, in fact, a vital blow at the divine right of kings; and works like Parsons' *Conference on the Next Succession* became textbooks for democratic writers. But on the ecclesiastical side their task was an impossible one. They had to prove the legitimate character of a papacy which would not surrender one jot or title of its ancient prerogative, and it was this which led Bellarmine to the theory of the indirect power. It is a vital doctrine, for in it, even if somewhat concealed by the polemic of the time, lie the real foundations of international law. Broadly speaking, the pope is regarded as standing to his subjects in England as the king of France to Frenchmen resident abroad. He has, that is to say, a reserve power of protection which maltreatment, or potential maltreatment, may call into play. Clearly, therefore, the papal attitude to a foreign sovereign will depend upon the religious laws he may feel constrained to operate.

It is a doctrine that brings comfort to men of diverse views. It enabled Parsons to lead the party of no compromise on the ground that the occupancy of the throne by a heretic immediately brings the reserve power into play. In enabled men like Roger Widdrington to argue that the loyalty of Catholics is, in theory at least, un-

assailable, since even by the Jesuits the life of the state is
admittedly divorced from that of the church.   The doctrine, of course, is the coronation of opportunism, and
Bishop Andrewes did not hesitate to urge that to argue
for potential power, the exercise of which is dependent
upon conduct of which the pope only can be judge, is destructive of the whole theory of the two kingdoms.   The
Catholic, in fact, is for the Protestant not less a traitor
because theory can put his power of treason a stage
further back.   The only comment we can make is the
inference drawn by Professor McIlwain.   The Jesuits
were not toying with principle in the sense of caring for
it lightly.   Their motive throughout was the recovery
of the papal kingdom, and if they suited their statesmanship to the hard demands of necessity, only the most bitter
will blame them, for they worked with the halter around
their necks.   "A sixteenth century Jesuit," as Professor
McIlwain remarks, "might be a traitor, but his is not the
character of a trimmer."   He might suit his sails to the
varying winds, but he had no doubt whatever of his harbor.

Certain at least it is that the work of the Jesuits in
England precipitated the controversy which produced
the main body of political theory in England for a generation.   They split the English Catholics into a party
whose attitude resembles that of the *Politiques* in France
and one which had the single ideal of restoring at any
cost the pope to his ancient kingdom.   They fought, as
any one who reads Christopher Bagshaw's *True Relation*
can see, with a bitterness that not even the antagonism
between Protestant and Catholic surpassed.   The ex-
tremists were converts to Rome and, like all converts,
optimistic.   Parsons himself seems never to have doubted
that England would lie prostrate beneath the heel of

Rome, could Philip but safely land his army. Naturally enough, it was to this party that the popes themselves inclined; and the victory of the Jesuits over the seculars virtually involved the resort of Elizabeth to persecution and the growing emergence of the idea of divine right. The indirect power came almost at once to involve the deposition of heretical kings; and the problem in England was more acute for all parties by reason of the obvious possibility that the succession might be disputed. And at a time when, in the face of the theory of separate powers, Elizabeth, despite her "etceteration," was most patently supreme governor of the church, it seemed clear enough that a thorough-going definition of allegiance was necessary when the stake was the English Kingdom. The Jesuits lay at the back of treason and plot. Their very determination was the parent of the divine right of kings.

The situation, in fact, was akin to that of Luther. When a divine institution refuses self-reformation, the divinity of the means of cure very obviously demands its proof. So Luther asserted the divine right of the German princes and, perhaps as an after-thought, the affinity of Rome with Anti-Christ. That Elizabeth, two generations later, had a dilemma to face hardly less tragic in nowise eased the Catholic position. "The historian," as Professor McIlwain says, "ought to see a clash of irreconcilable principles; a contest for absolute power over an undefined field by two *jure divino* authorities, the King and the Supreme Pontiff." There could be no settlement in an age where diversity was sin and unity the most admirable of virtues. It needed the bitter experience of civil war at home and foreign conflict abroad to make men willing to explore the possibilities of that toleration for which stout citizens of London like Leonard Busher

and forgotten enthusiasts like Samuel Richardson so
nobly contended. Even then it needed the drastic ur-
gency of William III to persuade an unwilling people to
the experiment.

III

It is in such a background that Professor McIlwain
sets James I and his ideas. Throughout his life the
effort of James is no more than a variation upon a single
theme. Its single virtue is that consistency against
which Sir Henry Maine uttered an admirable, if ironic,
warning; and, indeed, the dangers of consistency have
rarely been more evident than in the thorough-going
fashion in which James attempts the application of his
doctrine. Nor can there be any doubt as to the meaning
of James' absolutism. It was never altered by contact
with new environment, though as Welwood points out,
it may have originated in the circumstances of his youth.
Melville and Buchanan were likely by repulsion to con-
vince James of the nobility of his office; and the fate
of his parents may well have attracted him to theories
which, ideally at least, put kingship beyond the censure
of the mass of men. The divine right of kings meant to
James exactly what it said. "Kings," he wrote, "are
the breathing images of God upon earth," and he strove
to give the hard substance of fact to this conception.
He admitted no limitations. Even an evil king was sent
of God to punish his people. Inferior office was derived
from the royal will. Subjects had duties without rights.
Law was the affirmation of the king's desire. The power
of Parliament was the duty to offer its advice when asked.
And it is clear enough from James' relations with the
Puritans that he welcomed no doctrine and no institution

of which the underlying idea suggested even a penumbra of independence. Crown and state were interchangeable terms.

Professor McIlwain points out how much of Scoto-Romanism has gone into these conceptions, and it is clear enough that they are irreconcilable even with Tudor constitutionalism. They rest ultimately upon a basis of feudal theory that had already suffered disintegration under the forces of sixteenth-century nationalism and of which the obsolescence is made manifest in the Act of 1660 for the abolition of feudal tenures. They are incompatible with a constitution which had already witnessed the deposition of two kings and treasured up fundamental law over a period of four hundred years. Indeed, as Professor McIlwain says, the real root of James' difficulties lies in the fact that not even twenty years of difficult government enabled him to understand the English constitution. *The Trew Law of Free Monarchies* is his Bible, but neither Puritans nor lawyers could find comfort therein. He presupposed a people incapable of self-government and thereby misunderstood the political instinct of his generation. He was an absolutist amidst a people whose essential genius lay in the relativity of mitigation. The result was conflict and inevitable conflict; nor did the vigorous antagonism of his Parliaments teach him the meaning therein implied.

James' theory needs discussion from two angles. Broadly speaking, he was, in the first place, urging a special theory of prerogative. It was a dangerous effort, for prerogative has a history; and obstinate, if pedantic, lawyers were at his side to urge upon James that its meaning was to be discovered in its origins. Prerogative, as Professor McIlwain says, may have been high, but it worked within limits reasonably capable of effective definition. It was essentially a reserve power, to be used, in Blackstone's excellent phrase, "out of the ordinary course of common law." Prerogative, in fact, begins where the law ends; and it is over the vague hinterland of confused disturbance that sovereign prerogative is intended to act. No one can read Staunton or Sir Thomas Smith, who, after all, stand outside the controversy of James' reign and have no case to plead, without seeing that to them the essence of prerogative is just this admission of the supreme control of law. It is, indeed, the final case against James' theory that his opponents, whether lawyers like Coke and Selden, or parliamentarians like those who drew up the protest of 1621, should have used no argument not to be found in the precedents. Novelty begins only with the Long Parliament, and it is the natural offspring of royal, but impossible, demands. James thought of prerogative as identical with sovereignty and took it unto himself. But the fundamental idea that the sovereign power was the fusion of noble and popular wills with the king's determination had already been sanctioned by the practice of Elizabeth herself; and when James argued against that view, he was already too late. The limitation he admitted — the duty incumbent upon a king to care for the welfare of his subjects — was meaningless in the light of his own reign and that of his son. Parliament saw that a will limited only by its own sense of right is in fact not limited at all, and it responded in the natural fashion of men who had ancient and venerated documents capable of being interpreted in their support. The struggle which ensued was, as Professor McIlwain remarks, "in all its stages a contest between law and absolute power." What the issue might have been if

James had been a great statesman, willing to use men
like Bacon to translate the doctrines of Dr. Cowell into
the Byzantinism of fact they demanded, we cannot tell.
It is at least certain that his incapacity laid the secure
foundations of constitutional government.

IV

The constitutional struggle of James' reign is the
most important consequence of his ideas; yet, so far as
the theory of politics is concerned, it is secondary in significance to the controversy which arose out of his attempt to enforce an oath of allegiance upon his Catholic
subjects.   This effort is, in reality, the positive side of
Elizabeth's negative policy.   She did not attempt the
definition of disloyalty; it was only when book or act
revealed it that suppression followed.   James went a
step beyond.   The oath of allegiance was intended to
divide Catholics into those who could be trusted and
those who would refuse to admit the fullness of his power.
Professor McIlwain's discussion of this controversy is
by far the ablest, as it is the most original part of his
book.   It is difficult, indeed, to admit his view that the
oath is a step toward the acceptance of the two powers
and thus a stage in the history of toleration, for James'
attitude toward the Puritans and the zeal with which
he embraced the Anglo-Catholic cause show that he was
still an eager adherent of the ideal of uniformity.   As
Professor McIlwain himself says, James' "views of the
danger of hersey are in no respect different from those
of the Holy Office"; and in the general background of his
ideas, that implies the principles of territoriality in religion, which is at bottom logically fatal to dissent of
any kind.   The oath confirmed the Church of England

as the national church, and its implications are responsible for that frenzied assault upon nonconformity which reached its administrative zenith in the Clarendon Code.

James, in fact, taught the Anglican Church the value of political doctrine as a means to political victory; and he thereby sanctioned that policy of exclusion which made impossible comprehension on the one side and toleration on the other. A good Catholic may well have denied, as Widdrington and Barclay denied, the temporal power of Rome; but it is difficult in the extreme to see how he could in good faith have promised, as the fourteenth section of the enacting statute demands, not to bring converts to the church he believed to be the only church of Christ. Unquestionably, as Professor McIlwain argues, the object of the oath was to widen the gap between the Jesuits and their rivals, and to a large extent it succeeded in its aim. But the mere abstention of James from claiming religious supremacy in the oath, at a time when he was laboring to identify the pope with antiChrist, is hardly opening the path to more tolerant ways. The act may not touch the spiritual supremacy of Rome; what it does may be, as Professor McIlwain says, "to deny emphatically that the Pope can ever override this division [between secular and religious power] by exercising the secular power of deposition under pretext of a spiritual end." But James was himself here defining the boundaries of the spiritual merely to suit his own convenience; and, as Professor McIlwain himself admits, he was making his Catholic subjects accept his definition in terms so offensive as necessarily to pain any Catholic with a regard for the religious position of Rome.

This attitude, at least, seems to be confirmed by the debate which followed. The Catholic party was divided

at once into two great classes; and later discussion has
only confirmed the division. The controversy is, at
bottom, the most fundamental of all debates until our
own time — the problem of the temporal power of Rome;
for it is only with the birth of scientific theology in the
nineteenth century that we have the final argument for
the supremacy of the state. Catholics like Bellarmine,
who were convinced of the divine character of the Roman
mission and the nobility of any effort which secured its
triumph, could be answered only by a rigid historical
examination of the Roman claims. Those who, like
Widdrington, denied the temporal power of the papacy
and thus admitted that the oath was justifiable, were
in fact cutting at the root of that which gave Rome her
decisive influence in the affairs of men. And, for the
seventeenth century, the oath was a focal point in the
whole theory of the Counter-Reformation. "England,"
as Professor McIlwain points out, "was universally recognized then as the one corner of Christendom in which there
was still hope of checking the onward moving tide of the
Catholic reaction." This it is which explains the eager and
widespread interest which statesmen and scholars alike
could take in the debate. It was no unimportant task to
break lance with a king; and a war of pamphlets in which
James and Bellarmine, Casaubon and Du Perron, Widdrington and Parsons, were the protagonists, could hardly
fail of illumination. Nothing, certainly, in this epoch
throws so vivid a light upon the stakes at issue in the
struggle to which Luther had given birth.

Professor McIlwain gives us a careful analysis of the
historical succession of the pamphlets which, if less full
than the admirable account of Krebs, is amply sufficient
for the purpose. The argument on both sides is clear

enough. The position of James and his adherents, whether in England or in France, is that the purpose of the oath is the securing of civil allegiance. In the case of men like Widdrington there is no desire to belittle the spiritual power of Rome. Rather is there, not seldom with a tone reminiscent of Wyclif's teaching, an urgent sense that her greatness depends upon her willingness to free herself from the dangers of temporal interference. But suppose her insistent in claiming the right of such interference, and Widdrington goes on to deny at once its historicity and its value in the modern world. It is, in fact, the parent of political confusion and, almost in the language of the *Politiques* a generation before, Widdrington insists upon the self-sufficiency of the civil power and the dangerous tumult involved in the view that it should, if need be, perish for religion's sake. There is a clear notion throughout his argument that, after all, the roots of obedience are in the individual mind, that unlimited commands on one side or the other are bound to result in forcing disaster. The reader of it can hardly fail at times to be reminded of Newman's famous *Letter to the Duke of Norfolk* and again of that letter from Tyrrell to the Father-General of the Jesuits which is, perhaps, the ablest analysis of the psychological background of government in the whole range of English literature. Widdrington occupies the same ground relative to James and Bellarmine as Newman to Gladstone and Manning. He is anxious to minimize claims on both sides that moderation may result in an equitable adjustment. Professor McIlwain does him no more than justice when he insists upon "the remarkable keenness of his criticism and the force of his language." Not even Bellarmine himself was capable of more effective utterance.

It is difficult not to believe that the real strength of
James' position, his possession of force apart, lay in
the support afforded to him by the moderate Catholics.
Yet there was able argument from his Protestant adherents. His own efforts, as Professor McIlwain says,
would hardly have been noticed had his position been less
dignified; but the writings of Casaubon and Andrews and
Donne were not unworthy of their opponents. Mainly,
their effort is to show the unreality of a claim to loyal
allegiance which still admits the presence of a power outside; and they argue, with no little show of historic
justice behind them, the incompatibility of royal government with the pretensions of Rome. Nor does their effort
end with the contemporary character of the debate. The
immense volumes of Baronius were intended as nothing
so much as an answer to the Protestant interpretation of
early Christian history; wherefore Isaac Casaubon must
be set to analyze it, page by page and fact by fact, that
the learned may see in what unscholarly fashion the
claims of Rome are vindicated. The *Convocation Book*
of Bishop Overall was obviously drawn up in the heat
of this contest. It not only, as Professor McIlwain
says, "made an explicit denial of all the grounds on
which those claims were based, and of all the theories to
which they gave rise," but it proved to Archbishop Laud
"the supremacy of Kings and chief civil magistrates above
the High Priest from the creation to the end of the
Jewish estate," and Overall does not conceal that it is
the identification of Rome with anti-Christ that is his
main concern. Even when, in 1622, James set Laud to
answer the sophistries of Father Fisher it was to these
arguments that the prelate went for his main support.

The most brilliant of James' adversaries lay, however,

not in Rome but Paris.   Four years after the dagger of
Ravaillac had ended the great dreams of Henry IV the
States-General met for the last time before the Revolution.   Paris, as always, was ill-disposed to Ultramontane
theory; and its *cahier* had suggested the need of an oath
whereby the "impious and detestable" doctrine of the
right of deposition might be condemned by officials and
ecclesiastics.   Clearly enough, its adoption would have
raised in France a warfare of pamphlets not less acute
than that already raging; and the underlying Gallican-
ism of the French Church might well have rendered the
debate both dangerous and bitter.   Cardinal du Perron
was, therefore, delegated to soothe the anger of the
Third Estate.   The man who had already disquieted the
profound Protestantism of Casaubon was well fitted for
the task.   A convert to Rome, his memory was unfathom-
able, his dialectical power unsurpassed, and if his learning, as Andrews was later to show, left not a few loop-
holes for antagonists, it was yet profound enough to
raise no question of his fitness for the office.   It was with
one eye upon James and England that he wrote.   Virtually the oath condemns the church and must thus prove
the parent of schism.   It would create great conflict
between the demands of the state and the claims of conscience.   It is thus a seed which when sown is like to
destroy that union of church and throne in France upon
which the unity of the kingdom depends; and Perron
even argued that this was not the least motive by which
James himself was moved.   It was useless for Miron to
answer that the oath was a civil safeguard against the
religious cloak under which assassination was fostered.
The Third Estate might grumble, but the Council for-
bade discussion of the oath; and Perron's argument

alone survived to demand response from James and his adherents. The result was James' *Remonstrance for the Right of Kings,* perhaps the ablest of his works and a clear defence of his original position that the indirect power of Rome in logic spells royal dependence on the papacy.

It remained for a lawyer who stood between the claims of Rome and England to sum up the debate in a fashion of which the spirit stands nearest to our own day. Barclay's *De Potestate Papae* not merely influenced those Catholics whom the debate till 1609 had left in hesitation, but, as Professor McIlwain remarks, is "one of the most effective presentations against the temporal claims of the Pope." The book, indeed, did for the seventeenth century something of the work accomplished by Döllinger's *The Pope and the Council* in the great infallibilist controversy. It caused many, said the Archpriest Birkhead, "to stagger about the oath." The discussion is valuable not so much for any novel elements that it contributes, as for its clear perception, and that from the standpoint of a convinced Catholic, of the evils of the temporal power. Barclay saw without difficulty that if the Roman cause were upheld, the result would practically make the ecclesiastical world an *imperium in imperio.* The supposed papal control over kings, in any save the spiritual sense of prayer for the sinner, he stoutly denies from lack of scriptural authority. That, of course, upon which Barclay pinned his faith was the complete division of secular and religious worlds — a point of view which, logically worked out, would have cut at the root of James' own position. Bellarmine's answer to Barclay reasserts the logical necessity of unity and so discovers the apex of world-power in Rome. But restatement is not response; and though Bellarmine may have satisfied his own intelligence, he did not quiet the fears of the Catholic conscience in England. For, after all, not only had they an imperative desire for peace, not only were they, as 1588 had shown, most fiercely conscious of their nationality, but the picture of a church, as Barclay drew it, deriving its strength from the unearthly splendor of the spirit, could not but make an eager appeal where political necessity added thereto an attractiveness which spelt domestic comfort.

With the opening of the Thirty Years' War, the struggle was transferred from the arena of the mind; and material and economic exhaustion drove both parties to a compromise which it is doubtful if they would otherwise have made. The inevitable result was the slow development of the secular state. Uniformity proved to be too costly an ideal, and doctrines of right gave place to doctrines of expediency. It is not at all clear, as Dr. Figgis has insisted, that the result is unallowed gain, yet the vindication of the right to be wrong which is implied in this evolution is perhaps not less valuable than what has been lost. What was involved was, of course, the necessity of toleration. Men do not urge either that Transubstantiation or the Thirty-Nine Articles are not doctrines for which it would be worth while to die; but they are driven by experience to the admission that this is a question upon which difference of opinion is not merely possible but also possible without penalty. Sooner or later, that toleration makes the state neutral and thence passes logically into indifference. The passion for uniformity breeds persecution; persecution, so far from destroying, seems almost to provoke diversity of outlook; diversity of outlook is in turn the parent of knowledge. The controversy which the acts and writings of James produced is, in fact, the necessary prelude to modern freedom.

v

It is also more. It was fought upon an issue that is far from dead. The experience it engendered forced men to admit that it is a mistake to propagate religious creeds by force. Westphalia meant that the Roman Church would never again exert decisive political influence. But the passion for unity did not die; rather was it transferred to the sphere of the secular state. The churches have had to struggle against the control of the state in a fashion hardly different from that in which the states of the Middle Ages fought against the dominion of Rome; nor can they as yet be said to have succeeded. The Oxford Movement, the rise of the Free Church in Scotland, the Vatican controversy of 1874, the *Kulturkampf*, are all of them protests of a church which refuses, like the Reformation Church, to regard itself as the creature of an alien body. Nor has the state hesitated to use in its turn the doctrine of the indirect power. The famous Free Church of Scotland case is nothing so much as the assertion by the state that where property is dependent upon dogma, the secular courts will constitute themselves the judges of its disposition and that without regard to the basic tenets of the association involved. The state, in fact, constitutes itself the ultimate reserve power in a manner at no point dissimilar from that of Rome three centuries ago; and it may yet again become true, as it was true in the seventeenth century, that the protests of organized religion will break down the fabric of the sovereign state. Certainly the problem of voluntary associations in their connection with the political organ is the most urgent that confronts us.

Nor is this all. Such external relationships present a problem about which, in the perspective of recent political theory, there is no special reason to despair. But the internal relations of the state present questions for inquiry that suggest a singular resemblance to those of the Stuart time. We are no longer, at least in theory, dependent for our political decisions upon the will of a single man, even though the number upon whom resolution seems to rest is, in an ultimate analysis, curiously small. But while it has proved reasonably easy, at least since 1829, to maintain religious toleration, political toleration we have not yet secured. "There are in our day," wrote Lord Acton in 1877, "many educated men who think it right to persecute." The national state, at least, has thought itself emancipated from the need to tolerate dissent; and we penalize heterodox opinion in politics hardly less cheerfully than heresy was penalized in the Middle Ages. In affairs of state, in fact, we do not as yet admit that the duty of the individual is to contribute his best personality to the common good. Rather do we insist by government enactment that personality shall flow along certain preconceived channels. Yet that is in truth to destroy the uniqueness in which the essence of personality consists. It is to pursue exactly that image of uniformity against which the liberal thinkers of the Counter-Reformation were struggling. No state can be free, which penalizes thought. To make political authority commensurate with the bounds of mind, is to misread the history of a thousand years. For if liberty is not the protection of an initiative which, as Mr. Graham Wallas has pointed out, must be continuous if it is to be vital, it is not worth the cost of attainment. Yet this is an historical truth we have still to learn.

It is herein that work such as that of Professor Mc-Ilwain possesses its especial import. No man can realize the bearing of what Bellarmine and Widdrington, Andrewes and Du Perron were trying to teach, without a more exact understanding of the problems of our time. Politics are not merely vulgar, in Seeley's admirable phrase, unless they are liberalized by history; they are, in fact, in large part unintelligible. For there is a real sense in which the problems of politics are perennial, and if the answer of each generation is different, it yet deposits a tradition which determines the environment of our next response. Nothing is today more greatly needed than clarity upon ancient notions. Sovereignty, liberty, authority, personality — these are the words of which we want alike the history and the definition; or rather, we want the history because its substance is in fact the definition. No period has so illuminated these questions as the Counter-Reformation. It is in some sort the birthplace of the modern state. The history of its ideas is in a special way the history of our social origins; and we bear upon the external aspect of our political life the scars of the special experience encountered in that epoch. That is why an analysis of its fundamental ideas is little less than a public service.

THE END

INDEX

www.ingramcontent.com/pod-product-compliance
Lightning Source LLC
Chambersburg PA
CBHW020525270326
41927CB00006B/444